Let 'er RIP!

GARDNER DICKINSON

on golf

LONGSTREET PRESS
Atlanta, Georgia

Published by LONGSTREET PRESS, INC.,
a subsidiary of Cox Newspapers,
a division of Cox Enterprises, Inc.
2140 Newmarket Parkway
Suite 118
Marietta, Georgia 30067

Printed in the United States of America

1st printing, 1994

Library of Congress Catalog Number 94-77587

ISBN: 1-56352-175-X

This book was printed by Maple-Vail Book Manufacturing, York, PA.

Film preparation by Holland Graphics, Inc, Mableton, GA.

Jacket and book design by Jill Dible
Jacket background photo M.W. Thomas / Atlanta

The author gratefully acknowledges the use of the following poems: "It
Couldn't Be Done" by Edgar Guest; "The Quitter" by Robert W. Service;
"The Woman Who Understands" by Everard Jack Appleton; "Solitude" by
Ella Wheeler Wilcox; "Unsubdued" by S. E. Kiser; "Might Have Been" by
Grantland Rice; "Good Intentions" by St. Clair Adams; and "Can't" by
Edgar Guest.

Table of Contents

Foreword

In the world of golf publishing, rarely does a significant new book appear from an unexpected source, by someone other than a famous writer like Herbert Warren Wind or a star player like Jack Nicklaus. This is such a book. For more than fifty years, Gardner Dickinson has accumulated a priceless store of knowledge about the game of golf and how to play it. He has shared his wisdom and insights with many of his fellow pros, and with the relative handful of fortunate amateurs he has taught over the years, but, until now, not with the general golfing public.

Dickinson was a protégé of Ben Hogan's during the period when Hogan was at the very top of his game, which, to most people who follow golf, was the pinnacle of all golf. Gardner gained valuable knowledge about the game from Hogan, and later from Sam Snead, the two greatest players of that era, which, added to his own talent, helped him become a mainstay of the tour; he won seven tournaments and was selected for two Ryder Cup teams. Later, Gardner served as chairman of the tournament players' group, the instigator and forerunner of today's PGA Tour. He was recently inducted into both the Georgia and Alabama Sports Hall of Fame.

With prodding from fellow teachers and players, Gardner Dickinson was persuaded to set down his own very personal beliefs and frequently original ideas about golf. Only a handful of top players — Bob Jones, J. H. Taylor, Joyce Wethered and Henry Cotton — have actually written their own books (typically, such books are ghosted by professional writers). Dickinson is the first since Cotton to do so, using not the modern word processor, or even a typewriter, but an old-fashioned pencil and yellow pad. The style is entirely Gardner's own, and what emerges is an irresistible look inside professional golf, lucid insights into the mechanics of the game, wide-ranging and provocative opinions about everything in golf, including the inner workings of PGA Tour politics, and entertaining yarns about most of the great players of the past half-century. Running through the book is a thread of easy, self-deprecating humor. It is hard to imagine any golfer anywhere in the world putting this book down without having discovered an armful of treasures.

The book has the appearance of a miscellany of stories and fragments, and, indeed, can be read that way, but the parts hang together as a hardheaded though grudgingly affectionate view of the game by one of its most intelligent and fascinating characters. As any of his fellow players can tell you, Dickinson expresses himself with blunt, sometimes bristly candor, yet in his teaching he is the soul of patience and good humor, delivered with a healthy dose of sweet common sense about swing technique and theory. Each of these qualities, and more, is found in the book.

Gardner Dickinson was born in Dothan, Alabama, in 1927, the son of Fredericka Pilcher and Gardner Dickinson, Sr., who later became a well-known southern golf writer. Within a year, the Dickinson family moved to Augusta, Georgia, the home of the Masters, where they spent the next dozen years. When young Gardner was thirteen, they moved to Macon, Georgia, where he took up the game at age fourteen and soon became a crack amateur player. After a fine college career at Louisiana State University, where he earned a degree in clinical psychology, Gardner attended the University of Alabama where he did graduate work in psychology, then served in the U. S. Army as an infantry lieutenant before turning pro in 1952. Although slender and wiry, Dickinson was one of the longest hitters on tour, a product of two of the more useful gifts nature can bestow on a professional golfer — fast, supple muscles and an aggressive disposition.

Save for putting, Dickinson was the consummate professional — a long, accurate driver, an excellent iron player and a master of wedge and bunker play. As a boy in Augusta, he watched the great Bob Jones play; as a young

Gardner: Always struggling with the putter, 1972.

professional, he knew and competed against Arnold Palmer; in mid-career, he spent countless hours with Florida neighbors Cary Middlecoff and Jack Nicklaus, arguing and plumbing the mysteries of golf technique. As a seasoned pro, he competed against, among others, Palmer, Nicklaus, Middlecoff, Bobby Locke, Billy Casper, Dave Stockton and Ben Crenshaw, all of whom are counted among the great putters in history, without much of it rubbing off — he still couldn't putt worth a damn. In this book, he tells us why, offers a potent antidote, and follows that with nearly a hundred sensational swing tips and stroke-saving, on-course corrections, none of which, as far as I know, have been published before.

Not every reader, including this one, will agree with all of Gardner's opinions. But, in the blizzard of confusing detail, bland drivel and stale clichés comprising so much of what we read about golf these days, Gardner Dickinson's book is a welcome blast of fresh air.

— *Cal Brown*

Part
1

···

The Game
and Me

Lashing and Bashing

Sam Snead never liked to watch Ben Hogan's swing, he said, because Hogan was a lasher, and Sam, despite his great power and length, considered himself a swinger. If Sam had weighed only 135 pounds, as Hogan did, I sometimes wondered if he wouldn't have been a lasher, too. I was a lasher and basher myself, because I weighed about 125 pounds when I started on tour, and even less when I was learning the game. I swung at it with shoelaces, belt buckle and anything else I could find.

But I had to swing hard if I wanted to drive the ball a long way, which I did. Plus, I loved knocking the hell out of something or somebody, whether it was in football, fighting or golf. I think all little guys love that, and particularly enjoy knocking a bigger guy on his butt. I remember in grammer school that I'd try every kid in the class, and I could whip all of them until I reached the sixth grade. Then I met two boys named George Barrow and Bob Sanders, and they tore my fanny right off. They were much bigger, but I had beaten lots of boys bigger than I was. I couldn't beat George or Bob, though, and that was the end of that.

In high school, I adored football and preferred playing defense, where I could hit people, but soon it was apparent that my 125-pound frame would not cut it, so I turned to golf. I suppose the hitting urge just carried over naturally into my golf game. Though long, I devoted endless hours to gaining proficiency with all the clubs, and I was an exceptional putter. Quite rapidly, I developed into one of the best players in Macon, Georgia.

Sixteen-year-old Gardner Dickinson at Idle Hour Country Club, Macon, Georgia, 1944.

I enjoyed my reputation as a long hitter, although my aggressiveness in competition sometimes landed me in trouble. There was a good side to this, however, because it led to an incident that changed my career. In the spring of 1945, when I was a senior in high school, I received a special invitation to play in a PGA Tour event called the Iron Lung Open, being held at the Capital City Club in Atlanta. That was the week Byron Nelson broke the world record by shooting 263, a mark he lowered to 259 later in the year.

I'd won the Georgia State high school championship three years in a row, and thought I could play. Charlie Miller, my pro and mentor at Idle Hour Country Club in Macon, accompanied me to the tournament where we were joined in a practice round by Ed "Porky" Oliver, who was among the best and most popular players on tour. We came to a par-three of about 160 yards and, with the honor, I hit a nine-iron onto the green. Porky, my partner, asked what club I'd used, and I showed him the nine-iron.

Porky shot me a look and said: "See here, son, let me show you something." He selected a club and effortlessly put his ball about three feet from the cup. Then he showed me his club, a six-iron, and suggested that, in the future, I let the club do more of the work in my swing. That was the first time I realized that a nine-iron didn't have to travel 165 yards. Still, I didn't see any reason to back down with my driver. In the first round, I was playing quite well as we came to the eighth hole, an L-shaped par-four with a big lake reaching across the corner of the dogleg. Ordinarily, I would lay up here, but with a strong wind blowing from behind, I decided to try to carry the lake with my tee shot. I knocked the hell out of it, and the ball not only carried the lake but came down hot and bounced up to the green, running past one of the players who was preparing to putt. I was horrified that I might have disturbed one of the big-name players, and in my concern, I missed the putt for eagle. I finally caught up with the group ahead at the tenth tee, where I apologized to the fellow whose putting I had disturbed, which is how I met Fred Haas, Jr.

Freddie Haas was incredulous that I'd driven the green, because in those days I was about as big around as an Eversharp pencil. He asked my age, my experience, and where I planned to attend college. Well, I said, I'd love to attend LSU. Freddie said he would look into the possibility of getting me a scholarship, and, sure enough, he delivered. So that lucky

drive was the beginning of a wonderful relationship with Fred
Haas and with LSU.

Freddie took me under his wing, and I shall be forever
indebted to him and to his wife, Paula, for their hospitality
and for the wonderful opportunity to receive a formal education. On weekends, I'd hitchike to New Orleans and we'd
spend hours at Metairier Country Club (where Fred's dad
was the pro) working on my game. During that critical period of my development as a player, I learned a great deal
about golf. Freddie liked to hustle me for five bucks every
chance he could, but it was part of the learning process. He
opened my eyes about so many aspects of the game that
previously had escaped my notice, and he helped me understand what a golf swing is all about. Fred had a brilliant
mind, and I can think of no one today with more knowledge
of the intricacies and finer points of a swing than Fred
Haas.

In some ways, he was too intelligent for his own good.
Fred could never settle on *one* golf swing or *one* putting
stroke. Instead, he kept searching for perfection, and therefore made constant swing changes. Freddie studied equipment the same way he studied a golf swing, and accordingly
had an extensive knowledge of club design. He knew, for
example, that an offset club promoted hooking, and realizing that most average golfers are slicers, he proposed a
design for offset wood clubs to Ted Wolley of the Golfcraft
Company. The idea didn't sell very well then, but it does
now. Freddie was years ahead of everyone in other ways. He
designed an excellent line of putters, mostly mallets, that
were made in Claremont, California, and were used by
many of the tour players. Dick Mayer, a U.S. Open Champion, wielded one like a master, and Freddie wasn't bad with
the short stick himself.

When Fred graduated from LSU in 1937, he went to
work for the Sun Life Assurance Company of Canada, selling life insurance while pursuing his golf. He was a member
of the Million Dollar Round Table for a number of years,

which meant that he was not only smart but could talk a blue streak. His peers on the tour can attest to that. Freddie wrote many of the life insurance policies for the tour players, myself included, and one year, when I couldn't meet the premium payments, he paid them for *me*. I paid him back, but how's that for a friend?

Freddie introduced me to many interesting people, broadening my contacts and experience. One day at Metairie, he hollered over to a gent named Dr. Oschner. "Hey, Doc, come over and meet this young fellow," after which he whispered to me, "He's a pickpocket." I had no idea if he was serious or not, but I played along. I'd heard of Dr. Oschner's famous clinic in New Orleans because he was the fellow who'd operated on Ben Hogan's legs after his terrible cable car crash. I began watching him more closely, but a few minutes later he asked, "Is this your watch?" I was dumbfounded, and all I could do was nod.

"If I ever need to have an operation," I said, "you're the man I want to perform it, Doc. Those are the most sensitive pair of hands I've ever seen!"

Georgia Crack Shots

Growing up in Georgia was a lucky break. Like Texas, Georgia had so many fine players when I was starting out that the State Amateur Championship was nicknamed the "Little National Amateur." I still remember some of the great players of this period. Gene Dahlbender, Jr., from Atlanta, had the potential to be one of the greatest golfers of all time. He was scoring in the 60s when he was ten years old, a feat that landed him in the RKO Pathe News shorts in movie theaters, but "Dollie" had too much affection for partying, and I'm afraid his social life won out over golf. The same could be said of Hobart Manley, an irrepressible fellow from Savannah, who possessed great power and a golf swing that Bob Jones would have loved. Sadly, I don't think Hobart truly cared about golf, for whenever the party roll was called, he was the first to answer it.

Everybody in Georgia knew about W. L. Goodloe, Senior and Junior, the famous father and son duo from Valdosta. Nobody wanted to draw them in match-play events because they both could play like hell. While playing guard on Georgia Tech's football team, Junior earned the nickname "Dynamite." Only about five feet tall, he weighed over 230 pounds. He kept his blond hair in a crewcut and constantly had a big cigar sticking out of his mouth. He was very long off the tee and had the touch of a safe-cracker with his old Cash-in putter.

Dynamite Goodloe was invited to play in the Masters one year, after a strong showing in the U.S. Amateur. When he arrived at the Augusta National Golf Club he was assigned a black caddie, also about five feet tall and a good 240 pounds. The press immediately dubbed them "Dynamite" and "Dynamo," and their pictures appeared almost daily in the Georgia newspapers, waddling down the fairway together. As I recall, Dynamite led the amateur field after posting a 72 in the third round, and, when he teed off on Sunday, he had half of Georgia following after him. After pars at the first three holes, Dynamite hit a long iron onto the back of the slick green at the par-three fourth hole, one of the toughest at Augusta National. He left the green in shock after four-putting, then, after splashing in and out of Rae's Creek in the middle of the round, he staggered home with a score of 88. Monday morning, all the flags in Georgia were draped at half-mast.

Many other characters from those days come to mind. George Hamer, of Columbus, had perhaps even more potential than Dahlbender, but after winning the NCAA, the Southern Amateur and the All-American Amateur at Tam O'Shanter in Chicago all in one summer, he seemed to lose interest in the game and decided, instead, to run service stations in his home town. Columbus was a hotbed of fine players, including my college roommate, Sonny

**Young Gardner and college roommate Sonny Ellis at the 1947
Peach Blossom Tournament.**

Ellis, one of the finest putters and finest men I've ever
known. Jack and Billy Key, whose family owned a bank
there, were wonderful players, and so was Sonny Swift,
who was always willing to bet you a dollar or two. One of
the most beautiful swingers I've seen was Tommy Barnes,
from Atlanta, who seemingly could do it all, except putt.
When his putting was just fair, he still won everything in

the South. In Atlanta, too, were Luke Barnes, the Black brothers, Carling Dinkler and Morton Bright, good players all. From Rome came Alvin Everett, a former national left-handed champion, and also Jennings Gordon. From Augusta came Frank Mulherin and Bill Zimmerman, both tough competitors. In other words, when you teed it up almost anywhere in Georgia, it behooved you to identify your opponent before making any bets.

Good as these fellows were, though, I hesitate to say that any were better than Arnold Blum, because nobody was. Arnold was a Macon boy, and a little older than I, though we never met in competition until I was in college. Then, in one summer, we went at it three times in the space of five weeks. The first time, Arnold was the defending champion in the Georgia State Amateur, and I beat him at the Columbus Country Club. Two weeks later, we returned to the same course for the Southeastern Amateur, and Arnold beat me in the finals by something like three-and-two. A month later, we met in the finals of the Middle Georgia Amateur at Bowden Country Club in Macon. It was the greatest match I've ever seen, let alone been involved in.

Arnold had me three down going to the seventh hole. My dad was following the match with a friend of his, Red Floyd, the town barber, who liked a nip now and again. Red had a hip flask with him, and I heard him whisper to my dad, "Say, let's take a little nip every time the kid makes a birdie; maybe we'll bring him luck." Well, I birdied the next three holes, and seven of the last nine, including seventeen and eighteen, and barely managed to win the match, *one up*. By this time, Red and my dad had exceeded their limit. Ten birdies were more than they had bargained for and, drained as I was by the match, I had to chuckle at the sight of those two old birds trying to navigate the big hill on the eighteenth fairway. Arnold and I still talk about that match; he was a wonderful swinger who played in the Masters several times and was a member of two Walker Cup teams. He would be about seventy now, but even today, I doubt if I could beat him.

My First Lesson from Sam Snead

During my sophomore year at LSU, I won a little tournament that allowed me to play an exhibition with Sam Snead in Alexandria, Louisiana. It was the first time I had the privilege of playing with Sam. About the fourth hole, I hit a shot into a bunker and took my customary slash. In those days, I took them at their word — when they said blast, I excavated the whole bunker. Sam looked at me kind of funny, then said, "What the hell you trying to do, boy?" He jumped down in the bunker. "Lemme show you something," he said, and proceeded to explain how he let the club do most of the work when playing from sand.

"You're swinging too hard, your hands are too far in front, and you're digging too much," he said. "Take a full swing, but make it smoother. Try to carve a thin divot of sand out onto the green; you don't need to dig that much." That was the first time anybody had ever taught me anything about bunker play, and Sam's routine worked a whole lot better than the caveman technique I'd been using until then.

When we finished that day, Sam gave me a ride back to Baton Rouge, where he was catching a private plane. They had charged every one a buck apiece for the exhibition, and afterwards they handed Sam a brown paper bag full of money. On the drive over, Sam passed the bag to me and said, "There's supposed to be five hundred one-dollar bills in that sack. See if they're all there." It took forever to count the money, and when we got to Baton Rouge, Sam asked, "You don't mind if I don't take you out to school, do you? I'm running a little late to catch this private plane ride." I said it was okay. Sure enough, the plane was waiting for him and, as I was stowing his bag in the cargo bay, he reached over and shoved something in my pocket.

"Here, catch a cab back to school," he said. After the

plane was gone, I reached into my pocket and found eight one-dollar bills and six new Wilson golf balls. I put the balls in my golf bag, stuffed that eight in my pocket and hitch-hiked back to LSU. That day I learned how to play a bunker shot and became eight dollars richer.

Greatest Golf Shots — I

The next time I saw Sam Snead, I was a spectator, but I'll never forget it because he hit one of those shots that only Sam could play. My college teammate, Bud Timbrook, and I had bummed a ride to New Orleans to watch Sam play a match at the Lakewood Country Club. After winning three or four tournaments in a row, Sam had taken a short vacation from the tour to play a series of exhibitions.

It worked like this: Freddie Haas and Cary Middlecoff would go into town and find the best amateur around. They would pair Snead with the amateur, then, with Doc and Freddie as partners, they'd play winner-take-all for whatever purse they could drum up.

Freddie had enormous feet, in fact the biggest on tour until George Bayer came along (we used to kid George that he had to buy his shoes in a boat store). For obvious reasons, Fred's nickname on tour was "Foots." New Orleans was Freddie's hometown, which gave him a slight advantage at Lakewood, expecially since Sam had not previously seen the course. Well, they came to a hole that rose up sort of gradually, high enough so that you couldn't see all of the landing area. Freddie advised Sam to hit his drive just right of center, which he did, but when Sam reached his ball, it was resting in the middle of a long, flat fairway bunker.

"Thanks a lot, Foots," Sam growled. "I'll do the same for you when you come to Hot Springs."

"Well, darn it, Sam, I've never seen anybody within *seventy-five yards* of that bunker!" Freddie protested.

Bud and I stood on the edge of the bunker watching while Sam asked his caddie what he should hit. We guessed he was about 245 yards from the hole and wondered what kind of shot he would play. The caddie hadn't a clue, so finally Sam took out his one-iron, poured honey all over the swing, and flew the ball onto the putting surface, where it stopped eight feet behind the cup. I didn't dream anyone could hit golf shots like that, and to this day I haven't seen another to match it. But that was Snead. Then, if you can believe this, he left his putt short — not once but *twice*. Thee putts from eight feet for a miserable par.

Sam's partner that day was a man named Raymond Salmen, a nice young fellow from a wealthy family and a good putter, but he couldn't hit the ball very far — or, at least, not far enough to help Sam. Toward the end of the round, Sam looked over at Foots. "You boys really got old Sambo set up, don't you?" They did indeed take care of Sam pretty good that day, but I don't believe they got away with it too often.

The Price of Anger

We had a marvelous golf team at LSU. At one time, just after World War II had ended, we had eighteen players who could shoot par or better. Some of them, like Bud Timbrook and Jay Hebert, had seen active service, and we naturally looked up to these older fellows. Among the ex-servicemen was Mike Barbato, our golf coach, and no team ever had a better one. Mike counseled us, listened to our problems, gave us rides everywhere and encouraged us as much in life as in golf. When he came out of the Navy, Mike had practically no money, but because of his affection for people and his hustle, he became quite wealthy. Mike would wait for me every morning at the athletic office so he could give me a ride out to Westdale, the university's golf course. He lent me money so often that we began referring to it as the "National

Gardner's LSU team photo, 1946.

Debt," but I always managed to pay him back with the two-bit Nassau money I won.

Our affection for each other was genuine, and we became very close. Mike admired the way I worked on my game, and he loved to tell everyone about the ice storm we had in Baton Rouge one winter. Ice storms were rare in that part of Louisiana, but this one covered the course for almost a week. I was fed up with no practice, so I hunted up some old plywood signs, laid them down on the tenth fairway and beat balls for hours off those wooden slabs. When the ice finally melted, said Mike, I was the only guy on the team in shape and ready to play.

I had quite a temper in those days (which some of my contemporaries on tour might claim never entirely left me), and I'll never forget how it upped and grabbed me in the Louisiana Open one year when it was held at our Westdale course. I led the event after shooting a first round 66, but I teed off late the second day and quickly hooked my first three tee shots into Coach Barbato's yard, out of bounds. Fortunately for me at that time, the USGA, in their wisdom, had deemed that out-of-bounds and lost balls would suffer the penalty of distance only, so I was hitting four on my fourth drive. Nevertheless, this began a long, long day, and, standing on the last tee, a reachable par-five, I needed par for 80. After a good drive, I nailed a long iron to within two feet of the hold; then, even though putting uphill, I yipped the stroke. In a rage, I swatted the ball from the lip of the cup over the back of the green, down the bank, and across the old tennis court — out of bounds. But again the Rules of Golf came to my rescue. Because of the distance-only penalty then in effect, I was allowed to replace my ball where it originally rested on the lip of the cup, allowing me to hole out for the damndest par-five anyone ever made.

I didn't always escape so easily, though. The sixteenth hole at Westdale is a reachable par-five with a goofy green pitched way up in the air. When after three-putting the two previous greens I added number sixteen to the list, in a burst of anger I hurled my steel-shafted putter over the road toward the seventeenth tee. I had accomplished this feat quite easily on several previous occasions, but this time the putter struck three high-tension wires suspended above the road; the wires began sparking, then dropped to the ground where they hopped around starting little brush fires. Horrified at what I had done, I grew even sicker with the realization that school was about to let out, and that little kids walked home along that road. My playing companions wanted to flee, but I persuaded them to stay while I went to phone the power company. Still in my spikes, I clomped up on the porch of the only nearby house and asked to use the telephone. When I reached the power company and told them about the downed wires, they asked who I was. "Never mind," I told them, and hung up. As soon as I returned to the spot, my buddies all lit out, and I knew I had to find a place to hide.

I set up a vigil in a honeysuckle thicket nearby where I could watch the road and soon was joined by about ten million Louisiana swamp mosquitos. When the power company had finally repaired the fallen lines and left, I trudged back to the clubhouse in the pitch darkness, only to find it locked. So, seven miles back to the campus, walking in golf spikes and lugging my golf bag. I can tell you it was a long time before I threw another golf club — well, maybe a month.

Titanic

Titanic Thompson showed up at our golf shop one day. Of course, we knew who he was. Alvin "Titanic" Thompson was a legend, a notorious gambler and hustler with a history of betting on anything, whether it was cards, horses, golf or World Series games, but never unless he could find or create an edge. Titanic told us he was selling stock in an oil well, which we soon discovered was dry, and when that ploy failed he worked at getting some of us to play golf with him, but nobody would. He was accompanied by a twenty-two-year-old blond, and Titanic claimed he was seventy-six, which I have no reason to doubt.

In his younger days, Titanic would travel around with a "caddie" and hustle matches in every small town with a golf course. He'd find the best players in town, rig a match for a few dollars, and play right-handed, which he could do pretty well. Once he had the suckers hooked, he'd offer to play them left-handed, with his caddie as a partner. He didn't bother to tell them that he was a natural lefty, nor that the "caddie" was Dutch Harrison, then a fledgling tour pro and virtually unknown.

One morning I arrived at the golf shop and Coach Barbato informed me that I had a game that day. He and the LSU athletic director, T. P. "Skipper" Heard, would play a match against me and my partner. "Skipper and I are playing you and Titanic," Mike informed me.

"Well, that's just wonderful," I replied. "Are you trying to squeeze old Gardner?" I was on an athletic scholarship, and I knew enough not to beat the athletic director. But I couldn't back out, so off we went.

On the first hole, I hit a drive better than I meant to, leaving myself a short wedge to the green. I figured I'd better knock it over the green, which I did, and Titanic looked at me kind of funny. I continued to dog it most of the way around, until we were three down with four to go. Ti was a little suspicious by then, and there was a bunch of money on the line.

Before we teed off at the fifteenth, a short par-four, I turned to Mike and said, "If you guys can't hold this lead, the hell with you. I'm going to let 'er fly from here on in." The ground was hard as a brick and, with a helping wind, I almost drove the green and made birdie to win the hole. I reached the next hole, a par-five, with a drive and long iron and made another birdie, putting us one down and two to go. I drove the seventeenth green, another short par-four, and goosed two putts up for a third straight birdie , making us all even with the eighteenth to play. By this time, Skipper was giving me the red-eye, so I stood up on the tee and put an eight-knuckle grip on it, swung hard, and hooked the ball onto the road out of bounds. Ti looked at me with a crooked grin, and said, "Oh, that's how it is, is it?" He knew what I was doing. Titanic put his drive down the middle, knocked his second on the green, and Mike Barbato had to hole a five-footer to tie us. That broke us even, and no money changed hands that day — amazingly.

The Hebert Brothers

In college I had the good fortune to meet the Hebert brothers, and we became lifelong friends. Jay Hebert was just out of the service, having been wounded in the thigh while landing in the first wave of Marines on Iwo Jima. Jay was a very talented golfer, possessed of an extremely long backswing, as was his brother, Lionel. Jay's was a classic swing. He was one of the most beautiful long-iron players I've ever known, which is a most unusual trait in a young player.

Lionel Hebert's swing was even longer than Jay's. For a while, it kept him from scoring well; he couldn't hook the ball with regularity until he shortened it. So he went home from school to work on his swing — and his trumpet — and about a year later, he beat all of us *and* the pros in winning the Louisiana Open.

Jay and Lionel are two of the finest gentlemen in golf, and they became the only brothers in history to win the PGA Championship . After turning pro, they both played the winter tour before going to their club jobs in the north. When Jay left the Kahkwa Club in Erie, Pennsylvania, in 1957, Lionel took over as the pro. That summer, Lionel beat Dow Finsterwald to win the last PGA Championship played at match-play. He became a full-timer on the Tour shortly thereafter and played the Tour for some thirty years, winning six other Tour events. Jay won the title in 1960 at the Firestone Country Club in Akron, Ohio. Firestone requires many long-iron shots, which was right up Jay's alley. So was Pebble Beach, where Jay later won the Bing Crosby Tournament, among many others.

During one of our early years on tour, we found ourselves at the Las Vegas airport following the end of the Sahara Invitational. Jay asked me if I was "busted," because I seemed so grim. I was, but denied it. As Jay left the gate, he put his hand in my pocket and murmured, "That's what friends are for." I pulled out a check for five thousand dollars.

(L-R) Cary Middlecoff, Gardner Dickinson, and Jay Hebert in 1964.

What a gesture, and how did he know? Afterwards, I played quite well and tried to repay him, with interest, but he tore up that check and several more. Finally he accepted the repay of the original five thousand. Later I found a beautiful gold bracelet watch in a fine jewelry store and had it engraved so it couldn't be returned. I think, to this day, Jay still wears that watch, and I hope it still conveys to him my lifelong affection for him and his family.

Lionel and Jay served several terms on the PGA Tournament Committee, each serving as its chairman at different periods. Jay spearheaded the players' successful effort to win back our entrance fees from the tournament sponsors, and Lionel led our efforts to return the television rights from the sponsors to the players. These two changes gave the players the leverage to take control of their affairs and begin acting like businessmen. I don't know where the players would have ended up without the honest and unselfish actions of the Hebert brothers. If it were up to me, I'd put them in any Hall of Fame the PGA Tour might develop. But I'm getting a little ahead of my story.

Getting to Know Ben Hogan

During college, I played every tournament I could find that I could afford to enter, which wasn't that many because I couldn't afford very many. Still, I won thirty-seven tournaments before turning pro, and in 1951 I won every tournament I played in, which made me think I could beat somebody. When I turned pro in 1952, I discovered, as so many young hotshots do, that the level of competition out on the tour was a tad higher than I thought it was.

After Charlie Miller had started me in golf, and Freddie Haas had polished me into a good player and taught me to think, the fellow who had the profoundest effect on my game, and thus my life, was Ben Hogan. In the spring of 1953, I had a chance to play in the lucrative Pan American Open at the Club de Golf in Mexico City. Although only my third outing as a pro, I opened up pretty good for a rookie and was near the lead at the conclusion of two rounds. You can imagine my apprehension, though, when I learned that I would be paired for the third round with the great Ben Hogan, who was then at the very top of his game, and Art Wall, a phenomenal scorer and a rising star. Choking like a dog, and generally playing like someone who'd never held a club before, I proceeded to three-putt the first four greens. On the narrow sixth hole, I knocked an iron into the woods, then stormed off the tee and flew up the fairway. Hogan grabbed me by the shoulder, suggested I slow down, and advised me to move up to the ball more quickly and let instinct have a chance. I was genuinely startled even to be addressed by the "Wee Ice Mon" on the golf course, let alone given advice. In effect, his counsel was simply to "knock the hell out of it, and go get it."

I settled down, limiting myself to only six three-putt greens, and posted a 78 to Ben's rather easy 68. After we'd finished, Ben stopped by my locker and encouraged me to keep playing, expressing his belief that I would become a good player. The next morning he invited me to share the long cab ride from the Bamar Hotel to the Club de Golf. Noticing that I was petrified at the ten-way traffic circles with no stop signs, where the loudest horn "wins," he advised me to do as he did and look down at the floorboard. Neither one of us, as I recall, looked up until we arrived at the golf course.

The following week at the Colonial Invitational in Fort Worth, I followed Ben Hogan's every step, as a spectator. The fairways were not roped in those days, so I was able to stand right behind him all week. During Thursday's first round, he turned to me at the sixth fairway and handed me a small piece of paper. "Gardner, I don't know what your financial situation is, but if you run out of money, don't quit," he said quietly. "This is my unlisted phone number. You call me, and I'll get you some money." This was a tremendous boost to my confidence and ego, and though I went on to win a check in almost every event the rest of the year and thus never had to call on Ben for financial assistance, it made a huge difference to know that I could.

At the end of that 1953 season, I wrote Ben asking if he'd make an exception to his usual rule and watch me hit some balls. A buddy of mine named Harold Hall, from Columbia, South Carolina, a fine player and former Carolinas amateur champion, bet me that I'd never hear from Hogan, but that if I did, he would fly me out in his new airplane. About a month later, I received a letter from Ben agreeing to help me if I would come to Tamarisk Country Club in Palm Springs, California, where he'd taken a new job for the winter months. So off we went, Harold and I, in his Piper Tri-Pacer, a single-engine puddle-jumper that took four days to fly from South Carolina to the California desert.

My First Lesson with Hogan

In 1953, Ben Hogan had won just about everything in golf, including the Masters, the U.S. Open, and the British Open, and he might have won the PGA Championship, too, if the dates hadn't overlapped with the British. No one had ever heard of Hogan teaching, so all the Tamarisk members were mighty shocked when Ben walked out to the range with me to watch me hit balls. I did so for a good fifteen minutes without Ben uttering a word. Finally I couldn't stand it any longer and asked him what he thought. He mumbled something about "looking pretty good," then asked me if I had a "safe shot." I asked what he meant. "I mean the shot you would try just to put the ball somewhere on the green with that club, for your very life," he replied. Without hesitation, I played a rather low knockdown shot with an abbreviated follow-through, and Ben exclaimed, "Hell, yes!" He asked if I could fade that shot, and I admitted that I couldn't do so at will, so he proceeded to show me how. The next couple of hours were really fun.

We went back to Ben's private office, where he offered me a seat, then he asked if I would like to work for him that winter, the idea being that I would do all the teaching. I accepted, and he told me to report January 1. The next morning, Ben called me back into his office and, somewhat apologetically, informed me that the teaching pro from the previous season had gone over his head to the Board of Directors and had been reinstated. It didn't bother me particularly, for I really wanted to play the tour.

A month or so later, I was playing in the La Gorce Pro-Am in Miami and having a post-round beer with my partners in the grill room when I heard my name being paged. Picking up the telephone, I listened to a voice say, "Gardner, this is Ben in Palm Springs."

"Sure, Wamp," I replied, "and I'm Tom Mix." I hung up and returned to the table, certain that the caller was my pal, Fred Wampler, who never tired of putting me on. A few minutes later I was again paged, and this time when I answered the phone, the voice said, "Dammit, Gardner, don't hang up. This really is Ben, and I want to know if you still want that job." I almost jumped through the telephone accepting, and I showed up promptly on January 1.

A Famous First Pupil

That first day at Tamarisk, I was sitting at a table with Ben when Pat Martin, the resident pro, stopped by and said that he'd booked me a lesson in fifteen minutes. Ben asked, "Who the hell with?"

"Jack Benny," Pat replied. I had listened to Jack Benny on the radio all my life, and now I was about to give him a golf lesson.

"Oh, my God," said Hogan, "you better make it the best lesson of your life. You have to give it, because Benny is a friend of the teacher you're replacing." It seems that I was being put to the test.

Fifteen minutes later, Mr. Benny and I proceeded straight

to the ninth green, where Jack dropped a basket of balls beside a yawning bunker, beyond which was the green with the pin cut close to its near side. Benny said that the only shot he couldn't play was "that nice little flip wedge that comes down right by the hole." I informed him that he had lots of company and doubted that I could play it either, after four days driving cross-country. He insisted that I demonstrate the shot, and fortunately the good Lord was at home to answer my hasty prayer. I flipped the ball up about a foot from the hole, and Benny screamed: "That's it, that's it! Now, do it again." So I did, and put that one about six inches away. I explained the shot to Jack and suggested he try it. The first swing produced a sickening clunk and a ball streaked past my nose — a solid shank. "That shank's my entire problem," Benny wailed.

To this day, I cannot remember what I told him, but his next shot stopped five feet from the hole, and the next three were all inside the first one. With that, Jack picked up the balls, handed me a hundred-dollar bill, and we returned to the clubhouse. He marched into the bar, stood on a chair and demanded everyone's attention. "Ben has just hired us the world's best teacher," he announced. I nodded a little self-consciously, then sat down quietly beside Hogan.

"What the hell did you tell Benny?" he asked, and I muttered that I couldn't honestly remember. But I knew I had it made. Benny was an extraordinary man, not at all like his screen image, and from that moment on he took a personal interest in me and eventually we became fast friends.

A Spat with Groucho

That same week, Hogan told me he was going to Thunderbird, a neighboring course, to play with friends. "You're still new around here, so while I'm gone, Harpo will take care of you," Ben said, walking me over and introducing me to

Harpo Marx. In the movies, Harpo was a mute, but in real life he never stopped talking. He chattered on about everything and nothing, and finally he pointed to his new golf cart and told me to climb in. Well, I'd never seen a golf cart before, almost nobody had, since they had only been introduced at Thunderbird a year or two earlier and very few were in existence. Those early versions were quite primitive, and I was somewhat apprehensive.

Harpo drove the same way he talked — a mile a minute — and after whipping across a few hills at breakneck speed, I decided that I had had enough. I sent a silent promise to the Lord that if he would just let me out of the golf cart in one piece, I'd never enter another. Of course, I lied, but I was genuinely concerned for my safety.

Later on, Harpo introduced me to the other Marx brothers. Harpo, Gummo and Zeppo were delightful people, but Groucho was a miserable man. He made his living poking fun at other people and making them feel uncomfortable, and he was the same in person. One day, while I was giving Harpo a lesson, Groucho strode up behind us, impatient to play, and rudely interrupted. "C'mon, you're wasting your time with this guy," he snapped at Harpo. "He's a flunky and doesn't know anything about the golf swing." He kept on in this vein until, finally, I reached my boiling point. Though I was conscious of my status as a lowly assistant pro, I turned to Groucho and let him have it. I suggested that his remarks were out of line, his manners uncouth and his behavior surly. I may have included a colorful descriptive phrase or two.

Harpo and Gummo watched with fascination, and after Groucho left, they both applauded. Grinning from ear to ear, Harpo grabbed my hand. "Lemme shake your hand. Somebody should have done that to him forty years ago." Apparently his brothers weren't any fonder of him than I was, at that moment, but after I cooled down I realized I might be in big trouble. I went in to tell Hogan, and all he said was, "The hell with him. You did the right thing." We never heard another word about it.

Working for Hogan

Ben Hogan's daily routine at Tamarisk almost never varied. He would arrive at the club at about 9:30 each morning, walk into his office and draw the drapes to read his daily stack of mail. Then he'd remove his clubs, which he kept in a small closet behind three locked doors, and tromp out past the practice range toward the ninth fairway, where he would hit balls toward the tee. His shag caddie, whose name was Fuzzy, had the easiest job in golf, seldom needing to move more than three or four feet to collect the balls. One of the stories they told on Ben was that one of his shots had struck the caddie, knocking him down, and before Fuzzy could get up Hogan's next four shots landed on Fuzzy's prone body.

Hogan played a good-sized slice in those days, and one morning I saw him start a ball left of Fuzzy that, unlike all his other shots, failed to curve back. After hitting two more shots that flew absolutely straight, Ben slammed the club to the ground and stomped across the range, went into his office, and closed the door. Twenty minutes later he was back and had resumed hitting perfect shots with that nice little fade, indicating that he had figured out whatever he was doing wrong.

After hitting balls each day, Ben would go to the putting clock to practice his nemesis, putting, where he always seemed to stroke the ball pretty well. Interestingly, he would devote about half this practice time, or about thirty minutes, to putting with a split-handed grip. He made a lot of putts with that grip, but never once did he use it on the golf course. He was just too conventional.

Never have I seen anyone control the ball as Hogan did during that period; it was just beautiful to watch. A decent putter playing as he did from tee to green would have scored in the 50s almost every day, and Tamarisk was no pushover course. One day he shot 61 and the longest putt he had for birdie, or eagle, was five feet. He could place his drives almost anywhere he chose, it seemed. Doc Middlecoff finally said to him, "Hawk, we could save a lot of time if we just let you walk down the fairway and drop the ball where you want it."

The swing that produced Hogan's characteristic fade was developed when he was close to forty, and it continued into his mid-sixties. Slicing the ball as he did cost Ben a lot of yardage, and eventually he went back to drawing his shots. I asked him one day whether, if he had been able to control the draw, he would have played with a slice, and the answer was a firm "No." I think that Ben played his finest golf tee-to-green during his mid-fifties, but by then he was literally helpless on the greens. It was sad to watch.

In college, I'd earned a degree in clinical psychology and was a qualified tester in psychometrics, which is a fancy word for mental testing. When I went to work for Ben at Tamarisk, I though it would be fascinating to test his I.Q. Well, Ben wouldn't agree to sit down and take a Wechsler-Belleview test, so I began to slip verbal I.Q. questions into the conversation every few days. When he answered them, I dashed away to record his responses. I was unable to administer the manual dexterity portions of the test, but I think we can concede that Hogan was far above normal in that department. Even so, I calculated that Ben's I.Q. was in excess of 180, a score that would place him in the high genius category.

In observing him, I became convinced that Hogan had a photographic memory as well, and one night his wife, Valerie, confirmed my suspicions. Coupled with exceptional powers of observation, she said, Ben could recall details of the most trivial incidents. For example, leaving a party one night, he had asked Valerie if she could explain why the knobs on their host's desk drawers had been installed upside down. He surely did notice the damnedest things.

But Hogan's great powers of observation did fail him occasionally. At the 1953 British Open at Carnoustie in Scotland, he discovered the rough was so thick he couldn't escape from it, so he decided simply to avoid it for the entire tournament, which causes me to chuckle whenever I think about it. But he kept blowing shots over the greens and couldn't understand why. Finally he thought to check the height of the flagsticks and discovered that they were only five feet tall, instead of the seven feet that was standard back in the States. Shorter flagpoles give the illusion that you are farther from the hole, and Hogan had until then overlooked this important detail.

In the many practice rounds I played with him over the years, I noticed that Ben always tried to play the shot he knew best (which seemed to me to be all of them), the shot that offered the least risk, or the shot he had practiced most recently. One day, while playing Tamarisk, we noticed that all the pins were cut on the left sides of the green, and Ben growled, "The damn greenskeeper must be a hooker."

"What do you care?" I asked. "As straight as you hit it, you could aim for the pin even if it were on the edge of a cliff."

"Like hell," he replied. "Suppose I started it out there, and it didn't come back? Never start a ball in jail, on purpose, because it might stay there." There would be pins up ahead that he could shoot at, he said, and sure enough, there were. Years ago, Hogan had truly made a science of the game, analyzing its strategies thoroughly, a technique that has been explored by relatively few players since.

Hogan's Two Swings

I would imagine that I have watched Ben Hogan hit more practice balls than any man alive, so let me offer my impressions of his swing technique, and in the process perhaps lay some myths to rest.

Early in his career, from the late thirties to the mid-forties, Ben had a strong left-hand grip and a backswing so astoundingly long that his club pointed almost straight at the ground as he reached the top of his backswing, even more so than John Daly does today. I'm sure that Ben assumed, correctly, that he could hit the ball farther with this long backswing.

On his downswing, Ben swung with a pronounced lash forward, almost violent, with the bottom end of his spine moving laterally toward the target much more than happened with other players. This created an extremely late hit, so much so that by the time the club head struck the ball, the loft on Hogan's driver at impact was reduced to near zero. More often than not, the result was a hot, low, ducking hook which, said Ben, drove him nuts — and, indeed, very nearly drove him from the tour. Then around about 1947, while looking through an old golf book, he came across a photograph of a very fine ball-striker who, even though he had a strong grip, was unconcerned about overhooking his shots. Ben told me that he noticed the player's left wrist at the top of the backswing was wrinkled, a very different situation from his own flat-wristed position at the top of the swing.

As he experimented with putting some wrinkles in his left wrist, Ben gradually changed his grip so that his left hand showed about one and a half knuckles at address. At the same time, he let the right hand move more on top of the shaft so that the "V" formed by its thumb and forefinger pointed between his chin and left ear. He then moved the ball forward in his stance, and repositioned his hands at address so that they were about even with the ball, or even slightly behind it with a driver. Finally he assumed a distinctly closed stance at address, even on pitch shots, by withdrawing his right foot from the intended line of flight. I asked him why he pulled the right foot back out of the way, and he explained that he didn't want that leg in the way when he started his backswing. His hands could go back easily, he said, in the little channel he'd created. Ben aimed with his shoulders, not his feet, so the closed stance had

Ben Hogan, still smooth in 1989.

minimal effect on his targeting.

There was one more critical adjustment: when he wanted to fade the ball, Ben made sure he set the left wrist under the shaft at the top of the backswing. You can do this yourself by cupping your left wrist so that your knuckles are positioned over your wristwatch at the top of the swing. These set-up changes, plus the cupping of the left wrist, caused Hogan's clubface to become quite open at the top, which allowed him to unleash his tremendous forward slide, with its blinding speed, without fear of smothering or even hooking the shot.

In this final, brilliant product, Hogan had taken his biggest enemy, the huge forward slide, and turned it into his biggest asset. His flight pattern changed from a near unplayable hook to a gentle fade. With the changes he had made, he said, it was virtually impossible to hook. The beauty of the new method was that when he tried to hook the ball, the shots went straighter, instead of fading, and the more he tried to hook them, the straighter they flew. With this method, he once remarked, he could even slice the ball with a wedge.

Strangely, Ben felt that he had also succeeded in retarding his hip turn during the backswing, but even though I watched him hit many thousands of balls, I could never see any restriction or absence of hip turn, especially with the driver. When Ben was aiming drives toward the north, it always appeared to me that, when he reached the top of the swing, his belt buckle almost faced south. In other words, even the greatest don't always swing like they think they do.

Incidentally, Ben Hogan was a shaft swinger, not a clubhead swinger. By this I mean that he fixed his attention on the shaft, not the clubhead, nor on some part of his body. At address, he placed the clubface behind the ball the way he wanted it, and from there he simply concentrated on swinging the shaft.

Nothing's Funny Out There

While Ben Hogan's great book *The Modern Fundamentals of Golf* was beautifully conceived, superbly written with the help of Herb Wind, and handsomely illustrated by Tony Ravielli, I think it was, more than anything else, a system of defense against a low, ducking hook, a problem that afflicts very few golfers. During the time that I was teaching at the Breakers Hotel in Palm Beach, Florida, I taught Hogan's system quite faithfully. I probably helped about two-thirds of my students, but I was killing the other one-third. At the time, I thought they were uncoordinated, or just plain dumb, but I wish now that I could give them their money back.

In many ways, I made the mistake of trying to copy Hogan too closely during these formative years. I had no problem with hooking , as Ben did, and although I thought I knew a great deal about a golf swing, I didn't know enough to copy the strongest points of his technique. Instead, I copied many of his mannerisms, which didn't really help me.

Hogan came up the hard way and had always worked harder than most others did. I wasn't afraid to work, either, and so I modeled myself after his work habits. Ben was close-mouthed, and I was, too. Ben hardly ever smiled on a golf course, so naturally I didn't either. He told me that there wasn't anything funny out there, and I agreed with him. But I learned a lot about life, and a tremendous amount about golf and people, from Ben. I thought so much of him that I named a son after him, and I don't know how you could honor a man more than that.

People have said that I acted mean on occasions, or at least gave that appearance, and that this was another attempt to copy Hogan. There might be a grain of truth in that. One day a bunch of us were sitting around at a club in Fort Worth, when Denny "Tex" Lavender asked rhetorically if anyone knew why Hogan was so mean. Lavender was a golf pro who had grown up with Ben in Fort Worth, and, when none of us could answer, he told us how, as a kid, little Ben had a job selling papers at night in the railway station downtown.

Each night, it appears, he would sell all but two newspapers, which he tucked under his arm as he hitchhiked or walked all the way out to the Glen Garden Country Club where he was a caddie, along with Lavender and a tall boy named Byron Nelson. Young Ben would then spread one of the newspapers in the bottom of a deep bunker near the eighteenth green, cover himself with the other, and spend the night. He figured if he were the first in line at the caddie shack in the morning, he might get two loops in one day. When Byron and Denny sauntered in around 7:30 a.m. and saw little Ben first in line, the two bigger boys would toss him, stomping and scratching, to the end of the line. Denny claimed that this is what made Ben so mean later on, and not long ago when I visited with him, Ben confirmed the story.

For some reason, Ben Hogan was never mean to me. Maybe he figured I would scratch as hard as he did. Whatever the reason, he was my entrée to many fine places and interesting people. One of them was Marvin Leonard of Fort Worth, whose idea of a good time was to play golf for $25,000. Mr. Leonard had built the Colonial Country Club and started the Colonial Invitational, then had created a new club called Shady Oaks, where Ben hung out every day. One rainy afternoon, eight of us were in the grill room swapping stories when suddenly the rain stopped. Mr. Leonard suggested we play an eightsome, and off we went. As it happened, I was riding in Mr. Leonard's golf cart, and when we reached the first green, he drove right out on the putting surface to our balls.

"Mr. Leonard, we're driving on the green," I reported. "I know it," he said, "but we have balloon tires, so we're not hurting the green. Besides, we don't want to get our feet wet. And furthermore, we don't have any rules here." I assure you, though, that nobody else ever had nerve enough to drive out on the greens at Shady Oaks.

Hogan the Dance Champ

Later that summer of 1958, I returned to Fort Worth to have a damaged disc removed from my neck by Dr. Fred Rehfeldt, and afterwards I spent some time recuperating at Hogan's social club, the Rivercrest Country Club. When I was well enough, Ben invited my wife and me to dinner at the club, and that night I was astonished to discover that he was an accomplished dancer — in fact, one of the best I'd ever seen.

It turned out that Ben and Valerie had enrolled at Lavonia Bella's dance studio, a famous establishment in those parts, and that Ben had become one of Lavonia's prize pupils. After ordering all our entrées, Ben proceeded to amaze me by dancing beautifully not only with his wife Valerie, but with half the ladies at Rivercrest. He specialized in South American dances, cutting a smooth figure with the mambo, tango and cha-cha-cha, all within a floor space of about twelve inches. He just seemed to glide in rhythm to the music. When the band began packing up at about one a.m., Ben went over to the leader, slipped him some cash, and went on dancing for another hour. I think he danced every dance. I'd heard that Sam Snead was a pretty fine dancer, and I should have figured that Ben Hogan would be, too.

Fading It "From the Inside"

One day Ben Hogan invited me to Shady Oaks to watch him practice. We drove out to a remote spot on the little par-three course, and Ben started painting shots against the trees toward his shag caddie. For nearly twenty minutes he put on the damndest display of accuracy with his four-wood, the face of which he had recently painted white, until finally I told him that I had never seen anything to compare with his precision.

"Baloney, you can do just as well," he said, and handed me his four-wood. My neck was still full of stitches and I thought I'd better not, but Ben insisted. "Just hit it easy," he said. He'd been showing me how he faded the ball while still hitting it hard — in effect, the art of fading the ball "from the inside." I knew what I was in for, but if you think I was going to miss that piece of information you're very much mistaken.

Sure enough, I ripped out every stitch, for I never had and didn't then know how to "hit it easy." That night, my neck looked like a sumo wrestler's. I carry those neck scars to this day, but it was a small price for what I learned that day.

While I was recuperating from the operation, I spent a great deal of time in Hogan's factory in Fort Worth. Ben was in the process of getting his golf club company rolling, and I was anxious to leave Wilson Sporting Goods so I could establish myself with the Ben Hogan Company. When Ben started the company he was on top of the golfing world. His main source of financing was a Dallas oilman and friend, Pollard Simon. When Hogan finally produced some clubs, he was very displeased with the results and told Pollard that he'd start over rather than put an inferior model on the market.

Pollard, as I remember, wanted to recover some of his money and insisted that Ben market those first sets. Ben refused, and many of those clubs, I'm told, ended up in Japan. At any rate, the story goes that Hogan went to the bank, borrowed some $450,000, and bought out Pollard Simon. Marvin Leonard, Hogan's wealthy Fort Worth friend, put together a small group of investors who took Ben's name off the note and became limited partners. I believe Bing Crosby was one of the investors. The Ben Hogan Company went along doing pretty well, although it spent very little money on advertising. Hogan felt strongly that advertising expenses should come only from profits.

Pretty soon, a labor organizer showed up at the plant,

which angered Ben to no end. But he let the organizer wander around the plant for a while, and one morning I happened to be there when the workers decided to call an organizing meeting. Ben called for his employees' attention, and what he told them went something like this: "I understand that all of you fellows want to organize my business here and join a union. Well, that is certainly your privilege. If you'd like to pay a nice portion of your salaries to a union, be my guest. You obviously think that by organizing you're going to make a lot more money and, in effect, tell me, the boss, what you're going to do. Before you vote, let me tell *you* just one thing: I've already started over once, and I can and will do so again, if necessary. So far, neither I nor my investors has made one damned cent; when we do make some money, I'll see to it that you make some, too. Until that happens, you're not going to make one damn cent more than I can afford to pay you. And if any of you don't like those terms, you can go straight to the pay window and draw your severance pay, because in thirty minutes this plant *will be* operating full-blast again. Period!"

No one had anything else to say, and to my knowledge, no vote was ever held.

Years later, when American Machine and Foundry, Inc., purchased the Ben Hogan Company, the unions immediately moved in, and Ben offered to handle the union negotiations for AMF. As diversified as was AMF, though, they declined Ben's offer.

In the middle fifties, Ben had also taken a keen interest in the oil business. You could tell that he studied oil and gas exploration intensely because the walls of his office were covered with geologic maps. Rumor had it that Ben had dropped a considerable sum with an old wildcatter named Willard White, who apparently had brought in eleven straight dry holes. Marvin Leonard and some of Ben's buddies at Shady Oaks who were in the oil business came to me one day and expressed their concern with Hogan's dropping all that money with the wildcatter. They asked, bless them, if I would express their concerns to Ben. Like an idiot, I did approach Ben. He told me that he appreciated everyone's concern, but said he was merely investing "tax dollars" in those explorations, and that all that "six-footer" money was safely stashed away

As I reflect, those were great days for me. None was more fun than the day Ben asked me to come back out to the Hogan plant, and there, on a big table, were displayed four of the brand-new sets of Hogan clubs — irons and woods. "Go ahead, I'll give you first pick, and I'll take second," Ben told me. As I began eyeballing each club, Ben said, "Look at them, if you want to, but every club is exactly alike." And damned if they didn't appear to be just that.

After the long wait for Ben to perfect his line, I was really ready for those clubs. I promptly took them to Birmingham, Alabama, for the U.S. Open qualifying event. I hit all twenty-eight fairways and thirty-four of the thirty-six greens in regulation, and putted so horrendously that I failed to qualify. But I knew that I finally had a set of clubs with which I could really play.

'Hot' Shot at Colonial

For some reason, after my first year on tour I didn't play with Ben Hogan again until 1962 when we were paired in the first round of the Colonial Invitational. I was sailing along at two-under until we reached the fifth hole, which at that time was the toughest par-four in golf. The hole stretched more than 450 yards along a crowned fairway, doglegging to the right, with up ahead a little old green no more than 4,000 square feet in area and surrounded by bunkers and bare ground. Hitting from the old back tees, sensible players tried to fade a driver, or even a three-wood, to avoid the Trinity River on the right and a deep barranca on the left. Before the hole was shortened, any of us would gladly have taken four and run to the next tee.

Feeling cocky, I decided to shorten the hole all by myself by hitting a high *draw* over a big tree that sits at the corner of the dogleg beside the river. I put some sauce on it, but the ball hit the tree and bounced back into the river. As I stomped angrily from the tee, Hogan grabbed my shoulder, his steely eyes blazing: "Dammit, you tried to *hook* that ball into the fairway, didn't you?" I nodded. "Well, you got what you damn well deserved," he said, and I guess I did, for I knew better than to fool with Colonial's dreaded fifth hole.

When I dropped my ball behind the tree, though, it jumped up into a decent lie. I was lying about 240 yards from the green, but aiming right at that big barranca on the left. I turned to my caddie, Herman Mitchell, who later became such a familiar figure carrying Lee Trevino's bag, and told him, "Give me the driver." Herman asked if I'd lost my mind, but I told him to step aside. I caught the ball on all four screws. It sliced low around the tree and ran like a scalded dog right up onto the green, stopping ten feet from the hole. Ben took off his white cap and shouted, "Helluva shot," thereby astounding both me and the large gallery.

After escaping from jail, I couldn't miss that putt, and I didn't. The miraculous four went down on the scorecard, and on the way to the next tee, Ben quipped, "I tied you on that hole, you know," which made me feel better about the scolding he had given me.

The Crosby

On a typically rainy and blustery winter Monday on California's Monterey Peninsula, I found myself struggling around Pebble Beach trying to qualify for Bing Crosby's "Clambake," a tournament every young pro wanted to play. I was not playing very well but had scratched like hell all the way around, and, standing on the eighteenth tee, I was

(L-R) Gardner, Bing Crosby, and Ben Hogan at the "Clambake."

one under for the day. Barring disaster, I knew I'd earned a spot in the tournament.

I stayed down the right side of the fairway, away from the ocean, on this quite long par-five. My second shot left me a rather long third over a big pine which guards the right side of the green. I hit a terrific shot, clearing the pine safely and landing on the green about fifteen feet from the hole. I was a little miffed at Bing for not giving me an exemption, since we'd become pretty good friends at Tamarisk, where he was a member.

As I stood over my putt for birdie, I was astonished, then angered, to see our Tour Supervisor, Joe Black, walk over and place his foot over the hole. He then walked down my line and *stepped on the ball.* I was seriously considering bashing Joe with my putter when he grinned and told me I was already in the tournament. As I was playing the thirteenth hole, where Crosby has a home, Bing had looked out his window and spotted me trying to qualify in that storm. Evidently he had called PGA Headquarters at the Lodge and informed the officials that they *were* to enter Gardner Dickinson in the tournament, and they had done so.

I was both relieved and appreciative, but, at that point, I didn't really want an exemption. I had worked like hell all day long and had *earned* my way in. But I knew that Bing's heart, as usual, was in the right place.

Head to Head with Nicklaus

In 1969, I finally won the Colonial tournament, one of my biggest thrills in golf. For the final round on Sunday, on a very windy day, I was paired with Jack Nicklaus. I'd always been an excellent wind player because I normally kept the ball down, an advantage when playing against a high-ball hitter like Nicklaus. I managed to knock a few drives past him that day, and at the eighteenth, after he really tied into one, I followed with a lower screamer, one of my best.

"You little squirt, you got me again," Jack squeaked, and sure enough, when we reached our drives I was twenty yards in front of him. I chose a seven-iron for my approach and, using the knockdown shot that I had learned from Hogan, drilled the ball over the flag and settled it about fifteen feet past the hole. Glancing up at the huge gallery by the clubhouse, I spotted Ben standing alone on a fire escape perched on the side of the building. Neatly dressed in a suit, he bowed slightly and doffed his felt hat toward me. That single gesture made what seemed like a century of practicing all worthwhile.

More Hogan Memories

In 1954, I played in my first Masters tournament. In those days it was a true invitational event, and I had been fortunate enough to receive an invitation after finishing in the top sixteen at the U.S. Open the previous year. That Open was played at Oakmont, where I'd played the last two rounds directly behind Hogan, finishing 3-3-3-3, just as he did, which got me into the Masters.

Playing the big fade of his, Ben was having trouble in practice rounds with a large pine tree sticking out over the fairway on the left of the Augusta National's seventh tee. Two days in a row, he clipped one of the branches, and when he hit it again on the third day he grumbled, "I can't play this damn hole. I don't care how narrow they want to make it in the landing area, but at least give me a chance to start the ball off the tee." Later, as we sat in front of our lockers, Ben was still talking about that limb when Cliff Roberts, the longtime chairman of the Masters, stopped by. Hogan complained about the tree, whereupon Roberts invited Ben to show him. They jumped in a golf cart and out they went to number seven. The next day, the limb was gone.

Ben Hogan won the Masters three times, and damn near won three other times. In 1942, he and Byron Nelson tied at the end of four rounds, and Byron beat him by one stroke in one of the greatest play-offs in golfing history. After five holes, Hogan led by three shots. He then played the next eleven holes in one under par but still lost five strokes to Nelson. Ben lost another in 1946, again by one stroke, when he three-putted the seventy-second green from eight feet, and in 1954 Sam Snead beat him in another play-off after they'd tied, just one

Ben Hogan (L) and Gardner at the 1954 Masters.

shot ahead of Billy Joe Patton, the sensational amateur. And who will ever forget Hogan's spine-chilling performance in the third round of the 1967 Masters, when he shot 30 on the back nine at the age of fifty-five? When his score of 66 was posted on the leader boards, galleries all over the course rose to their feet in a moving tribute to Ben's skill and courage.

An Unforgettable Scene

I recall another day, too, when Hogan was nearing the end of his career and had become a basket case on the greens. He, George Knudson and I were paired in the first two rounds of the Carling Open at Cuzzy Mingola's rolling Pleasant Valley course near Worcester, Massachusetts. The Boston area is real golf country, and Pleasant Valley always draws enormous crowds, but I don't believe I've ever seen so many people on a golf course. There must have been fifty thousand fans lining that first fairway when we teed off, and on some holes they were literally hanging out of the trees.

Hogan put on a magnificent display of golf that day, knocking down every flag, along with a pitiful exhibition of putting, yipping virtually every putt. As we moved down each of the eighteen fairways, packed tee to green with people, they cheered as Ben passed and many placed their hats over their hearts. It was the damndest thing I've ever witnessed.

The sound of the applause, sustained and echoing among the trees, was eerie: it made the hair stand up on the back of my neck. Ben trudged down the fairway, obviously embarrassed, all the while looking down while tipping his cap. At dinner that night, I asked Ben what had gone through his mind. He was completely flabbergasted, he said, and didn't know how to respond to such a tribute, so he just tipped his cap and kept going. I can tell you that it wasn't easy for George and me to continue to play, because both of us had goose bumps and misty eyes.

The Supreme Thrill

It took three years on tour before I won my first tournament, a period of time that now doesn't seem quite so long as it appeared to me then. I've won several tournaments that were richer, or more important, and played on two Rider Cup teams among many wonderful experiences in golf, but I don't think anything can equal the thrill of breaking through with that first victory.

Mine came at the 1956 Miami Beach Open, at Bayshore, after ten hard days of practice on my long game and my putting at Seminole, near my home in North Palm Beach. I began the final round five shots behind the leaders and awoke on Sunday morning to the cheerful sight of strong winds that were bending the palm trees close to the ground, conditions that were right up my alley. I was paired with Jimmy Demaret and Mike Souchak, fellows I admired and both great players, which was a good break for me.

At the sixteenth hole, a little 315-yard, well-trapped beauty, I nailed the driver and, aided by the following wind, the ball somehow avoided the bunkers in front and bounded right up onto the green. I holed the eagle putt, and as we were walking to the seventeenth tee, I overheard Demaret remark to Souchak, "You know, this skinny little dude might win this thing."

Pumped up like never before, I made an easy par on seventeen and, playing against the wind at the par-five eighteenth, killed my drive, then burned a four-wood onto the green, goosed my first putt up close and holed the next one for birdie. Fortunately none of the leaders matched my birdie at the last hole, making me the winner by one shot over Billy Maxwell. On the long drive up the next evening, to Wilmington, North Carolina, the tires on our car never touched the highway.

Golf's Greatest-Ever Swinger

Sometime in the sixties, I approached Sam Snead while he was knocking balls around the putting clock at one of the tournaments and asked him, rather hesitantly, if he would

Sam Snead and Gardner teamed up in the National Four-Ball Tournament, 1970.

be my partner in the upcoming PGA Four-Ball tournament. Sam grinned, and said, "You bet! We'll have a go."

Sam was, and still is, so very talented that it's an education just to be around him, and I was delighted that he had agreed to team up. Even then, Sam was the player nobody wanted to play a $50,000 Nassau against. Thus began a long and lucrative relationship .

There are many very intelligent people who believe that Samuel Jackson Snead may have been the greatest swinger of a golf club who ever stepped on a golf course. To me, Sam was a more powerful Bobby Jones, and, with the possible exception of putting, he set the modern standard of excellence for every club in the bag. He could hit them *all* better than anyone else, although he did occasionally have some problems with the driver. He'd hit twelve beauties, very long and straight, then maybe a couple over the fence.

But Sam looked better hitting one over the fence than anybody else did hitting their Sunday best. He had a gorgeous grip, his thick hands molded beautifully to the club, and he never had to fool with changing it. As I've described earlier, he was masterful with a one-iron and could hit it with control at least 250 yards. He could also hit a one-iron 150 yards, and up in the air, if you please.

Try that some time.

Most fans liked to watch Snead's tremendous drives, or those effortless, towering one-irons, but personally I enjoyed watching him "cut up" a little six-iron from 135 yards to within two feet of the pin, or feather a soft pitch in to a hard green, as Sam loved to say, "like a butterfly with sore feet." Not many people remember that Snead was the best bunker player in the game, and I could not tell you how many times he chipped in from off the green.

If that isn't enough for you, Sam was also, by his peers' reckoning, the world's premier wedge player. He probably acquired this skill because he hit so damn many huge drives. He would drop those little wedge shots so gently and so stiff it made your mouth water; you couldn't detect a conscious hit when he played the shot. But with as much God-given talent as he obviously possessed, don't think that Sam didn't work at his game. He hit almost as many practice balls as Ben Hogan, and, when not on tour, still played thirty-six holes of golf most days.

Snead knows as much about a golf swing as anyone I've met. He can accidentally pass out more sound, simple information than a clubhouse full of Leadbetters, Ballards or Haneys could contrive in a lifetime. Sam's technical knowledge is immense, although I don't think he pays much attention to all the fancy terms you hear about, nor most of the fads and foolishness that pass for golf instruction these days. Sam is generous in sharing his knowledge with others, but he's smart enough to know that you can't put a Volkswagen engine in a Cadillac and expect it to run like a Cadillac.

One of my favorite Snead stories concerns a pro-am partner who asked Sam how he could "spin back" a three-iron shot like the Old Master. Sam stared at the man for a moment, then asked, "How far do you hit a three-iron?"

"Oh, about 150 yards," the fellow replied.

Sam grinned. "Then why the hell do you want it to back up?"

Snead taught me how important temper is in championship golf. As any of his contemporaries will tell you, Sam had one, but he understood that it can work for you as well as against you. I don't think there's ever been a player worth a damn who didn't have a temper, but the great ones learn how to control it, how to make it work for them. Jack Nicklaus has been a superb example of this, too.

Sam Snead was living proof of the importance of a long swing. Even though his swing shortened as he passed into his sixties and seventies, Sam always had a full, flowing backswing. Like everyone else's, his swing would shorten sometimes when he tried to steer the ball, particularly with his drives. Practicing one time at La Costa for the CBS Classic, I remember Sam's drives landing in the deep rough because, in my opinion, he had shortened his swing.

"Well, I guess everybody has to get old," I finally said.

Sam's eyes narrowed. "What do you mean?"

"I remember when you used to swing that driver back at least to horizontal, but you can't get it up there anymore," I said.

"You watch this backswing," Sam declared. He took the club back at least a foot farther, and blistered a long, straight one down the middle.

I stared at him. "You mean you can swing like that, and you don't?" Thereafter, Sam gave me the whole swing.

We played for some years as partners and enjoyed considerable success. Our first victory came in the CBS Golf Classic in 1967 at Firestone Country Club in Akron, Ohio,

Gardner and Sam Snead (C) being interviewed by Cary Middlecoff (R) after winning the 1967 CBS Golf Classic.

a made-for-television show. We managed to beat Julius Boros and Don January, one up, in the final on a day plagued by high wind and sleet. We finished in the dusk, and quite a finish it was. We hit four great drives, then four wonderful second shots to Firestone's long par-four finishing hole. Boros holed his putt, a twenty-footer, and then it was my turn. Although I was closer to the hole, Sam elected to putt first and drained a twelve-footer to close out the match. Afterwards, I bought a case of Moet & Chandon to celebrate, and Sam, who rarely drank, even helped me polish it off. I got him drunk twice on the way to San Diego.

Victory in the Legends

Our victory in the first Legends of Golf is probably the one people remember best. This was another event staged for television, created by Fred Raphael and Jimmy Demaret to showcase the famous players who had passed the age of fifty. Some of these legendary players, like Snead and Demaret, were in their sixties, and Gene Sarazen was in his seventies, but they still could hit all the shots, and none had lost the desire to compete. A few still competed on the regular tour, but most were headed for the limbo that overtakes players in their fifties and sixties. Raphael and Demaret sensed that there was an audience for an event that brought all of the great names together and showcased their talents and personalities. How right they were, because, as we've seen, the Legends of Golf gave birth to the enormously successful Senior Tour. No one, including Demaret and Raphael, had any idea how successful it would become.

That first Legends tournament in 1978 was a real jump starter because of the dramatic finish. Sam Snead birdied the last three holes, which was vintage Snead and great television, enabling us to edge the great Australian pair of Kel Nagle and Peter Thomson by a single stroke. The seventeenth hole at Onion Creek is a little uphill par-three of about 145 yards, and on the final day the pin was cut in the back of the top level of the two-tiered green. Sam always asked me to play first because if I hit the fairway or the green, which I usually did, he could then freewheel it and go for the flag, or for distance. Slightly keyed up, I crushed a nine-iron and flew the ball onto the green about twenty-five feet left of the hole. Sam asked what club I had hit, and I told him.

"Shoot, I'm your partner," Sam said, not believing it. "What the hell did you hit?" I showed him the nine-iron with the divot-dirt still on it, and Sam just shook his head. He changed clubs twice, then feathered a shot up toward the flagstick that nearly went in. He stuck the club in my face, and I saw that it was a five-iron. For the most part, you see, Snead and Hogan seldom hit their iron shots head on, but rather slid the leading edge up under the ball at impact, which I called *clipping* the ball, so that the shot would come down soft and light. Too bad Greg Norman never got to witness that shot.

On the last hole, a par-five, I pitched up pretty close, well inside of my partner. But Sam, the old scene-stealer, wanted to putt first, and he poured it right in for his third consecutive birdie and the victory. Champions always seem to find a way to win, and Sam did it more often than anyone else. We played as a team in the Legends for a couple more years, but eventually Sam dumped me for three-putting so many times — and I can't blame him, either.

Some golf writers have suggested that Snead can't be considered among the greatest players of all time because of his failure to win a U.S. Open. Anyone dumb enough to draw that conclusion hasn't bothered to study his golf history and consequently deserves little consideration as a writer about the game. It's a dirty shame that Sam didn't win the Open — just one of those tricks fate sometimes plays. He finished second four times, but if you had asked every contestant in those Opens to name the best player in the world at the time, I imagine most of them would have picked Sam Snead.

Several years ago, at a Senior Tour dinner honoring Sam, we presented him with ninety-four medals, respresenting the ninety-four official tournaments he won during his career (although Sam said we were about thirty-five short, because that's how many he won before the PGA and the so-called golf writers started keeping records). To give you some idea of what a great player and winner Sam Snead was, the next guy on the list, Jack Nicklaus, has won seventy-one official tournaments.

There have been some bad knocks on Sam's take-me-or-leave-me personality, and maybe prior to my knowing him some of them were valid. But since 1953, I think you'd have to place Sam among the world's good guys. He's pleased many a man and offended damn few, and I think it's about time the sports world gave him his due, while he's still with us.

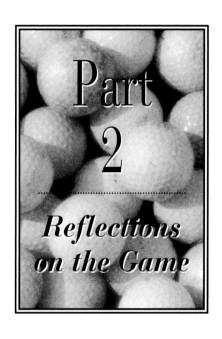

Part 2

2

Reflections
on the Game

On Gurus and Other Nostrums

It never ceases to amaze me how naive the average touring pro is, and I include members of both the men's and ladies' tours in that assessment. The plain truth is that pros, as a group, are not much different from average weekend golfers in their search for swing nostrums and cures. To reach either professional tour, a player's skills must be in the top one-tenth of one percent of all golfers in the world. Yet for instruction and advice, they travel long distances and pay big money to see instructors who, let us be frank, never could play the game well.

One of the currently popular golf teachers, David Lead-better, was asked why he had never been a top player. "I was just too much of a perfectionist to play well," he replied. I had to chuckle, because all the golf perfectionists I know either play on tour now or have in the past.

Should you come to me for instruction, you figure, correctly, that I know a few things about golf that you don't know. I'm certain that good golf is played by feel, and I also know that winning feel is produced by a knowledge of good mechanics that work under pressure. The more experience one has of playing with good mechanics and a winning feel, under tournament pressure, the better chance one has of being able to pass that feeling on to someone else. If that were not the case, I would merely be passing along warmed-over ideas that I've picked up second-hand by reading what others have written, by listening to what someone has told me, or by guessing what it feels like to play winning golf. Even worse, I might simply be experimenting on people.

Such teaching "resources" might work for the average golfer, but for those on tour, or with tour potential, I think I'd want to see a Toney Penna, or a Byron Nelson, or a Cary Middlecoff, or a Bob Toski, or a Jackie Burke — someone who has compiled a record as a winning player.

I just don't see how you can impart that winning feel if you have never personally experienced it. If you'd never experienced an orgasm, how could you possibly explain it?

Swing Merchants and Myths

There's an old saying, "Them that can play, play; and them that can't, teach." This isn't always the case, but too many would-be "star" instructors hang out a teaching sign, then offer students some sort of preconceived notion of what all golf swings should look like. God only knows where they pick up these ideas. But then, myths are much easier to peddle than reality.

Generally speaking, if you find a teacher who keeps talking about "the" golf swing, you'd better get away from him, *quickly*. On the other hand, pay close attention to the fellow who talks about "a" golf swing. I would be suspicious of anyone who claims there is one way to swing a golf club, because I know it simply is not true. If you doubt this, turn on your television any weekend and watch the world's best players. No two of them swing alike.

Not everyone is an athletic genius, nor does everyone think alike, so asking a student to learn a preconceived template for a golf swing, or to follow a rigid system is, in my opinion, an invitation to failure. You'll be able to systematize golf instruction the day you're able to clone people, along with their coordination and their intelligence.

We hear a good deal of talk from these so-called experts about "basic fundamentals," a term that to me is both redundant and inaccurate. It implies that all great players do things identically, such as, say, grip the club in a certain way. We might all agree that a left-hand grip that shows one and a half or two knuckles is desirable, but it is certainly not mandatory. If it were, Gene Sarazen, Paul Azinger, Grier Jones, Bernhard Langer, Dan Sikes, Judy Rankin, Lee Trevino, and Fred Couples couldn't possibly have played championship golf, because all of them had or have three-knuckle grips, or stronger.

In my time, I've observed a large number of ambitious young players trying to "curl under," that is, rotate the left wrist under the shaft during the first two feet of backswing. These poor fellows wind up with a flat left wrist at the top of their swings, with the clubface dead shut. Only a few players are gifted enough, and strong enough, to play from so shut-faced a position. Two very likeable but misinformed non-playing golf professionals devised this gizmo twenty years or more ago as part of a system they called " Square-to-Square." They forgot to add "to Oblivion" at the end of the title, because most golfers who tried their system were led in to golfing purgatory. Later one of the authors publicly retracted his advice, admitting he had been wrong, which, in my opinion, takes a big man.

Heat and Gas

The present worldwide fascination with non-playing gurus is hard to explain. For me, it rose to dizzying heights when I opened a copy of *Golf Digest* and saw an article entitled, "How to Handle the Pressure of Tournament Golf," by Peter Kostis. Now, *Golf Digest* is, in my opinion, the best of the golf publications — but Peter Kostis, indeed. This is the same fellow we see on national television demonstrating golf shots in a feature dubbed, "The Art of Playing." It is my understanding that Kostis shoots at his best in the mid-70s, although I have been unable to locate any record of his performance on any tour. In the television feature, we see Kostis demonstrating a backswing that is some two feet longer than his normal swing, but unfortunately we are not shown where his shots land, which, to me at least, is fairly important. Incidentally, I was intrigued to see that this program was sponsored in part by a company called Acushnet, which happens to make a pretty good golf ball called Titleist, and which for years announced in its ads, "Remember, no one is paid to play Titleist."

Soon I expect Peter Kostis will tell us what it's like preparing to drive from the first tee at Augusta National in your first Masters . . . mouth dry, hands shaking, knees locked for fear that if you bent them your thighs would collapse and you'd pitch to the ground. That sort of thing is called "heat" by my generation of tour players. I'd like to see Kostis stand on the last tee of any tour event, needing a par-four to win, and describe the slender ribbon of fairway surrounded by monstrous rough, the tiny green perched between Alcatraz and Sing Sing, and the enormous psychic effort required to force any kind of workable swing in the circumstances.

"Gas," we used to call it, because you never knew until it happened who would survive and who would pass out. No one who hasn't *been* there can possibly know what taking gas feels like, just as no one who hasn't *played* under that kind of pressure can truly understand what makes a golf swing that will stand up to it.

I suppose we must have empathy for the non-playing teachers, since our own organization, The PGA of America, is promoting a standardized system that, in theory, its membership can teach to everyone. Indeed, we now have a PGA Teaching Manual, which was several years in compilation by another non-playing guru, Dr. Gary Wiren. In his teachings, it has been reported that the good doctor concerns himself with things like whether the left lobe of the brain controls the backswing or the downswing. I have been told that he has predicted that the ultimate "swing of the future" will begin only after the golfer has carefully *placed* the club at the top of the backswing, then visually checked to see that his top of swing position is correct before allowing the club to descend.

Well, maybe so, but I doubt that anyone reading this now will ever see a day when the world's best players use such a method. I have to believe that the downswing is influenced by *how* the club arrives at the top, and that *how* it gets there also plays a considerable role in establishing the rhythm of a swing. But, more to the point, I doubt seriously if the PGA, or anyone else, can teach a fellow to teach from a book. Not even this one.

A Simple, Elegant 'Secret'

Non-playing ace teacher David Leadbetter, mentioned earlier, has become quite popular today by advocating that golfers strap their elbows closely to their sides; that in the downswing they move to the left rather than forward; and that they restrain the use of the hands. It seems improbable to me that he could sell a world-class player on such ideas, for, in effect, he is saying that *all* the great players and teachers who preceded him were crazy as hell. It is difficult to imagine a sane person seeking to play good golf by trying to restrain the use of the hands in a golf swing. Indeed, if there is a truism in golf, it might be this: *Do not allow the body to take your swing to a place where you can't get at the ball with your hands, at the proper time.* That proposition is worth committing to memory, because it embodies one of the simplest, most elegant "secrets" of golfing technique.

Most of our golf periodicals pound the public with the names of successful tour players who have been helped by non-playing gurus, but the magazines would do an equally valuable service if they also reported the golfing cemetery created by these same teachers. I can assure you that more than a few bodies are buried there.

If you are a truly gifted player, or someone with tour potential, I would leave you with this thought: Can you imagine Ben Hogan taking lessons from one of these gurus?

Jack Nicklaus

Jack Nicklaus has always referred to his great friend Jack Grout as his "lifelong teacher." From personal observation of the two at work together, I would say that "teaching," in the formal sense, was the wrong word for their later relationship. You don't win twenty major championships without knowing how to play golf. What Nicklaus sought and received from Grout, pretty much from the time Jack turned pro, was mostly affirmation and confirmation that he was still applying the fundamentals that he had learned from Grout in his teens. Jack Grout, who had played the tour in his youth with Ben Hogan and Byron Nelson, also provided tremendous encouragement and support to Jack, much in the manner of a fine coach.

Although throughout his career Nicklaus has always been ready to listen to tips from players he respected, the first time he really worked with anyone but Grout came in early 1980, following his then worst-ever competitive year, in an effort to rebuild a winning game. He was successful in this, because in 1980, after being written off for at least the third time, he won the 1980 U.S. Open and PGA Championship.

His teacher of choice was a good friend from his amateur and early tour days, Phil Rodgers, who had achieved a fair amount of success himself in both these arenas, largely through his superlative short game. It was the short game that Phil and Jack mostly worked on, particularly the little flip wedges and chip shots, with Jack Grout always in the wings as overall counselor, booster and long-game supervisor.

Rodgers had once been a protégé of Paul Runyan, a small

but tenacious player who was a leading money-winner in the mid-thirties, and twice the PGA champion. Because of his short stature and inability to match the distances his rivals could achieve, Paul had developed a remarkable short game. A superb fairway-wood player, he became so deadly around the greens that his contemporaries called him "Little Poison." Later Runyan became a respected teacher and is still in great demand. His short game technique is based on eliminating all wrist action in chipping and putting. He is also an advocate of the split-grip putting style.

Runyan had been quoted as saying that as great a player as Jack Nicklaus was, around the green he was a ten-handicapper, and one day Jack asked me about Paul's short game system. I explained it as best I could, recommended he buy a copy of Paul's book, and, after he did, suggested he see Runyan himself. As I recall, Jack saw Paul on one of his West Coast trips but ended up with Rodgers, who was perhaps the leading disciple and tour-playing exponent of Runyan's short-game methods. I must tell you that Phil worked wonders with Jack's short game, even though Runyan told me later that Rodgers had "out-Runyaned" Paul himself. Phil added a few touches of his own. Rodgers had developed a very wristy flip wedge shot that he dubbed the "whirly-bird." While Jack was still learning this effective but dangerous shot, he produced a number of silly-looking "poops" around the greens, much to the horror of the purists in the galleries.

Eventually Jack mastered that shot and other new ones, and I thought he improved tremendously around the greens. At the very least, Rodgers had caused Nicklaus to practice his short game a great deal more than he ever had before.

After Jack Grout passed away, Nicklaus worked for a while with Peter Kostis, the well-spoken, ambitious fellow who taught in Boca Raton not far from the Nicklaus home, and who had helped Jack's son, Jackie, then aspiring to play the tour. Kostis was a protégé of Jim Flick and had worked his way up in the *Golf Digest* instruction schools before setting out on his own to attract clients among the tour pros. Although it seemed to me that Jack's swing began to shorten noticeably as he worked with Kostis, the relationship persisted until Jack decided Peter's approach to the game was a little too "mechanical" for him.

Not long after that, Jim Flick offered some thoughts to Nicklaus during a tournament in Arizona that apparently sounded very much like what Jack Grout had taught him since childhood. From this alliance emerged the Nicklaus-Flick Golf School, a commercial venture based in North Palm Beach. Some time after that, Nicklaus worked with yet another non-playing guru by the name of Rick Smith, once again as the result of a recommendation from another son, Gary, who is also an aspiring tour pro.

What is so puzzling to me in all of this is the picture of the greatest golfer in history lending an ear to instructors who cannot possibly know a fraction of what Jack knows about the game of golf. The main change in Nicklaus's game from the glory years, apart from putting, is that his backswing is two feet shorter than it used to be. In his younger days, Jack would swing back far enough that the club was slightly below horizontal, and pointed slightly across the line. Also in those days he used to swing forty percent harder than he now does.

Jack had a great gift that no one talks about: He arrived at the top of his swing with the wrists fully cocked, but damned if you could tell *where* he cocked them. Everything was smoothly integrated. In fact, his wrists broke quite late in the upswing, but you had a hard time seeing exactly where or how this happened.

Everyone talked about Jack's flying right elbow and how terrible it was, but I never thought it was a fault. I think Jack simply had the idea, very early in his career, of making the swing arc straighter than anyone before him. By that I mean that he swung the club more upright, and therefore kept it closer to the target line longer than anyone else. If you're strong enough to keep the club on that straighter path and still deliver its head to the ball at great speed —

which Jack certainly can — how can it be wrong?

Study Nicklaus's swing and you will see that his left knee goes straight out as the backswing starts; it's almost the first move he makes. (Ben Hogan did the same thing.) When the left knee moves out like that, it allows the right side to move out of the way, clearing room for a full, free backswing. Like Hogan, Jack created a little channel that allowed his arms and hands to swing down on an inside path with maximum speed.

But, all talk of technique aside, the real key to Jack's success was his fantastic ability to score. His drives sometimes went in the rough, but he could plow the ball out of the tallest grass and get it on the green; bad lies simply didn't affect him as much as they did others. Jack also got tremendous height with his one-iron and two-iron, which meant that he could stop them better than his rivals. And, of course, there was his putting. He was magnificent on the greens. Jack had the ability to will himself to putt just as well under pressure, or perhaps better, than when he was playing a casual round.

Jack Nicklaus and Gardner doing equipment research and development, circa 1986.

There is no denying that Jack Nicklaus's record is second to none, but his swing was considered unusual when he appeared on the scene. His extremely upright plane was very difficult to copy, but copy it they did; or, at least they tried to, whether or not they had Jack's great strength. But Nicklaus buried every cat that came along, and, I'm convinced, could bury some more if he truly wanted to. I remember that Johnny Miller would have us believe that he almost invented the game and played the best golf of all time when he won a few winter tour events in the mid-1970s that Jack didn't enter.

Then along would come Big Jack in the next few events and bury Miller, and we'd hear no more from Johnny for quite a while. I think Johnny, who was a beautiful player, had truly convinced himself that he was the only player who has *ever* put all his second shots within ten feet of the pins. Well, there were many tournaments in which even I could do that, but the big difference was that Johnny could *make* almost all those eight to ten footers. Then, we'd hear a great deal from Tom Weiskopf who, it seemed, spent half his life suggesting to writers that his beautiful golf swing was just as good as, if not better than, Nicklaus's. Jack then came out and buried ol' Tom, and that was the end of that. Though he never said so, that must have tickled the hell out of Big Jack.

'Skanking'

In its simplest form, winning at the highest levels of golf is the ability to make a number. Players who are successful on tour seem to have a facility for adjusting quickly to any conditions in which they find themselves. Patience is certainly a virtue in golf (Nicklaus believes it's his top competitive weapon), but I believe what separates the champions from the good ones is the ability to adjust very quickly to any type of weather, wind, fast or slow greens, lousy caddies, bad breaks, unruly fans, and any other irritations and inconveniences. Champions display this ability in every round they play, and those who would be champions need to develop it.

Most successful players carry around in their mental computers little tricks or gimmicks, learned from experience, that will immediately stop, for example, hooking, or slicing. When the player hits that "hook button," his computer better spit out a non-hook correction, and one that works right now. And he better have several more at the ready, in case the first one doesn't work instantly. Indeed, that's one of the reasons we practice so much — to discover and file away such information for future competitive use.

The class players, those fellows who seldom post 76 or 77 on their bad days, have a special technique for those times when nothing seems to be working. Through the use of carefully nurtured, heat-proof swing keys, they can almost always get around in no more than 72 or 73 strokes. The techniques vary from player to player, but on tour, everyone refers to the process as a "skank" swing. A skank swing is one that will get your ball somewhere in or very close to the fairway, and somewhere on or near to the green, so that the highest score you're likely to make is a bogey.

Some players are great skankers, some appear to be permanent skankers, and some don't have a clue about skanking. I'm not sure that I can tell you how to come up with an effective skank swing, but one of my techniques on really bad days was simply to punch the ball around the course. When my rhythm was off, or I felt uncoordinated, I found that if I purposely hit the ball lower, I didn't seem to hit it as far off-line as with my normal trajectory. Also — though I confess I don't know how to do this on purpose — I found that, with a driver, "necked" tee shots and those hit toward the sole plate didn't go very far but usually ended up in play. In my case, gripping the club down the shaft, as much as three or four inches, helped on those days when I could barely do anything correctly, including write my name legibly.

The Greatest Triumvirate

How would golfers of the past stack up against today's players? Who are the greatest players you've seen? You'd be surprised how many times people ask me questions like these.

Quite frankly, I don't see how you can compare golfers from different eras by any objective standards, so, even though I've gained some strong impressions over the past fifty years, I'm afraid my opinion, like anyone else's, is purely subjective. I'm confident , however, that my contemporaries would be disappointed if I tried to beat around the bush, so for what it's worth, I'm compelled to say that, measured purely by tee-to-green standards, I don't see any Ben Hogans, Sam Sneads or Byron Nelsons on the horizon. This may rankle some of the big names in golf today, but I repeat that I simply don't see a player who could be compared with those three, for either the tournament performance or the pure ball-striking proficiency they achieved, day after day, week after week, and year after year for so much of their lives.

A doyen is a leader, an expert, a virtuoso, an artist, a master. Well, those guys were doyens of a generation of professional American golfers who just never seemed to hit shots as far off line as the leading players do today. They'd have cut their throats if they had to go find some of the balls hit by today's supposed superstars. Hogan, Nelson and Snead dominated an era that included players like Jimmy Demaret, Ralph Guldahl, Lloyd Mangrum, Henry Picard and, later, Jackie Burke, Cary Middlecoff and Julius Boros. This "Greatest Triumvirate" was so good that any one of them could putt just "average" and still win, because their games didn't revolve around the putter. Consider that Byron Nelson won eleven tournaments in a row, and nineteen in one calendar year. Shortly thereafter, Ben Hogan won thirteen tournaments and Snead eleven in a single year.

They were that much better than the rest.

When Nelson, Snead and Hogan achieved their peaks, they were in their middle to late thirties, relatively late in life compared with many of today's top players. Hogan told me once that you weren't supposed to know anything about golf until after you were thirty-five, which I guess was because Ben was about thirty-six before he finally figured out his own game. I can tell you that Nicklaus knew a lot about golf before he was thirty-five. Long before.

As all of us know, Jack Nicklaus was very strong physically, but it's hard to say he was any stronger than Sam Snead. The good Lord only puts a body like Snead's down here about once every thousand years. Sam could beat you at anything — the fifty-yard dash, shooting, wrestling, tossing pennies, basketball, or pool, you name it. Even at age eighty he is still a physical marvel.

The generation of Hogan, Nelson and Snead seemed to work harder at their games than my generation did, and definitely more than most of Jack's generation. Part of the answer may be that there were fewer tournaments then, and so the players couldn't compete nearly as often as today's players do. Logic suggests that players back then had more time to analyze their games and learn new techniques. They developed a pride and confidence in their ability to play just the right shot, in any conditions and in any conceivable circumstance.

Everyone knows about Ben Hogan's work ethic, and surely no one ever worked harder, but nobody ever talked much about Sam Snead pounding balls. Perhaps he didn't work as long on some things as Ben did, but perhaps he didn't need to. If he didn't play thirty-six holes each day, he'd play eighteen and spend the rest of it practicing. Every day on tour, I'd see him practice some phase of his game, even chipping from the fringe. Most of us neglected that, but not Sam. Consequently, Sam chipped in a lot because he *owned* that shot.

I noticed that Sam rarely chipped the same way twice.

Didn't he follow any special method for chipping, I asked him? "Hell, no, it's whatever I feel like," he replied. Bob Jones was much the same in this regard. Jones said that if he felt a hook coming on, he wasn't about to stand up there and face left. "I'm going to face right," he said. "I'm going to *join* that hook."

One reason why Snead maybe didn't hit as many balls as Hogan was he caught on so much quicker than most. With Sam, it didn't take many repetitions. I think Hogan knew that he needed more repetitions to master a move, and I always felt that it took more for me, too. I guess I operated on the theory that if a little bit is good, then a whole lot just has to be better. That isn't necessarily so, because I've prac- ticed myself into and out of more good swings and more good putting strokes than you can possibly imagine. I believed that if I stayed out there and worked hard I would automatically get better, and that's just not so. I didn't have sense enough to practice until I "had it," and then go home to sleep on it — as Nicklaus, for one, always had the sense and self-discipline to do. (Or was Jack, maybe, a little lazy?)

Sam Snead's golf swing became the world's model, replac- ing Bob Jones's swing, and if today's and tomorrow's young players want to copy a golf swing, I suggest they dig up some of Sam's old films. He possessed Jones's beautiful, seemingly effortless rhythm, but with much more power. Snead appeared to be perfection itself, and I guess he came as close to it as anyone has. Jimmy Demaret paid Sam the ultimate compliment when some silly golf writer asked him, "Just how good is this fellow Snead?" Jimmy shook his head and chuckled, "Son, Sam hits *every* shot the way the rest of us wish we could hit just one before we die."

Byron Nelson was hard to figure. Although Snead, Nelson, and Hogan were born in the same year, 1912, Byron reached his prime a little earlier than the other two, and, of course, he all but retired well before he was forty. We all knew he was great because he won all those tournaments, but it went past that with Nelson. When Byron was in his

Gardner gets a wedge lesson from the master, Byron Nelson, circa 1985.

prime, he hit more shots cold stiff to the hole than anyone who has ever played, except maybe Snead. I mean cold stiff kick-aways. It was almost as though Byron were starting out each day three or four under par. He was a magnificent driver, perhaps not quite as long as Hogan or Snead but long enough, and a superb long-iron player, maybe the best there ever was. Byron had that big dip down into the ball, so his swing wasn't as pretty to watch as Sam's, but his shots were. When Byron was "on," I don't think there has been anyone better.

Hogan controlled the ball better, day after day, than anyone in the world. Although he might not have knocked as many cold stiff as Nelson did, I feel confident that Ben put more shots within eight feet or better than anyone in history. Hogan's tempo was a little faster, but if you discounted that tempo, Ben's swing, to me, was just as gorgeous as Sam's.

He looked absolutely wonderful at address, put the club in a beautiful position at the top, and his head didn't move an iota coming down. He had a magnificent full finish, the back of the right hand facing the hole, as it should. Incidentally, when you rank the greatest iron players of all time, you can start with Hogan, Nelson and Snead. They were all marvelous. They never seemed to hit their irons a flat, head-on blow, but rather seemed to clip the ball, which produced a much softer and more controlled flight. When I hit a seven-iron, Hogan would frequently hit a five from the same spot, and Sam might even hit a four. But you just try to get inside them.

By one of those odd coincidences, Snead, Nelson, and Hogan appeared on the scene at the same time, and, between them, they defined the art of hitting a golf ball. Nothing I have seen leads me to think that we will someday learn something about a golf swing that they didn't know. I doubt if ever again anyone will combine such physical gifts with the cold, driving will of Hogan, the fierce competitive heart of Nelson, or the raw appetite and killer instinct of Snead. A thousand years from now, if someone comes along with Snead's swing, or Hogan's, you can be damned sure that you'll be watching the best player of that era, or any other. There are just so many things you can do with a golf club, and they could do them all.

There was a presence about those three players that no one else had. They impressed me as being so far superior to the rest of us that to consider ourselves in the same league was unthinkable. They just made you feel inadequate, comparing what they could do, and did week after week, to your own game. When any of those fellows put a club in his hands and waggled it, you knew. Once in a while, I would get the same feeling about Cary Middlecoff.

Nobody else in my lifetime has made me feel like that. I don't know why, but I never felt that way about Jack Nicklaus, and I certainly should have because he has the best record of them all. But I never felt that, if I played my very best, it wasn't possible to beat Nicklaus, which is how I always felt about Nelson, Snead and Hogan. I don't give a damn what I did, I wasn't as good as they were — and maybe Middlecoff, sometimes. In the 1940s, long after he had ended his career, I used to watch Bob Jones play a few holes at Augusta National. He was certainly not a contender then, but he had that same aura.

Hogan the Gamesman

I don't think these great golfers deliberately intimidated others, although I know from personal experience that they were not above some good-natured gamesmanship. This was a side that Ben Hogan rarely showed to the public, but it was there.

I can remember warming up before a practice round at the 1965 PGA Championship at Laurel Valley, in Ligonier, Pennsylvania, the year Dave Marr beat out Bill Casper and Jack Nicklaus and a fellow named Dickinson. It was hot as Hades on the range, and Hogan called over to the Hebert brothers and me, saying that he was ready to play. Jay Hebert asked Ben if he had put up a ball on the first tee, to mark our place in line.

"What do you mean?" Ben asked. He knew exactly what Jay meant.

"Did you put a ball up there to mark our place in line?"

"No. Did you?"

"Hell, we won't get to tee off for an hour or two," said Jay.

"Baloney," said Hogan, and off he went to the first tee, with the three of us trailing behind. Seeing the long line at the tee, I said, "C'mon, Ben, we might as well go putt."

"Hell, no, I've already putted," said Hogan, and he walked up on the tee itself and placed his foot on the right tee marker. Well, now, here are all these little old club pros, teeing off in waves, and I know this is going to be fun.

Each group insisted that Hogan and his foursome tee off in front of them, but Ben waved them on, saying, "Oh, no. Go right ahead. I'll wait my turn."

I have never seen golf pros make swings like I saw that day. Ben laid those steely blues of his on those poor fellas, then kept on staring at each one as he drove off. Pretty soon their hands began to tremble, their throats to clog and their waggles reduced themselves to wiggles. As each addressed the ball, Ben would turn to me, close his eyes and silently shake his head. Sure enough, here came the sky balls and duck-hooks. Balls fell everywhere — right rough, left rough, sometimes not even a hundred yards from the tee. It was pathetic. For twenty minutes no one, as I recall, hit a decent drive. Finally one of the club pros came up to Ben and said, "Mr. Hogan, you just stopped this practice round. If you don't tee off in front of me, nobody else will get to play today." So off we finally went. Although I never asked him about it, I could tell Ben enjoyed intimidating those fellows. But he affected all of us that way, even when he wasn't trying.

As the captain of the 1967 Ryder Cup team, held at the Champions Club in Houston, Ben pulled up in his golf cart beside the third tee to watch us during a practice round. His wife Valerie was sitting beside him, and he was dressed in coat and tie, felt hat, creased trousers and polished shoes. I managed to hit a good drive, and then it was Johnny Pott's turn. Hogan stared at him unsmilingly. Johnny couldn't stand it.

"Hey, Cap'n, Mister Ben," he said, with that big wide grin of his, "can you do me a favor? You got anything else to do today?" Hogan asked why. "Well, I sure would like for you to follow me the rest of the day," said Johnny. Again, Hogan asked why. "Looky here, Mister Hawk, if I can hit it with you sitting there watching, I ain't gonna worry about those darn British."

Pott proceeded to hit the worst-looking snap hook imaginable, smiled weakly and said, "See what I mean?" I guess

Johnny thought that if he could play under that kind of pressure, he could play under any.

There was a droll side to Ben Hogan, too, that he would allow people to see occasionally. At the Houston Open one year when the pairings came out, journeyman pro Ron Cerrudo discovered to his dismay that he'd been paired the first two rounds with Hogan. "Oh, no!" wailed Cerrudo. "Has anybody got any gray flannels?" Ron was from Southern California and wore all those wild, zooty threads — trick clothes, we called them — and he was worried that Hogan might disapprove. Word got back to Ben about his concern.

The next day, Cerrudo walked out in a very subdued outfit, looking pretty nice despite his big mop of hair. Walking up to Ben, who was leaning on a club smoking a cigarette, he stuck out his hand and stammered, "Mister Hogan, I'm Ron Cerrudo."

Hogan ignored the handshake and said, "I know who you are, son." Then he looked at Ron for a long moment and said, "You're a hooker, aren't you?" Cerrudo nodded. "Well, I'm a fader," Ben continued. "You see that line going right down the middle of the fairway?" There was no such line, but Rod nodded vigorously. "You just stay on the left of that line, and I'll stay on the right of it, and we'll be fine," said Hogan.

"Yes sir, I sure will," replied Cerrudo, whereupon Ben decided that enough was enough, cracked a smile, put his arm around the youngster and shook his hand.

In that same tournament, however, Ben one day really tore into the late George Knudson for what he regarded as the Canadian's unsightly appearance. We were in the locker-room, where Ben was getting a massage for his bad legs, when George strolled by, red handlebar mustache, dark glasses, the trick clothes, hair sticking up all over his head.

"Knudson," Hogan's voice thundered. George turned around. "Is that you, George?"

Knudson peered intently, then replied: "Yes sir, Mister

Hogan." George idolized Ben.

"C'mere," growled Hogan. We could hear the whole thing as Ben proceeded to chew a hole right through poor old George. "Dammit, you're a disgrace not only to the tour, but to humanity. You look just awful. As lucky as you are to be playing out here, you ought to be ashamed of yourself. You know all those ole guys who wear striped ties and blazers, the guys you think are fuddy-duddies? They're the ones putting up the money so you can play. You ought to show them how grateful you are by showing up on the first tee dressed in black tie and tuxedo."

For nearly fifteen minutes Ben chewed on George unmercifully, and you could have heard a pin drop in that lockerroom, it was so quiet. No one dared say a thing, because we knew Ben wasn't kidding. The next day, Knudson showed up with a short haircut, a somber outfit and no mustache.

Not long after that, the Colonial Country Club in Fort Worth held an anniversary dinner for past champions, with Hogan serving as the master of ceremonies. In addition to the past champions, the club had invited the Air Force aerobatics team, the Thunderbirds.

Ben rose, lifted his glass in welcome, and said, "Ladies and gentlemen, I want you all to look around the room at this fine gathering. All of these people are great champions, and they all have one thing in common." He paused, while everyone wondered what he was going to say next. "They all have a nice haircut," he said, and sat down.

Ben thought gray was a loud color. I told him that gray wasn't a color at all. "Oh, yes it is," he said. People think that Ben never wore anything but gray or brown, but he would sometimes wear navy blue, white and even yellow. He wore Allen Solly shirts made of Pima cotton, the most expensive you could buy in those days. He never had them washed, always dry-cleaned. His white caps were made by Cavanaugh on Park Avenue in New York, the priciest hatter in the world at the time. I know, because in the summer of

1953, Fred Wampler and I ordered a dozen apiece. Wamp had peeked inside Ben's cap during lunch one day and found out they were made by Cavanaugh, so we called and told them to send us each a dozen of the same caps Hogan ordered, and to be sure to give us his price, too. Hogan probably got his free, but they charged us twenty-five dollars apiece, and sent them C.O.D., too. I can tell you that after we got over the shock, we took good care of those caps; they must have lasted us five years apiece.

The Irrepressible Mr. Penna

Toney Penna

By the time my generation reached the pro tour in the early 1950s, Toney Penna was an established figure in American golf. Anthony Geraldo Penna was born in Naples, Italy, and received very little formal education, which gave little hint of his eventual influence on the game and the pro tour. His family immigrated to the the United States, settling in Harrison, New York, where Toney began caddying at a young age. From caddie, Toney moved up to apprentice clubmaker to Alex Smith, the famous pro at the Westchester Biltmore hotel and golf complex outside New York City. Smith had won two U.S. Opens, and his brother Willie had won another. A third brother, Macdonald, was twice runner-up in the national championship.

Later Toney worked for Tommy Armour and "Wild Bill" Melhorn, so his golfing pedigree was close to impeccable. Toney became a good player and a regular performer on the pro tour, winning several tournaments, including the prestigious North and South championship at Pinehurst No. 2 in North Carolina. In 1934 he was hired by Clarence Rickey, the head of MacGregor Golf Company, to be an "emissary" for MacGregor on the pro tour. In 1937 Rickey asked Penna to help design a new line of clubs. Toney's flair for design was quickly evident, and for the next twenty-five years, he designed all of MacGregor's club lines. He produced a series of winners, including the Tommy Armour irons and woods, the classic Tommy Armour putter, and the popular "MT" irons. His wood club designs became the standard for the industry. Even players from rival golf companies played Toney Penna's drivers, and he became the most copied man in the golf business. I'm not certain of this, but I think that every tournament Ben Hogan won was with a set of clubs designed by Toney Penna, and I am certain that Jack Nicklaus had his best years while playing Penna-designed clubs.

Toney continued to play the tour while working for MacGregor, during which time he signed what I think was the finest group of players ever assembled on one staff. They included Ben Hogan, Byron Nelson, Jimmy Demaret, Jackie Burke, Bob Hamilton, Vic Ghezzi, Bob Toski, Dow Finsterwald, Doug Ford, Herman Barron, Dave Douglas, Craig Wood, Tommy Armour, Clayton Haefner, Mike Souchak, George Fazio, Jack Nicklaus, and Louise Suggs from the Ladies PGA.

Although small statured, Toney loved clothes and wore them well. Like his friend Jimmy Demaret, he sometimes traveled with a steamer trunk full of apparel containing up to seventy-five pairs of slacks, forty pairs of shoes, and dozens of hats, caps and tams. Toney had an irrepressible, generous nature, of which some fellows sometimes took advantage. At one tournament, the hotel manager gave Toney a suite and sent up a large supply of liquor. Word got around that Penna had a stash of booze, and pretty soon

Willie Goggin and George Low, two large fellows who *would* take a drink, knocked on Toney's door and demanded some of the liquid cheer. Toney denied he had any, so Goggin and Low searched the suite. When they couldn't find any bottles, they grabbed Penna by the arms and feet, bumped out the window-screen, and held Toney from the window, twenty floors above the pavement. Toney screamed that it was in his steamer trunk, told the two pranksters to take it and get out. Toney is convinced that hanging out of that window caused his hair to fall out.

On another occasion, Toney and Jimmy Demaret were sharing a suite. Toney played early, returned to the hotel and was showering when he heard a knock at the door. Throwing a towel around himself, Toney answered the door, and there stood Demaret, who grabbed the towel and shoved Toney into the hall. Jimmy jumped inside the room and slammed the door, leaving Penna to pound on the door and holler for admittance. Jimmy refused, however, and then Toney heard the elevator stop at his floor. Quickly he squirmed into a little broom closet across the hall, and, when the people left, he resumed pounding on the door. Demaret picked up the telephone and called the house detective, informing him that a crazy little man was running around naked in the hall, trying to knock down his door. If he couldn't find the maniac when he arrived, Demaret told the house detective, then look in the broom closet. Up came the detective and pulled Toney from the closet. "Please, officer, that is my room, and this joke's gone far enough," Penna pleaded. "Just knock on the door and Mr. Demaret will confirm that I belong in the room." The detective knocked and, when Demaret opened the door, asked if he knew Toney. "Officer, I've never seen this guy in my life," said Demaret with a perfectly straight face.

Toney Penna has lived in the north end of the Palm Beaches for about forty years, as have I, and as a consequence, we've played hundreds of rounds of golf together. Toney has a beautiful home overlooking the beach at

Jupiter, and until recently, he was in the habit of hitting practice balls from his lawn out into the ocean. Before his health began to decline, Toney was always full of energy and strong opinions, combined with a delightful and sometimes wicked sense of humor. He drove around in a large Cadillac, whose license plate bore the letters "L.F.F." When a fellow asked Toney what these letters referred to, Toney grinned and replied, "Let the f——r fly." In a way, the title of this book was inspired by my friend, Toney Penna.

In the early to mid-1960s, I had not played very well on tour, and Toney had begun offering suggestions he thought might be helpful to my game. One day at his house, we were hitting balls into the ocean when Toney suddenly asked how I stood financially. I admitted that I was not exactly flush, and, before I could finish, Toney asked if I would like to join the MacGregor Tour Staff. I leaped at his offer. Toney picked up his outside telephone and called Bob Rickey, the head of MacGregor Golf, and told Rickey that he had just signed me to a contract for $3,500 per year. I overheard some noise from Rickey, but Toney said I had already signed, and furthermore, he was sending me up to the Mac-Gregor plant in Cincinnati to have new clubs made.

Then Toney dialed his friend, Al Heiman, owner of the Hamilton Tailoring Company, also in Cincinnati. Toney wanted Big Al to put me on his staff, too, make me all the nice clothes I wanted, and pay me $1,500 a year. In those days, Toney Penna got things done.

In fifteen minutes, I was $5,000 richer, and I played like hell after that. Several years later, Toney left MacGregor, and with investments from Al Heiman, Perry Como, Bob Hope and Tommy Lo Presti, he started his own Penna Golf Company in Jupiter. Toney made some wonderful golf clubs before he sold out.

Well, Toney helped my golf swing a great deal. In my zeal to copy Ben Hogan, I had weakened my grip and learned to fade the ball. Inevitably, this had shortened my backswing. Toney strengthened my grip about two knuckles, added about three feet to my backswing length and taught me how to hook a ball again. I picked up about forty yards off the tee, which I had gradually lost — although, I confess that, with that hook, the squirrels in the left woods hated to see me tee off. Many of the things I teach today I learned from Toney Penna.

Three Underrated Golfers

As I look back on the history of golf in this century, it seems apparent to me that Byron Nelson, Cary Middlecoff and Bill Casper are players who have never received the recognition they deserve. To me, all three are certainly among the game's all-time greats.

Byron got more recognition than the others, but people seem to think he cut his career too short to merit the highest consideration. Indeed, it's even been claimed that he retired in trepidation over Ben Hogan and Sam Snead returning from the military after World War II. That's baloney.

The truth is that Byron retired for medical reasons, which I know for a fact as I was a witness to his screaming nerves. I was in the men's room at the city course in New Orleans in 1946, a tournament that Byron won that year, when he came rushing in and threw up his breakfast in the urinal, the victim of an incredibly nervous stomach. But I don't think it matters when he retired, and I know it didn't matter who Nelson played. He beat all of them, and he might have beaten all of them today, too. He had a marvelous grip, he looked wonderful at address, and he possessed great balance. He was one of the all-time dominant figures of the game.

Billy Casper came out as a hooker, then became a fader, and won the U.S. Open playing both ways. He went back to hooking again as a senior, and won there, too. Everyone marvels at his putting, which they have every reason to do, but Billy could really play from tee to green. He had great

Cary Middlecoff, circa 1958.

hands, he was a good driver, an excellent iron player, a magnificent wedge player, and a fine thinker, steady and very cool under pressure. He was a helluva player; he just didn't seem to have any friends. Tommy Bolt said that Casper was the only guy who played the tour for twenty-five years and never made a pal. He didn't seem to want any buddies, said Bolt. Whether he did or didn't, Bill was an awesome talent who won over fifty tournaments, including two U.S. Opens along with the Masters and five Vardon Trophies. He was selected for eight Ryder Cup teams. If that record doesn't qualify for recognition, then shame on all of us.

Doc Middlecoff was not quite the longest and not quite the straightest driver I've seen, but when you combine the two, I'm certain he was the longest straightest driver of my lifetime.

When I was playing the tour regularly, if you could manage to finish ahead of Middlecoff, you would grab one helluva big check. For years Cary was the man to beat every week, and to be regarded that way by your peers meant that you were, indeed, a great player.

So it puzzles me why Doc is so seldom mentioned among golf's greats, because he should be. Perhaps his reputation as a slow player detracted somewhat from people's judgment of his shotmaking prowess, and there is no doubt that he was at times terribly slow. But he kept beating your brains out, and after a while, you began to wonder if maybe you, too, shouldn't take a little more time with your shots. Doc affected many of us that way.

Greatest Golf Shots - II

Not only was Cary Middlecoff the greatest driver in the game, he was a marvelous long-iron player, perhaps one of the best ever, and he could putt with anyone. I won't tell you about the six-footer he drained under pressure to win the U.S. Open, or the seventy-five footer he snaked in at the thirteenth while winning the Masters. Let me tell you about a shot he hit in the Houston Open in the 1950s — and, yes, he won that one, too. I'd finished my round and had wandered back out to the sixteenth hole, a long par-five, to see if anyone could reach it in two. We'd all tried, but no one had come close all week.

Along came Middlecoff, who hit a wonderful drive but turned around in disgust when he got to the ball and said, "Look at that, there's a damn log behind my ball." That was exactly the situation, meaning he would have to hit the limb before he hit the ball. Somewhat disconcerted, he took out the three-wood and waggled and waggled and then waggled some more. Suddenly, he jerked back and asked in a sharp voice, "Where's that camera? Who's got the camera?" Everybody froze but there were no camera noises where I was standing. Finally, Doc addressed the ball, took some more waggles, then he finally swung and mashed the limb up against the ball so that the damn thing flew out of there just as far and straight as if he had caught the ball flush. I'll bet he hit it 290 yards, right up on the edge of the green. Now, Cary could hit his long fairway woods just about as far as he could hit the driver, but that was ridiculous. That was the closest I'd ever seen anybody to that green in two. It was an unbelievable shot. In fact, Doc and I have talked about that shot many times since, and it's still unbelievable to me.

Middlecoff played what is, in my opinion, one of the greatest rounds of golf ever witnessed when he shot a 68 in some of the nastiest weather the Bing Crosby tournament has ever experienced. In the final round at Pebble Beach, I holed every putt that I looked at and scored 74 in the worst gale and rainstorm I've ever played in. I thought I played a helluva round. Our group was right behind Hogan and Crosby, and I believe Ben shot 83, trying his utmost on every shot. At the ninth hole, that long par-four along the ocean, I hit a driver, three-wood and five-iron, and I hit them all just as hard as I could. Middlecoff reached the green with a two-iron — in two. It didn't seem possible that anyone could shoot 68 under those conditions, and I wondered if maybe Doc hadn't cut across somewhere and left out a couple holes. But he was capable of that kind of brilliance.

Doc Middlecoff was well-educated and very intelligent,

which made him a natural choice as chairman of our tournament committee at the time we demanded, and got, our entrance fees back from the tournament sponsors. Doc was also an excellent television commentator for CBS, but he made the mistake of asking for a salary increase, whereupon they fired him. (The same thing happened to Bob Goalby when he asked NBC for a raise, costing us two of the best commentators in the business.) But it's as a player that I remember Cary Middlecoff, because the image was indelible and the record endures. I know that if I had to make a list of the ten greatest players of the century, Doc's name would be on it.

My Favorite Caddie

When I first joined the tour in 1953, a player was not allowed to use the same caddie two weeks in a row, so we employed high school kids in the summer months and the rest of the year had to settle mostly for a mixture of winos and bums. It got pretty old having to conduct a caddie-training program each week on the winter tour; even if your bum showed up, you never knew when he might step on your ball or forget to pick up a club, and you could just about count on his trailing you by a hundred yards down every fairway.

Eventually, however, I was lucky to meet the world's best caddie. In those days, we usually opened the tour with the Los Angelos Open at the public Rancho Park course, and on this particular occasion I was peeved to find no player parking area near the clubhouse. I'd parked far away up on a hill and was lugging my bags back toward the clubhouse when a big, fat black man approached and said,

"Mr. Gardner, I sho' would like to caddie for you this week."

I looked at him and said, "Man, you couldn't make it up and down all those hills out there."

He bristled back, "What the hell do you mean? Man, I'm an ath-ah-leet."

I asked him what game he played and he replied baseball. I inquired if he was, by chance, a catcher.

"Yeah, how'd you know dat?" he said.

I allowed that with his build he didn't exactly look like a twinkle-toed shortstop, and we both cracked a smile, and that's how I met Herman Mitchell. Finally I said, "Here, take this bag and we'll give it a go, but only for today," and Herman waddled on up the hill with me.

When we got out on the course, I asked Mitch, as I later called him, to pace off the yardage on each hole. Every time I checked his count he was within a yard or two of my own measurement, so before long I trusted him to supply the yardages while I concentrated on my own game. Later that day I went to Jack Tuthill, our fine tour supervisor, and asked him what he'd do to me if I used Mitch every week. Jack said he thought that would be against tour regulations. I acknowledged that I thought so, too, but said I couldn't find a written version of the rule anywhere. The next day "Tut" told me that I was correct and said that he couldn't prevent Mitch caddying for me every week. "Take a good look at this fat guy," I told him, "because he'll be on my bag from now on."

By the time of the Bing Crosby tournament at Pebble Beach a few weeks later, practically every player had hired his own regular caddie. For the first time since maybe the 1930s or early 1940s we had professional caddies again. As a result, though, caddies became much more expensive, to the point where today I'm not certain I did the tour a favor. I'm not even sure it was a fair practice, for there were damn few Herman Mitchells out there.

Mitch became the best damn caddie a man ever had, as well as a fast friend. You can see him today as Lee Trevino's caddie and in some of Trevino's television commercials. I'm glad to see that Lee has persuaded him to slim down some. Mitch will always be number one on my list. If I could have played as well as he thought I could, I imagine I might have beaten Hogan's and Snead's best ball.

Favorite Golf Courses

Tournament professionals are constantly asked their opinions about golf courses. When a member asks, "What do you think of our course?" he is not anxious to hear criticism of his course. Ed "Porky" Oliver came up with the best reply to these inquiries. "I think it's the finest course of its type I've ever played," he would reply. That always covered it. My own opinions about golf courses are colored somewhat by the fact that I tend to be overly critical of golf course design.

Still, if I had to play a golf course every day for the rest of my life, I think I'd choose the Seminole Golf Club in North Palm Beach, one of Donald Ross's finest designs. It has everything a golfer could want in terms of strategy, shot value and playing variety, and it's a sound test of skill, especially when the wind is up. Its setting alongside the Atlantic Ocean is ideal, and it boasts one of America's classiest clubhouse and locker rooms. Unfortunately, Seminole has a policy that golf professionals are ineligible for membership and, by implication, inferior, a throwback to the attitudes of the 1920s that Walter Hagen did so much to change. But that aside, I've played perhaps a hundred rounds at Seminole during my lifetime, and it always left me with the same feeling — I couldn't wait to get out there the next day.

Another marvelous course is Cypress Point on the Monterey Peninsula in California. It is not the monster of its famous neighbor, Pebble Beach, especially not for today's best players, but if you added about forty yards to some of those holes, you'd have a monster. Then it might play as it did some sixty years ago, the way the architect envisioned its being played with the equipment available at the time. Cypress Point is always in marvelous condition, and its famous sixteenth hole over the ocean is the shortest par-four I've ever seen that is labeled a par-three. Should you know a member of this exclusive club, be certain you prevail upon him or her to allow you to play this jewel.

One of my favorite courses is Winged Foot in Mamaroneck, New York, the site of many national championships. Pete Dye and his imitators should look closely at the two excellent courses here, for they prove that one does not require bunkers and water hazards extending for 450 yards or more, nor railroad ties surrounding the greens, in order to present a great test of golf. Winged Foot, designed by A. W. Tillinghast, is rightly known as a golfer's club because it's tough but fair for any class of golfer. Almost across the street from Winged Foot is another tremendous Tillinghast course called Quaker Ridge. Its greens are perhaps a shade less severe, but its demand for great striking is every bit as high, and it's always been a personal favorite of mine.

In the late 1950s I played a course in Detroit with Lloyd Mangrum during qualifying for the U.S. Open. I remember Lloyd saying, "The USGA wouldn't need to 'trick up' this baby. They could just run up the flag and say, 'Let's go.'" The name of the club is the Country Club of Detroit, and it may be the finest layout I've every played. Another great course is at Kirtland Golf Club, a relatively unknown course outside Cleveland. Eddie Meister, the fine amateur, used to run Kirtland, which is an old Donald Ross design. I played it only once, to my regret, but it left an impression.

Chicago is crammed with wonderful courses, the most illustrious of which, I suppose, is Medinah No. 3, which has hosted a number of U.S. Opens. It's a very difficult course, with narrow, tree-lined fairways everywhere, but with the exception of a few blind shots and the tilted seventeenth green, I wouldn't change a thing. Another course I admire is the *old* course at Colonial Country Club in Fort Worth, Texas. The present course lost much of its toughness and charm when changes dictated by the Flood Control District were made, among which were enlarging the greens. I'm not the only touring pro who thought that the old, par-70 Colonial was the hardest course in the world on which to match par — in competition and without tricking it up.

When I lived in Augusta, Georgia, the Augusta National course, where the Masters is played, was considered the third best course in town, behind the Augusta Country Club and Forest Hills, a splendid Donald Ross course built alongside the Forest Hills Ricker Hotel. The layout has changed somewhat, but when Ross turned the course over to the owner, William E. Bush, it was a gem. During World War II, the hotel was operated as an Army hospital and the course was known as the Armed Forces Golf Club. Three holes were abandoned and replaced with three ordinary holes. Quite frankly, I never saw many things the Army improved, except for our country's security, but I suppose that's what the Army is supposed to do.

Golf Course Architects

The subject of golf architects and their designs is among my principal sources of irritation. Whenever I see some of these modern "masterpieces," my reaction is, "Come back quickly, Donald Ross. The world of golf needs you since apparently you didn't train anyone before you left." I've been told that Ross designed over six hundred golf courses in America, and I've yet to run across a bad one. Now, if you design six hundred courses, they can't all be great. Last summer, I saw a Donald Ross course I didn't much like, but who knows how many well-meaning greens chairmen had contributed their two-cent changes?

Donald Ross shaped my architectural thinking. He didn't like blind shots; I hate them. He believed in proportion — big hole, big green; little hole, little green. To me, that's just logic. Nor did Ross seem to buy the idea that "golf was not intended to be fair," a theory to which many present-day course planners subscribe. Apparently they believe there are no limits to what you can do to a golfer. I suppose foremost among this school is Pete Dye, along with his family. Among them, they've butchered more good ground than Sherman did while marching through Georgia. Ostensibly, they are advocates of "target golf," although I seem to remember Jack Nicklaus commenting that he had not yet figured out how to stop a golf ball on the hood of a car with a two-iron, which is what Pete Dye's designs often require. Still, Pete must be able to talk pretty well since he greatly influenced many of Jack's future designs.

In my opinion, the architectural field today is wide open. If I had a nice piece of ground and didn't want to design my own course, I don't know whom I would hire. Surely Bob Cupp, but I'd watch him. All the architects seem to be interested in building monuments to themselves, or they just don't care. Perhaps they don't know any better. Most of them don't realize that the average golfer comes closer to playing croquet than golf, if you consider the amount of time his ball spends in the air. These so-called architects haven't been on the lesson tee with Joe and Josephine Hacker to observe how poorly the average golfer strikes the ball; nor do they care, any more than they care about the owners who have to finance and maintain the monsters they build.

Quite often they will take a thickly wooded area and carve out a swatch of trees one hundred yards wide in order to build fairway "waste bunkers," for the love of heaven, and apparently for aesthetics. Have you ever seen a beautiful sand trap? I haven't. Bunkers require sand at up to $35 per ton, while trees are beautiful, strategic, and require no maintenance at all. More and more we see today's architects building par-threes of 220 to 240 yards, a length which the ordinary member would play as a par-four. I dislike par-threes that long, particularly since most courses have fourteen other holes to show everybody how strong we are.

Pete Dye once told me that his primary aim in design was to *fool the golfer*. What a beautiful premise. Dye designs courses just as a frustrated touring pro would, and I guess he is one. He seems to be saying, "I'll show you guys that you're not as good as you think you are." Pete has a very independent mind. He doesn't believe in golf course plans, preferring to build courses by "eye" until he gets it right. Some banks require plans in order to secure financing, but Pete tosses the plans in the trash bin the day construction begins. I thought for a long time that he and Deane Beman might be "in cahoots," because of all the work Beman provided for Dye in connection with the PGA Tour courses. Lately, however, Beman seems to favor his own greenskeeper, Bobby Weed, as the Tour's architect; perhaps Bobby works for less and pays more attention to Deane's wishes.

Currently the architect hailed as the best is Tom Fazio, George's nephew. His Black Diamond Ranch in Central Florida has been acclaimed by golfers and golfwriters alike and shows that Tom has, indeed, improved. Some of his work in South Florida is suspect, however, especially at Lloyd Ecclestone's PGA National Resort. Not everyone was thrilled with its so-called Champions Course, which was vastly altered by, of all people, Jack Nicklaus. If you thought it was a bad course before, you should try it now. Such are the politics of the PGA of America and its developers.

Why doesn't someone come along and build golf courses based on good sense and logic, with smallish greens that emphasize good iron play instead of putting, which is demanded by the huge greens on so many of the courses we see? Large greens have always slowed up the game because it takes more time to three-putt than to two-putt. Why not return to fairways of less generous width — say, thirty yards wide — and let's find out who can drive straight instead of just slugging away? Why don't we find out who among the pros can hit his long irons? And is there anything wrong with having an occasional flat putt? Or a halfway level practice putting clock? And why shouldn't the greens on par-five holes be the smallest on the course, since even the hacker's third shot is the shortest he'll have all day?

If you think about it for a moment, what a golf course architect really does is to tell you, and me, *how* golf is *supposed* to be played on a particular piece of ground (according to him). But what are his credentials for telling us how to play the game? Has he himself ever been able to hit the particular shots he is requiring of you and me? Where did he acquire his expertise to know how we should play? I think you'll find that most golf architects have never played the game very well, nor do they possess the skill to play the shots they ask of us. Jack Nicklaus is an exception, and so is Arnold Palmer, although I'm told that Arnold has little involvement with the design of courses bearing his name. The vast majority of golf designers, the Trent Joneses, the Dick Wilsons, the Fazios, the Joe Lees, the Maples, the Desmond Muirheads, the George Cobbs, all were, or are, relatively mediocre players who have elevated themselves into positions of authority mainly through the liberal application of B.S. and marmalade. There is no other explanation, and I resent their telling me how the game should be played almost as much as I do the stuffed shirts and novices from the USGA telling me how to play U.S. Open courses.

The Unruly Rulesmakers

The United States Golf Association does many good things for the game of golf, but running the national championship and making logical rules are not among them. So far as I know, I've never met a member of the USGA Executive Committee I didn't like or respect for his or her overall intelligence. But when this august group convenes, something must happen, because they deliver such outright frivolous and irrational decisions, particularly as pertain to the Rules of Golf. The fact is, the USGA changes the rules quite regularly, depending on who's currently in office, yet tries to justify these changes by an appeal to antiquity, which is a logical fallacy. That just won't fly with intelligent people, and there are other intelligent people who love and want to preserve the game of golf.

In the summer of 1940, when I first started in golf and Franklin Roosevelt was president of the United States, the penalty for both out-of-bounds and lost ball was distance only; in effect, a one-stroke penalty. In the ensuing years, with changes in the USGA Executive Committee, the penalty for both infractions became stroke and distance; in effect, two strokes. If memory serves me correctly, another Executive Committee changed it back to distance only before finally settling, once again, on stroke and distance, which is the rule we play under today. In other words, somebody decided you were a better golfer if you whiffed the ball completely than if you drove it three hundred yards, but one inch out of bounds. That doesn't make sense.

Upon my graduation from Lanier High School in Macon, Georgia, I received a full golf scholarship to Louisiana State University, but was dismayed to learn that the USGA had just passed a rule prohibiting a young man from attending college on a golf scholarship.

Well, after much soul-searching I decided I was accepting the scholarship anyway, and the USGA could go to hell. Shortly thereafter, when it became obvious the prohibition was being ignored by so many, the rule was rescinded. Had the USGA stuck to its guns, think of how many fine young men would not have attended college.

The USGA has tried some goofy ideas at times. One of these was the rule passed some years ago stating that a ball on the putting surface could be cleaned only once. But this was unfair to early-morning golfers, whose balls tend to pick up sand and debris from the dew-covered greens. The pro tour refused to abide by this rule, and pretty soon it, too, was rescinded. Another rule specified that a player could not fix ball marks on his line, nor wipe mud from his ball. This one contained more inequities than you can count; morning players encounter wetter greens, which produce deeper ball marks and more debris, whereas afternoon players don't normally have to contend with this condition.

In the late 1950s, as I recall it, the USGA sent committee-man John Winter to the New Orleans Open to admonish the touring pros for passing a local rule that allowed players to clean the ball and repair ball marks. In a players' meeting one night, we nailed Mr. Winter to the boards on this one. The next day, Jack Tuthill, our outstanding tournament director, drove Winter around the course to see for himself. The best shots to the greens spun the most and consequently picked up the most Louisiana black gumbo. The balls would have been virtually impossible to putt if uncleaned. Winter understood immediately, returned to the USGA headquarters and had both rules changed, bless him.

Another example of unruly rulesmaking occurred at the Masters and involved Arnold Palmer. There is a long-standing rule against hitting the sand in anger, or far any other reason, after having struck a shot leaving the ball in the sand. The penalty for this infraction is two shots, and we all know it. On this occasion, Arnold put his second shot in a greenside bunker, then "pooped" his sand shot and left it there. He slammed his wedge into the sand in disgust. I know the feeling well. Arnold looked up and saw Jack Tuthill standing there: "I guess that's two shots, huh?" Tuthill, then the head of our tour staff, was serving as a rules official, as he did in many Masters tournaments. His one word reply was enough: "Yes."

But no sooner had Tuthill spoken than another Masters official ran over from the other side of the green, and a big conference ensued as other officials from the USGA joined the fray. They decided Palmer was not to be penalized. They ignored the rule. Tuthill was flabbergasted and told the USGA officials that he would never again penalize a player for hitting the sand in anger. To save face, they afterwards changed the rule. Imagine our surprise when they reinstated the two-shot penalty several years later. Appeal to antiquity, huh?

This brings me to the U.S. Open, a tournament conducted by the USGA for our national championship. Apparently the

USGA had in mind that their tournaments should be a test of endurance, as well as skill — or, perhaps, *instead* of skill. For many years, the USGA refused to play on Sunday, requiring the players to walk the 36 holes on Saturday, which amounts to approximately fifteen miles in the summer heat. Had not television money dictated an eighteen-hole finish on Sunday, I suspect we'd still be playing a double-round on the last day.

The U.S. Open is a beauty. Sometimes it appears as though the USGA bluebloods believe golf pros should have a golf bag slung over each shoulder and a bottle of Mogen David in each hip pocket. They've staged their tournament and taken us to such garden spots as The County Club in Brookline, Massachusetts, where, during tournament week, the members draped their antique settees and chairs with white sheets and forbade the pros to sit down. It's incongruous what the professionals put up with from the USGA.

In PGA Tour events, the field is cut to seventy players and ties after two rounds, since summertime daylight assures they can finish. The wise old USGA cuts to sixty and ties. It is interested only in determining one champion, and the hell with the rest of us.

Well, in a way, the pros have asked for it by not making any strong demands of the USGA. And yet we realize that the USGA is fully dependent on the U.S. Open for most of its financial support. The Open is primarily a venue for professionals; if the pros didn't play, the USGA would have a pretty thin treasury. We pros are the only group in the world who play strictly by the rules, yet we're constantly badgered about them.

The USGA tees up a starting field of 156 players. Can you think of twenty-six players in the world who truly belong in the U.S. Open who do not play the PGA Tour regularly? I think not. So instead of busting our butts and pocketbooks trying to prove to the dear old USGA that we're good enough to tee it up in their championship — something we've already proved to the PGA Tour — why not demand that the

USGA earmark 130 spots for American tour players? We'd see to it that they get the 130 best players.

Of course, such a system would eliminate untold thousands of dollars in entry fees, furnished by the thousands of golfers now padding the qualifying fields all over the country. In 1993, nearly ten thousand golfers, amateurs and pros alike, paid forty dollars apiece to enter the qualifying rounds. That's the kind of arithmetic the USGA likes.

From the Other Side of the Ropes

For the last fifteen years or so, I have been sitting or standing outside of the gallery ropes, observing tournament golf the way most other Americans do. It probably won't surprise you, although it did me, that things look very different than they seemed to me when I was competing. I've learned a lot that I never knew before I began watching from the other side of the ropes, which leads me to suggest that our would-be champions should spend some time outside the ropes. I truly believe they might learn something there.

For example, I was struck by how close tournament golf is to life itself. It's a constant struggle in which you work for a prize, and those who sacrifice the most and work the hardest and think the best are the ones who succeed, just as in life. Some would say luck is a factor in both life and golf, but luck is a sucker's bet. I'm one of those who believes, "The harder I work, the luckier I get."

Winners and true champions are almost always strong possibilities. With few exceptions, the most successful players are selfish, egotistic, combative and utterly indifferent to the well-being of their fellow man, and care even less about the well-being of their fellow competitors. Champions find a way to win. They don't settle for putts that "rim out." "In" is all they accept.

Another thing I've observed from behind the ropes is

That Dickinson stare: No smiles here.

how really simple the game appears, quite different from the view we get when the club is in our hands. I'm not sure which view is the correct one, but I suspect that the one from outside the ropes comes closest to reality. In other words, golf is not as complicated as it's sometimes made out to be.

When I return home after observing my wife Judy's tournaments, my attitude and understanding is much improved. I go about my practice in an entirely different way than I did during my days on tour. It now seems a much simpler task to drive a ball down a fairway, or to place an iron shot on the green, than it ever did previously. I suspect that this view is not only a better one but also a truer one. One thing hasn't changed, though; putting still seems very difficult to me, even from the other side of the ropes.

The people I've met in the gallery have also opened my eyes, not only in their lack of sophistication about the intricacies of tournament golf but in the sometimes peculiar ways they have of judging the players. I know one thing I'd do differently if I wanted the gallery's approval, and that is to *smile* every time I possibly could. Smiling seemed such a difficult task for me in my days on the tour, for I seldom thought of doing it, and most of the time I didn't feel like it, either. About the only funny thing I could think of out there were some of the strange shots I hit, but I rarely laughed at them. Now, though, as a member of the gallery myself, I disapprove of players who constantly frown or who fail to react pleasantly even when they hold a long putt.

So if I had it to do over, I'd punch that smile button far more often, and maybe after I faked it for a while, I'd actually begin to enjoy it. I've discovered that if you smile or grin during the course of making a golf stroke, it is virtually impossible to be tense or jerky-fast, although I seldom practice this way myself since it does seem so silly.

In watching tournaments from outside the ropes, I've observed that the wildest drivers usually hit the ball very high when they drive it far off-line. On the other hand, the most accurate drivers, if they are long hitters, tend to hit the ball much lower. To hit the ball high requires more trunk action, and I'm sure that those who use a great deal of body action find it more difficult to time the swing correctly. The ball may go higher, but the woods are full of high-ball hitters.

Finally, I think the gallery can read the players quite well. They can sense when a player is about to hit a good shot, or a poor one. It's not only the player's mood but the subtle gestures he makes, even his body language, that telegraphs this. I think if I were a player again, I might fake confidence for a while, even if I didn't feel it, and pretty soon I might actually gain some.

Part 3

Learning the Game

The Beginning of a Golf Swing

I was introduced to golf on a regular basis in the summer of 1940, just a couple months short of my fourteenth birthday. We had just moved from Augusta to Macon, Georgia, and my dad, a good player, had joined the Idle Hour Country Club, an old Donald Ross beauty. He paid two dollars for my first lesson from our club pro, Charlie Miller, who had learned his golf from Jock Hutchison. That was the last time Charlie charged me for a lesson. Thereafter he took me under his wing, and over the next few years taught me the intricacies of the game.

In that first lesson, in just one hour, Charlie taught me how to hook and slice a golf ball, and also how to hit both high and low shots. He urged me to do my homework and to practice. Well, practice I did, and within four months I broke 80 on the par-70 Idle Hour course. Then, after eleven months, I broke 70. I really worked at it, keeping the air full of balls and divots almost every day. I mention my success only to emphasize the importance of a fine teacher and a determined pupil. Charlie Miller had a beautiful, long and powerful swing and was the finest club teacher I have ever heard of. Whenever I wasn't in school, I'd watch him give lessons, then try on my own swing the things I'd heard him teach his pupils. Charlie seemed to get to the root of golfers' problems faster than anyone I've ever known. I'd experiment with each new solution I heard, and they were many and varied, and sometimes I'd try them out on my buddies, Jack Gillon and Jack McCommon. If they worked, I'd file them away, and if not, I'd discard them. Thus, by watching

Charlie Miller (L, wearing tie), Ben Hogan, and Byron Nelson (driving).

a great teacher at work, did I start to become a good teacher myself.

Why, you might ask, did I have such success at the game so quickly, even though I weighed only 115 pounds? Well, despite my small stature I had very strong hands, wrists and fingers, as well as strong stomach and back muscles. In other words, I had almost all the ingredients for a strong and powerful golf swing. Plus, I loved to compete. I wanted to beat the hell out of everybody, and to that end was practically fearless.

I think Charlie Miller soon recognized my quickness of muscle and passion for the game, figured I could be a good player, and decided to help me as much as he could. Charlie taught me how to use my hands and arms in a golf swing, and, above all, to hit the ball with the *head of the club*, rather than with my body. There are so many deep, dark, and complicated golf theories around today that we often forget that the object of the action is simply to strike the ball squarely, solidly, and fast with the head of the club.

To illustrate how important the hands and arms are in a golf swing, Charlie would bet the members at Idle Hour that he could break 75 while playing each shot sitting on a spectator's seat cane. Leg action was not possible, yet his tee shots were within ten yards of his normal driving distance. Charlie could also shoot 75 standing on either foot, or playing left-handed. From all this I learned the importance of hand action, early and well.

Charlie also advocated a long or full backswing, for he knew that a long swing gives a golfer time to coil his maximum power and to get set for the downswing. There have been a few very good golfers with short swings, such as Harry Cooper and Doug Sanders, but in my opinion no great players. So why would anyone beginning to learn this great game start out behind the eight-ball with a short swing? I almost cry when I see youngsters using a short swing, for they'll pay a heavy price for it later. I can assure them that Old Father Time will shorten that swing for them.

Let me repeat that the most important lessons I learned from Charlie were to use my arms and hands in golf, and to hit the ball with the clubhead. Therein lie the beginnings of my golf swing, and a half century later I have no hesitation in saying that this is the beginning and the end of everything we learn in golf. If you take nothing more from this book, try to remember that.

There are very few things in my later adult life that I boast about, but I'd own a lot more real estate today if I'd felt about my tournament golf game the way I feel about my ability to teach our game. Teaching is something I *know* I can do, and I would take a back seat to no one in that department. Bring them on — all of them.

Address Your Problem

When I was playing the tour, many of the guys would come to me for help in working out their swing problems. In diagnosing their trouble seldom did I have to start with actual swing mechanics. Almost every time I was able to help someone, I noticed that the player had changed something in his address position, which had changed something in his swing, usually for the worse.

How very often was I paired with a player who was driving long and straight and knocking all the flags down, and then a few weeks later had to watch this same fellow who now seemed incapable of hitting a single decent shot.

This used to puzzle me, but close observation and deduction eventually led me to the conclusion that the player had merely changed his position at address, which by changing his "feel" changed his entire swing. Moving the ball only an inch or two forward in the stance, for example, can produce changes in a swing because it changes the set-up, often with disastrous results. On the other hand, when the set-up change can be detected and corrected, a swing can fall back into place quickly and dramatically. Therefore, if you want to play to your top level, it behooves you to understand how the set-up affects a swing, and to know the set-up procedure that works best for you.

Once we set the swing in motion, athletic ability really counts, but even great athletic talent can be negated by a poor set-up. I have never seen a golfer who addressed the ball in a basically acceptable manner who did not eventually play good shots. I admit that I've seen some golfers play very well who looked just awful at address, but I just assumed they were exceptionally talented, and wondered how well they could have played if they had started from a better set-up.

I can assure you that the address is *the* most important element of a golf swing, since *how* you stand up to the ball determines, for the most part, what *will* happen when things start moving. Ben Hogan once told me that it takes absolutely no talent to address a ball properly, but that it does require a good deal of knowledge. In my own case, I think I discovered what was the best set-up for me, and whenever I could get strong and secure at address, I invariably played my best.

It may surprise you that good players — even great players — occasionally stray from their best set-up. Even though I know exactly what to do at address, I still do not get it right every day. Even when I was playing regularly on tour, there were times I couldn't feel comfortable at address.

Then, you ask, what chance does the average player have? Well, in my opinion — and in Hogan's too — the more knowledge of the principles of the set-up you have, the better your chances. I feel so strongly about the importance of the set-up that I'm going to explain it in some detail. Perhaps some of my thoughts will help you understand your own game better, and might even make golf a little easier.

The Grip

Just as I am certain there is no "correct" way to play golf, I'm equally sure that there is no single "correct" grip. The purpose of any golf grip is to secure the club and its face in precisely the position we want it to return to the ball at impact. Any old sort of grip may do this occasionally, but a good grip makes it much more likely to happen time after time after time.

Gene Sarazen and Gardner at the Masters, circa 1956.

Everyone who has ever read a golf book or magazine surely knows that there are essentially three grips we can employ: the Vardon overlapping, the interlocking, and the ten-fingered or baseball grip. Frankly, I don't like any of them, but since I haven't been able to invent a better one, I use history's most popular version, the Vardon overlapping grip, in which four fingers of the right hand are placed on the shaft, with the little finger hooked around the left forefinger. Rather then letting the little finger ride piggyback on top of the left forefinger, I think you can create a more secure and powerful feeling by separating the left forefinger from the middle finger so that the right pinky finger can be hooked *behind* it.

I much prefer this grip to the interlocking grip, in which the right forefinger and the little finger of the left hand are interlocked, meaning that another finger is dropped off the shaft, which feels less secure to me. Because both Jack Nicklaus and Gene Sarazen have played magnificently with the interlocking grip, and both have small hands, I assume it would help others with small hands.

The other arrangement seen occasionally is the ten-fingered or baseball grip, in which all ten fingers hold the club. I wouldn't give you two cents for the baseball grip because I want my hands working together, not fighting one another. However, I must admit that great athletes like Bob Rosburg, Art Wall and Beth Daniel have used this grip beautifully. Personally, I like to get my hands as close together as possible, pulling my right hand up to my left, which the overlapping grip helps me do better than the other two.

The following point is, I feel, extremely important. In gripping with the left hand, I believe that the club should be placed *under* the heel, or callus pad, of the hand. This means that the club should lie more toward the finger-end of the palm than diagonally across the palm. Should you grip too much in the palm of the left hand, you'd essentially be playing golf with only the right hand.

I've noticed that most golfers grip the club at least partially in the palm of the right hand, instead of altogether in the fingers. The problem with semi-palm grip is that it makes cocking the wrists in the backswing very difficult. In my opinion, if you don't cock the wrists sufficiently going back you might as well take up bowling. In the golf schools I taught over the years, I had to move almost every student's left-hand grip more toward the fingers. When they got used to the change, every one of those students thought they'd suddenly grown some new muscles.

On everybody's right hand, at the very bottom of the fingers just before the palm starts, lies an almost straight line. The club should lie straight across this little line, not diagonally across the fingers. That frees the hands and wrists to function naturally, permitting maximum cocking of the wrists in the backswing, plus the freedom to lash or whip the club through the impact area. If you have placed the right hand properly across the roots of the fingers, it will feel as though the hand is riding fairly high over the shaft. The lowest point in a good right-hand grip is the bottom of the right forefinger, which is placed in a sort of "trigger" position. The completed right-hand grip should give you the feeling that you can reach down between your legs and fire a pistol into the gound behind you.

The feeling you should be trying to establish in a good grip is that neither hand is dominant, but rather that your two hands are unified in a balanced, neutral position. You'll achieve this more easily by placing the left thumb either directly on top of the shaft, or slightly to the right, with the right thumb to the left side of the shaft, *never* on top of it.

From the experience in playing in over two thousand pro-amateur events, I have come to believe that the average golfer might be better off by employing a "strong" left-hand grip. This means that as he looks down at his grip, without changing the angle of his chin, the good player should see at least two knuckles of the left hand, and the average player probably three. Logically, I've never understood why the club can't be returned squarely to the ball at impact even when using a four-knuckle grip, providing the grip looks the same at impact as it did at address. I've never felt that one had to supinate, or turn the left knuckles down to the ground in the downswing, in order to close the face or attain maximum power.

I do feel strongly that the right hand should be pulled up against the left as far as comfortably possible, while leaving the right forefinger in the "trigger" position. I've found that most of the shut-face players over the years — those who have the face of the club aiming at the sky at the top of the swing — employ a right-hand grip that is too strong, or too far *under* the shaft. Often, moving the right hand more on top will eliminate the closing of the clubface at the top of the backswing, and thereby neutralize any tendency towards hooking.

You might have heard some of the pros refer to a Harley-

Davidson grip. The term is used on tour to describe a golfer who holds the club with a strong left-hand grip and the right hand riding well over and on top of the left in a "weak" position. In my view, this is sort of a neutral arrangement, and is really not too bad. If the left thumb is placed just slightly to the right of center, such a grip feels much stronger without really promoting a hook.

Grip Pressure

I'm often asked how tightly I grip a golf club. I usually suggest that the club be held tightly enough that it won't slip or turn, but not tight enough that the weight of the clubhead can't be felt during the swing.

Hold a club out in front of you at arm's length, as tight as you possibly can, with your forearms rigid. Gripping a club this tightly, I do not believe you could possibly tell me how much the clubhead weighed. Now, relax your grip pressure until you can feel the weight of the clubhead in your hands. That's how tightly I grip a golf club. I do so because common sense tells me that if you can't feel the weight of the clubhead during the swing, then you don't know where the clubhead is during the swing and therefore you can't possibly know *what* to do with it.

As to the specifics of grip pressure, I agree with most of the conventional wisdom that advises gripping firmly with the last three fingers of the left hand, and applying the same firm pressure with the middle two fingers of the right hand. The key word here is firm, not tight. When the fingers grip too tightly, the small muscles of the wrist and forearms tighten as well, and thereby lose much of their flexibility and speed in downswing.

Ever notice the grips of the great tee-to-green players? They looked like they were molded on the club. I can close my eyes and still see the the powerful yet sensitive-looking grips of Jack

Nicklaus, Sam Snead, Ben Hogan, Byron Nelson, and my good friend and classical swinger Jay Hebert. Their great swings were built on steel foundations, not made of chewing gum. If I could do any youngster a favor, I would give him a sound grip and have him build his swing around it. It's tough to build skyscrapers on a chewing-gum foundation.

However you grip the club, if you are hooking or slicing too much out on the course, go ahead and change your grip. It seems perfectly sensible to me to strengthen or weaken the grip if doing so is necessary in the midst of a round in order to make a score. Then, when the round is over, you can head for the practice range, the research and development department, and look for what was *really* wrong.

Head Position

What's the best way to look at the ball at address? I've often wished I could climb inside Ben Hogan's or Jack Nicklaus's head on a full shot, or look out of Bobby Locke's eyes at a putt to see what the champions see. I can only surmise, but I doubt they'd see the same picture I do.

Ideally, for most iron shots, I think the head should be placed almost *over* the hands, while in the more sweeping motion with the woods it should be positioned a little *behind* the hands, or more toward the right foot. In both cases the head should be inclined so that you are looking directly at the ball from the center of your eyes. I would caution against dropping the chin so low toward the chest that you are looking at the ball through the tops of your eyes, or raising your chin so high that you're forced to look out of the bottom of your eyes. I've observed that golfers who carry the chin high have flattish backswings, and I suspect that those who carry the chin too low tend to swing too upright.

The chin should be inclined slightly to the right, but never to the point where your nose prevents you from seeing the ball with your right eye. Despite that, I strongly suggest that a golfer sight with the left eye, if possible — in fact, if I were naturally right-eye dominant, I think I'd try to make myself left-eyed for golf.

The chin should be tilted toward the right foot and should remain at precisely the same angle until the ball is struck. Tilting the chin slightly to the right is the position of champions — look at Snead and Nicklaus — and the reason is that it clears the way for the shoulders to turn in the backswing: it acts as an axle for the swing, a fixed point around which the clubhead can be accelerated to each person's maximum controllable speed.

Most of the great winners and ball-strikers have angled the chin in just such a manner. Bob Jones's head was noticeably angled to the right, as was Ben Hogan's, Sam Snead's and Jack Nicklaus's. Nicklaus's cocked chin, I'm confident, came from Alex Morrison through his lifelong teacher, Jack Grout.

Ball Placement

Let me suggest that there is no absolutely correct place from which to play the ball, if only because every golfer is built differently. Some people have a wide stance, others a narrow one; some people are tall, others short. In a general sense, I would agree that the ball should be played pretty much opposite the left heel with the driver, and that as you move down through the shorter clubs the ball should move progressively back toward the middle of your stance. But the exact position will vary from one player to the next, which means you would be well advised to seek professional help in working out the correct ball position for you.

Were I asked to name the *one* fault that I observe in most golfers, I'm confident I'd vote for the *ball being played too far forward in the stance.* In fact, many golfers play the damned ball so far forward that they almost have to dive towards it on the downswing, causing all sorts of problems. One of those problems is that the backswing is often shortened, golfers being naturally reluctant to turn their backs fully to the hole when the ball is played too far forward.

I remember the old Scotsman saying, "Laddie, there will be no 'ooks from the left foot," an observation that is based on simple physics. I can assure you that it's much easier to draw or hook the ball when it's placed farther back in the stance. Yes, I know how you feel when you move the ball back — you sense that you're going to push the shot right, and you're afraid you won't get the ball airborne. Well, just try moving the ball back an inch or two in your stance, hit some shots like that, being certain that your body does not move too far forward in the downswing, then report back to me.

Where should the head be positioned in relation to the ball? I've observed that most of the game's great iron players could spit straight down on their grips at address, except possibly when using the long irons. But with the driver, the head should be positioned more toward the right foot, since you're not trying to take a divot with that club, but rather to sweep the ball cleanly off the tee.

Distance from Ball and Posture

How far away from the ball we stand is dictated largely by our posture. Seldom do we see good golfing posture, which I assure you is one reason we see so many poor golf swings. For example, when I see golfers slumping over, as though their diaphragm had collapsed, the problem is usually not bending properly from the waist — "bowing to the queen," I sometimes call it. There have been a few good players who appeared to stand with their heads back over their heels, but for most golfers I believe the head cannot be too far out toward the ball at address — provided that the back remains relatively straight and the weight remains centered in the feet, not out towards the toes. I also think the player's fanny should stick out slightly behind his heels. In fact, the position of a good shortstop in baseball — inclined from the waist, hands on thighs waiting for the ball to be hit — is pretty close to what we're looking for, except we should not bend quite as far.

With good posture established, I think most players will get the best results standing so that the cap end of the driver grip is no more than eight or nine inches from their waist. This provides plenty of room for the arms to swing to and fro without reaching for the ball. It also seems to me a good idea to keep this distance as the clubs shorten. Certain variation shots, such as high pitches and some sand shots, can be made easier by standing quite a bit farther from the ball.

On most shots, I believe that the arms should hang easily and naturally from the shoulders once we've bent from the waist. When the arms are overextended, the muscles become stressed, which tends to inhibit free swinging.

For all normal shots, the hands should hang at least as far forward as the inside of the left thigh; with a driver, however, they should be a little closer to the middle of the legs. On iron shots, I strongly believe that the club should be shoved sufficiently far forward that the player can "feel" the ball against the clubface at address, and the ball should be grounded toward the heel of the iron, where the sweetspot always is.

Woods should be addressed at exactly that spot where we hope to contact the ball, at the lowest point of its arc. In playing irons into stiff breezes, I found it very helpful to set my hands forward of the ball and to actually touch the back of the ball — but very carefully — with the bottom edge of the iron. Even if this might promote an occasional thin shot, chances are that, into the wind, it'll turn out pretty good.

To conclude by covering a rather obvious point, if your stance is too wide, you make it very difficult to turn your body back and through. Should your stance be too narrow, chances are you'll feel wobbly during the swing and you risk your swing motion overpowering your base, causing a loss of balance.

Alignment

Alignment is an absolutely essential part of establishing an effective golf swing and should be considered fundamental to the preparation of every shot. Like many players who have a natural tendency to draw or hook the ball, I have always been inclined to align myself somewhat to the right. It doesn't take a rocket scientist to figure out that the more you aim to the right, the less likely you are to hit straight shots, because, if you did, they would all land to the right of the target.

When I wanted a straight shot, I was obliged to "pull" my swing back on line. This is not a fatal flaw, if you are very talented and if it is done in small degrees. Sam Snead played that way all his life, but Sam's pulling action was very slight, and his remarkable coordination and rhythm allowed him to play closer to the edge than most players could handle.

The opposite is true for golfers who tend to fade or slice the ball. To accommodate the left-to-right flight pattern, they naturally tend to aim left at address, then, when they want to hit a straight shot, they must develop a pushing action to get the swing back on line. Lee Trevino plays that way and does it magnificently, but it takes a real genius to play consistently well with this method.

Eventually, I determined to do something about my own tendency to align myself to the right. The system I devised, which works better than any other I've found, is as follows:

Begin by placing the clubhead on the ground behind the ball in the precise position you hope to return it at impact, and then secure it there with your grip, which we will assume is sound. After waggling the club, the clubface should return to precisely the same position in which it started.

That's the last time you should look at the ball until you have arrived at your final address position. Take your stance while looking directly at the *target*, not at the ball. You will find that you can trust your eyes to align yourself with reasonable accuracy. Should you look down and see that the ball is too far forward or back in the stance, or too far away, look back up at your target and make the necessary correction.

When I began correcting my misalignment, I found that I'd been lining up so far to the right for so long that, in order to aim myself properly, I had to force myself to pick out a target about ten yards to the left of where I really wanted to hit the shot. An observer can be very helpful in checking whether you are actually aligning yourself as you *think* you are.

Watch carefully and notice how many golfers take their stance while looking at the ball rather than the target. How can they possibly be properly aligned, unless they have an eye in their left ear?

Ben Hogan once told me that if he were forced to assume the alignment and posture of the average golfer, he'd have had a hell of a time beating him. That's how important address alignment and posture were to one of the game's greatest thinkers.

In summary, if you are correctly aligned each time you set up to a shot but still have problems, you can be confident that aiming and aligning has nothing to do with your troubles, and thus can look elsewhere for the solution.

Weight Distribution

When addressing a short-iron shot, anything from wedge through eight-iron, I set so much weight on my left side I feel as though I scarcely need my right leg. I have found there is no need to shift any weight to the right side in the backswing, but rather simply turn around on the left leg. With the middle irons, five through seven, I think you should have about sixty-five to seventy percent of the weight on the left leg, and again I think that weight relationship should not change at all during the backswing.

But, you protest, aren't you describing a reverse weight shift on the backswing, supposedly one of the worst things a golfer can do? Well, what I'm advocating is maybe half a reverse pivot, because I'm certainly not recommending that a golfer shift his weight back to the right side on the downswing.

The keys are playing the ball farther forward in the stance than is normal and not shifting any weight to the right in the backswing. Then all you have to do is turn the left side out of the way on the downswing, rather than charging forward onto the left foot. If you've never tried this before, you might need some supervision — provided, that is, you can find anyone with a clue as to what I'm talking about.

With the longer irons, two through four, the weight at address should approach a fifty-fifty distribution. It is not absolutely essential that a divot be taken with these clubs, but the best long-iron players seem to at least scratch the ground. I also believe in a fifty-fifty weight distribution with the driver, with the hands held about even with the ball at address. Don't forget that we generally want a sweeping swing with the driver, that we're not trying to make a divot in the ground.

With the fairway woods, I noticed that Ben Hogan took a divot when he was trying to get the ball close to the pin and wanted some backspin, but he swept his three-wood on the par-five holes when he was after maximum distance and wanted maximum roll. Incidentally, a straighter fairway wood player than Ben never existed.

The Importance of the Address

Why should we be so particular about the way we address the ball? It's pretty obvious, if you think about it.

In golf we stand to the side of the ball, not astride it. We swing a stick around our bodies and hope to strike the ball flush, with maximum speed. The object of a sound address position, then, is to arrange the body in such a way that best promotes these goals.

You can spot a good address position a mile away. I remember once walking out on the course to watch Ben Hogan play his way in, after my round was over. To my surprise, there were about fifty fellow players out there with me, watching the Hawk. I found myself standing in the gallery beside a little old lady who obviously knew little about golf, but nevertheless nudged her companion and pointed to Hogan: "You can tell he's going to hit the ball beautifully, just by the way he stands up there," she said. How right she was.

Good players seem to telegraph that they are going to hit the ball well. Recently, watching Arnold Palmer on television, I was reminded how beautifully he has always addressed the ball. His set-up clearly previews the powerful bash which is about to occur, and there's no doubt it's helped him produce fantastic results for many, many years.

Who were the best in this department? Certainly Ben Hogan, Sam Snead and Byron Nelson rank at the top of my all-time list. So do Jack Nicklaus, Tom Watson, Palmer and Cary Middlecoff, when he eventually got set. All of them address the ball in a way that gives them the best chance of releasing their full power with the least amount of interference. In my view, they were or are all great ball strikers mainly as a result of their sound address positions.

How a golfer stands up to the ball determines what's *possible*, and also what's *likely*. With perseverance, and attention to detail, I'm confident that you, too, can look like any of these fellows at address. It's only when the club starts in motion that they're liable to beat you.

The Waggle

You will certainly have noticed that most fine players waggle the club a time or two prior to starting the swing. The waggle can be thought of as a tiny practice backswing, performed with the hands and wrists simply by moving the clubhead a few inches or so *behind* the ball. I think Ben Hogan described the waggle beautifully in his book, *The Modern Fundamentals of Golf*, as a bridge between the address and the start of the backswing, and I'd suggest the reader look it up and apply his technique.

A proper waggle gives life to the wrists and forearms, makes them ready to go, while also helping the golfer start his swing from a dynamic motion rather than a static position. I remember Byron Nelson used a two-handed, stiff-wristed waggle, the only great player I've seen to use this method. I'm certain this made sense for Byron, since I'm told that he felt excessive use of the wrists had contributed to his occasional bouts with the shakes. Byron's waggle, for some folks, is still pretty good stuff.

Starting the Backswing

Most of the good players I've seen start the backswing with the move we know as the forward press. I know what it looks like, and I know what it feels like, but like many others before me, I have difficulty describing it. But I shall try, since I think most serious golfers need a forward press.

The forward press is a small, rhythmic movement in the direction of the target that helps you recoil sort of smoothly into the backswing motion. Most players shift the tailbone or right knee slightly toward the hole, and most of them also ease the hands slightly, about one to three inches, that way, too. Immediately this has been done, the club starts swinging back without hesitation in a sort of smooth recoil action.

Since we are looking for the least amount of variation possible, you should try to use the same forward pressing motion every time.

Getting It Up There/ The Backswing

Personally, I believe that a golf club is started back from the ball with the hands and arms. I like to have the feeling that both hands work together and that their initiation of the move happens only very slightly before other parts of the body get involved.

This allows the shoulders, hips and legs to *follow* the clubhead, rather than leading it, all the way to the top of the swing.

You may recall that this philosophy derives from Charlie Miller teaching me that the purpose of a golf swing is to hit the ball with the clubhead, using the hands and arms, and to that end the legs and body must play a supporting, but always a subordinate, role.

In the early 1900s, instructors taught golfers to drag the club's grip end away before the clubhead with the left hand and arm, which meant that the hands started back a milli-second *before* the clubhead moved. This action was necessitated by the high torquing tendencies of hickory shafts, which caused the clubface to twist open during the swing. The idea was that the dragging technique kept the clubface square longer, sort of looking at the ball more, which prevented a quick pick-up of the club while still allowing full cocking of the wrists without fear of leaving the clubface open. It certainly wasn't at all a bad move.

If you'd like to experience this feeling, place a tee peg directly behind the clubhead at address and start the backswing by dragging the club away with your hands. By the time the clubhead has knocked the tee from the ground, you'll find that your hands will be a little farther back than the clubhead, creating a mini-lag.

In an outstanding book by Ken Bowden and Dick Aultman entitled *The Methods of Golf's Masters* (later republished as *The Masters of Golf*), one thing was quite obvious from the sequence photos of history's greatest players. In almost every case, there was a definite little clubhead lag during the first few feet of the backswing, as evidenced by the slight bending *back* of the club shaft. This certainly indicates to me that the hands were initially moving earlier, or faster than the clubhead, however slightly. The only exception was Lee Trevino, who will certainly go down in history as one of the great shotmakers, but whose swing, nevertheless, I have never seen anyone yet try to copy. Lee's method was entirely his own, and if we are to study a golf swing scientifically, should we not study the swings of history's greatest players to find the few common swing elements that they all employed?

The Shoulders

Of all the harmful notions in golf instruction, the one most likely to produce mischief is the idea that the shoulders control a golf swing. I spend a good deal of time on the LPGA Tour with my wife Judy, and I have noticed that many of the young gals take the club back completely with their shoulders. Apparently, their goal is to eliminate hand action almost entirely from their swings.

Of all the great players with whom I've discussed this subject, I can't recall a single one who recommended the conscious use of the shoulders to control a swing. On the other hand, I cannot recall a single fine golfer I've known or watched who did not believe that the *hands and the arms control the swing.* Since we already know that the arms and wrists supply virtually all of the power, too, it follows that the big muscles of the body must be willing to "give." From start to finish, the large muscles of the shoulders, back, hips and legs must yield to allow the smaller and faster muscles of the arms and hands to swing the club freely.

The idea that women, of all golfers, would in any way restrain or restrict the biggest source of power in a golf swing, or even think of doing so, is ludicrous. Besides, using the hands is the only part of the game that's any fun. It is a mystery to me how such a trend could catch on, and a great pity that sincere but inexperienced golfers are the victims.

I don't really mind if some of the non-playing ignoramuses who claim to be ace teachers try their experiments on old men and gullible tour pros, but when they start spreading their snake oil on women and youngsters, they deserve to be horsewhipped.

Farther Back

Where the wrists break in the backswing is largely a matter of personal preference, plus the type of shot being attempted. With the possible exception of short pitch shots, I never liked to see players break up the swing arc right off the ball by cocking the wrists too early in the upward swing. But I am convinced that they must break the wrists and that the more fully they do so the better. Ideally, I think the wrists should remain unbroken and travelling sideways almost to hip-height, then should break up fairly quickly while the shoulder turn is bringing the hands slightly to the inside. I also believe that the hip turn should begin almost as soon as the club starts back. The same timing applies to the left knee, which should move almost straight out and thus a little less toward the right knee than most golfers think. Finally, I believe that almost all of the body's turning should take place during the *first half* of the backswing, leaving the action to be completed by a lifting of the arms as the wrists are broken further by the momentum of the clubhead.

At the top of the backswing, the toe of the club ideally should hang toward the ground in a slightly open position. There are those who prefer to see the face turned up toward the sky ever so slightly and regard this as a square position. In my view, that position is slightly closed, but it can be effctive. When the clubface at the top points directly at the sky, the face is dead shut, which makes a free release almost impossible, requiring instead a very tight grip and some dif-ficult maneuvering of the body and club through the impact zone. Arnold Palmer and Lee Trevino are regarded as shut-face players, but both are very strong physically. I often wonder just how good they might have been had they learned to play with the clubface more open at the top?

This may rattle the cages of orthodoxy, but I believe the most important element of a backswing is this: For a num-ber of years, I've noticed that almost all the good golfers, when playing at their best, cross the line at the top of the backswing. That is, on full shots their shaft is angled at least slightly toward the right rough at the top of the swing. From this angle at the top a player can easily deliver the club into the ball slightly from the inside. If the shaft is pointing to the left rough at the top, a position we refer to as laid off, it is very difficult to deliver the club on any path except from the outside. The club can be laid off by too flat a shoulder turn, or by fanning open the clubface at the beginning of the swing. A common feature of the laid-off swing is that the player's head moves back toward the heels during the backswing.

I've never believed that a player must push his hands and the club high over the head to be successful. I think that ear-high or the top of the head is about right. History tells us that the best drivers over the years have swung the club shaft back to about a horizontal position. If you can't presently do that, then work on it, and don't give up on it.

As you get older, old Father Time will shorten that back-swing for you, but you must fight that shortening. The long swingers have *always* been the best; thus, if you have a short swing at a young age, you don't have much to look forward to.

If I am fortunate enough to be around to start my twin boys, Barron and Spencer, into golf, you can be sure that they'll both have long backswings. And you can bet that their right elbows will be *above* the horizontal at the top of the backswing. I won't be teaching any of this arms strapped-to-the-sides business. That's like playing in a straitjacket. Jack Nicklaus modified his flying right elbow and looked more conventional, but it cost him forty yards.

Left vs. Right

Let me confront one of the age-old debates in golf, the role of the left versus the right side during a swing. I've often wondered why we've been taught to guide a swing with the left arm, the left hand, and the left side. Since most of us are right-handed, how do you suppose such a radical idea evolved?

One can only speculate, but I imagine that many years ago, perhaps in Scotland, some old fellow who happened to be thinking about his left hand beat his pals one day, and since anyone who makes two pars in a row automatically qualifies as a teacher, figured he'd better keep on conscious-ly using his left hand in the swing. He figured out that a two-handed swing would be more powerful and manageable than a one-handed one. Thereafter, we heard left, left and left for so long that many of us simply forgot to use our more powerful and natural side, the *right*.

I don't think it matters much whether your dominant hand is the right or the left in golf. After all, for right-handed players the backswing takes place entirely on the right side

of the body and the part of the downswing that really matters takes place on the right side of the body, too. Could I
not much more easily — and more reliably — put the club
back where I wanted it by using the arm which is already on
the right side, rather than reaching all the way across the
chest to put it here with the left? Food for thought.

If you *hold* the club firmly with the left hand and *direct*
the club with the right, the left will go back with the right,
and the swing will be directed by the stronger and natural
part of the body.

The Left Heel

Over the years, the single worst piece of information
passed on to golfers is to keep the left foot planted solidly on
the ground all the way to the top of the backswing. This
might apply with some of the shorter shots, but not when
length is needed and *never* with a driver. If a golfer has a
full backswing and keeps his left heel down, he will surely
drop his left side down, too, as he swings back, and from
that position he's in trouble. The correct idea is to try to
hold the left side up during the backswing , in order to keep
the body as level as possible. You can possibly hit solid short
irons when dropping the left side and keeping the left foot
flat, but you'll have a tough time with a driver, a club with
which most of us don't want to take a divot. Ask Bruce
Crampton or Bobby Nichols, neither of who lifted their left
heels, as I remember, and both of whom have been subject
to spells of wild driving.

I don't recall seeing a consistently long straight driver
who lasted any length of time who didn't have his left heel
at least slightly off the ground at the top of the backswing.
This prevents dropping the left side so much that it cramps
the swing and inhibits a powerful sweep forward into the
ball. In both playing and teaching, I've found that the *earlier*

the left heel leaves the ground in the backswing, the better. This allows the left side to remain up and level during the backswing, which provides plenty of room for the club to release in the hitting zone.

The Downswing

For many years, I made it a point on tour to ask the players with the best golf swings, day in and day out, what they thought started the club down from the top. When Sam Snead told me the same thing that Charlie Miller had taught me originally, I quit asking anybody else that question. What Sam did, or even thought he did, was good enough for me.

Sam told me that he pulled the club down with "the same damn thing I took it back with, mah hands." Further, he said, "Mah hands are the only thing I've got aholt of the club with, and they're the only things that know how much the club weighs, or where it is. Mah hips don't know, mah shoulders don't know and mah legs and feet don't know. They gotta move some to let mah hands and arms swing the club where they want to, with speed. Other than that, they've gotta be dumb."

I have studied for hours pictures of the world's great players, and watched them in action for years, and almost always I see a bending *back* of the shaft and clubhead as the club starts down, which could scarcely have been caused by a movement of the hips or legs. It is caused by a small pulling down of the hands, with, in good players, the body "giving" towards the target to accommodate the action of the hands and club.

Imagine a baseball pitcher at the top of his windup saying, "Okay, legs and feet, start me down toward the plate, then when we get to just the right place, now, arms and hands, turn loose the ball." Baloney! Throwing a hard, straight pitch is an integrated motion where all the parts blend, so that the arm can sling the ball across home plate.

If the club has been taken back slightly inside, a player has a better chance to follow a similar inside path on the downswing, provided he doesn't interfere by getting too active with the body, expecially with the shoulders. Because we stand to the side of the ball, the club should approach the ball along this inside path and momentarily coincide with the target line as it strikes the ball, then swing back inside as it moves past impact. That's what is meant by the swing going from inside to square to inside.

It is a myth that the club travels straight along the target line for more than a centimeter or so at the bottom of the swing, although it appears to do so in the swings of some players like Ben Hogan and Lee Trevino. The club is in contact with the ball for only the tiniest fraction of a second, and it begins moving inside again the moment the ball is struck. If you doubt it, just look at the divots left by the good players. It has been my experience that once the club has started down, any *conscious* attempt to direct the swing will only slow it up or screw it up.

One of the worst pieces of advice I've ever heard is to urge golfers to groove a "late hit." I've never had it explained to my satisfaction just why hitting the ball with the clubhead quite late in the swing will make the ball go farther or straighter. I know it will make the ball go lower, and maybe start considerably more to the left, but that's about all this harmful piece of advice will accomplish. I won't mention names, but the two players in my memory who hit the latest were absolutely the worst and wildest drivers I ever saw.

Ben Hogan exhibited rather a late hit with his old swing of the early 1940s. A young kid saw a picture of Ben just short of impact, with the shaft pointing almost straight up, and carried it around for years. When he finally met Ben, he whipped out the picture and asked, "Where do you think that one went, Mr. Hogan?" Ben replied, "I have no idea, but I know it wasn't very high."

Swing Finishes

Unless they are swinging one of the longer irons, the best iron players in the world *never* wrap the club around the back of the neck when they finish. Rather, should they drop the club from their hands as they finish the swing, the club would hit the ground on the left side of their bodies. This signifies to me that they have eliminated excessive belly action and other body motion from the swing, a very desirable goal, to my way of thinking. Too much body action slows down the clubhead. When I hit a driver all-out, I don't

A good swing finish at the Masters, 1968.

want any part of my body doing anything that would slow down the club until it slams me in the back, with force.

Here's a little drill that may help you eliminate excessive body action, particularly shoulder action, in the downswing. Using a short iron, try to finish the shot with the clubshaft pointing directly at the hole and both arms extended to their fullest, *parallel* to the ground. If you drop the club immediately, you will find that the clubhead usually hits the ground much farther to the left of the intended line than you would have imagined, which indicates you have swung it incorrectly, using too much shoulder action in the downswing.

A Dissenting View

This next little jewel may blow a few minds, but it is the result of an intensive study I have conducted for many years.

I had always been taught that a golfer should try to turn the majority of his weight onto the right leg in the backswing with both irons and woods, and I sure as hell tried. Over time, I found that this weight-shifting was far more successful with a driver than with the irons. I began to watch and watch again all the players who played the best iron shots, and I came to the conclusion that, despite what these players *thought* they were doing, they actually shifted no more than half of their weight to the right leg. In effect, they had achieved about a fifty-fifty weight distribution at the top of the swing.

What was noticeable in the swings of almost all the successful players was the fact that their thighs seemed to be leaning toward the hole, however slightly, when they reached the top of the backswing. Only after this became clear to me did I begin to understand the term "turning out of the way" in the downswing — there was no need for these players to move forward onto their left sides since they were already there. I was always skeptical of the notion that a side-to-side movement during a swing produced power, or even direction. Rather, it seemed to me that a coiling, torquelike motion produced more power. Watch a discus man or a hammer thrower if you doubt it. Those athletes really know the power sources and moves.

Almost without exception, golf's great masters employed a full backswing with the longer clubs, and, by observation, none seemed to be balanced on his right leg at the top of the swing. Check it out. See how much weight you can shift to the right when both thighs are already inclined toward the hole. Damned little, I'd say. A lot of missed iron shots by good players are caused by moving the tailbone too far toward the hole before impact. As I've observed, it's an unnecessary move when the tailbone is already over that way.

Sand Play

If there is an area of golf about which I feel particularly qualified to speak, it is sand play. For a number of years, I don't think there was a better bunker player in the world than I. Herman Mitchell, my caddie, can tell you how many guys I've run out of a bunker at a dollar a shot. When I say this I'm not trying to boast, but simply saying I was among the best.

The very best I ever saw was Johnny Revolta, the fellow who taught me the most about sand play. He was in the category of fabulous. And so was Sam Snead, who may have been the best of all time. Ben Hogan was marvelous on really long blasts, and Jackie Burke didn't take a back seat to many. More recently, Gary Player and Julius Boros were fabulous, as is today's Nick Faldo. Many more come to mind, but the fellows I've named were world-class sand players. Interestingly, I noticed one common denominator in all of them — *none* used a short backswing when playing from bunkers.

Gardner Dickinson: One of the best out of the sand.

This may sound overly simple, but I think the first essential of good sand play is owning a good sand wedge. I always preferred a sand club with the leading edge sticking out in *front* of the hosel. That feature made it much easier for me to slip the leading edge up under the ball and, consequently, produce a higher flight. Perhaps it was tougher to pitch shots from grass with that sort of club, but I found it greatly simplified sand play. Incidentally, I don't believe that any of the great sand players mentioned above used a sand wedge in which the leading edge was offset or goose-necked behind the hosel.

For years, the Wilson company made the best sand irons. Their old R-20 and R-90 models captured the largest share of the market because they possessed superior flanges, and still do. My personal preference was a 1953 Wilson Topnotch with the word "Harmonized" on the back. Another beautiful sand iron was the first of the Hogan "Specials," which came out in the 1960s. Also, Toney Penna made a real beauty he called the "Pin Grabber."

I really had no choice about learning my lessons in the sand. From an early age, we would stage bunker contests for money and soda pops. Later on, when I joined the tour these little games continued, with the competition somewhat stiffer. For instance, I recall the little dollar-a-shot sand games at Seminole when it seemed like I was always giving the party. My opponents included Hogan, Claude Harmon, Bob Sweeney and Chris Dunphy, who ran the place with a firm hand and might have been the best of the bunch. As a young pro, I came out to Seminole quite often and quite early to work on my bunker play, sometimes with Chris's help.

My own set-up and technique for sand play is not exactly orthodox, but I can assure you it is effective for me. I do not advocate that anyone copy my method but will describe it in the event it might help someone else.

I play the ball in *front* of my left foot, which keeps me from moving to the right as I swing back. My shoulders are opened to the target considerably, and I pull my right foot back out of the way in a distinctly closed stance. Off a full backswing, I make no effort to cut across the ball, but rather swing through on my normal arc and path. After Chris Dunphy suggested I hold the clubhead about six inches above the sand at address, I was suddenly in business and no longer giving the party every day.

If I had a secret that made it all work, it was this: The last thing I did was to stare at the hole, then I kept my mental focus on the *hole* during the entire swing — I could still "see" the hole in my mind's eye all throughout the swing — sort of an afterimage. If I deviated from this, I seldom got the distance right.

Here are a few more tips I've gleaned from nearly fifty years of sand play:

• At address, hold the leading edge of the club directly over the spot where you plan for it to *enter* the sand. Not many people know to do this; if they position the club otherwise and still hit a good shot, it's more a matter of luck than judgment.

• In loose or heavy sand I suggest that you keep the clubhead low for a longer time as you swing back. It's difficult to get any distance from the heavy stuff when you pick the club straight up, and particularly if you pound directly down into it.

• On hard, wet sand, the trick is to keep the clubface a little squarer than normal, rather than opening the blade. Then spank the sand smartly down behind the ball in order to force the blade through the sand underneath it. This will keep you from bouncing the club off the firm sand and blading the shot.

Shanking: The Cause and Cure

If you want to empty a room full of golfers, just mention the word "shank." By common assent, shanking is the most dreaded and embarrassing affliction in golf. Most golfers believe the shanks are contagious, and, as Henry Longhurst said, "When you've had 'em, you've got 'em," implying that the condition is irreversible. Can the shanks be cured? Sure they can. I was once the world's worst shanker, so, by necessity, I made quite a study of the mechanics of shanking. Eventually I discovered what I believe is the single fault committed by *all* shankers.

When I turned pro in 1952, my first job was as the second assistant to head pro Harry Dee at the Dellwood Country Club in New Jersey. My old pal and former roommate at Louisiana State, Bud Timbrook, was the first assistant. Naturally, I became second assistant teaching pro. One day a fellow from Long Island showed up for a lesson and proceeded to tell me about all the famous teachers who had tried to help him with his problem, to no avail. I asked him to hit a few shots with a wedge, and the first one cleared out every one stationed to the right of us. A solid shank.

After moving him forward about five yards so he wouldn't maim the other range rats, I told him of my terrible shanking problem as a youngster. I explained to him that all shankers seem to have one fault in common: As they approach impact, they drop the shoulder cage and head. In other words, the shoulder cage is closer to the ground than the height at which they started at address. This drop of the upper body, of necessity, causes the left arm to bend at the elbow during impact. The result is that the heel, or hosel, of the club leads the way, and off to the right she zings. If the left arm were kept straight, the golfer would stick the club in the ground behind the ball, so, naturally, the body compensates for this by bending the left elbow.

I had found that if the shoulders are kept "up" in the downswing, almost as if you're trying to skull the shot, it's almost impossible to shank. I made sure this fellow understood this, and, after a few practice swings, the next shot he hit was a pull-hook. That's a sure sign you're coming out of the shanks. This fellow didn't shank another ball for an hour, and left elated. There must be a secret international society of shankers, because, from that moment on, strangers would call asking for the pro who could cure shanking. My original shanker from Long Island was obviously spreading the gospel. Soon thereafter, my colleagues begain referring to me as "The Shankmaster."

Little Jewels

An old philosopher once said that success is not a destination but a journey, an aphorism that well might be applied to golf. Indeed, after fifty years in the game, I'm sure that golf is a journey in the sense of being a process of discovery, of painful trial and error, of constant learning. Along the way, we accumulate a few hundred or even a few thousand little bits of information and experience which gradually blend into the body of knowledge we use to play the game and to improve at it.

When you've been deeply involved in the game for half a century, as I have, you come to believe you've seen and heard just about everything — all the dozens of theories and hundreds of little variations, all the gimmicks and so-called "secrets" that are peddled about. Some of them work, but unfortunately many of them do not — at least not on a permanent basis. Thus, personally, I do not believe there is any substitute for sound fundamentals, nor for sustained, informed practice. Nevertheless, I'm happy to pass along some of the quick little tips that have worked for me, both as a player and in my teaching — with the warning that they are not recommended for unskilled or novice golfers who have yet to master the fundamentals of sound gripping, set-up and swinging.

Release

Sooner or later, someone is sure to mention the "late hit," implying that it is a desirable feature of a golf swing. This person will explain the advantages of saving all the power until the last possible instant, and advise that you restrain from hitting until as late as possible in the swing. Well, that's just so much bunkum. Instead, try the following, being sure you have plenty of room so that you don't injure anyone, and perhaps using an old club at first.

Take a normal stance and swing the club back at your customary pace until it reaches the top of the backswing. As you reach the hitting zone in the downswing, try to *throw* the club up in the air and toward your target. If you swing with your normal speed, you will probably swing the club far to the left and behind you. If you persist and finally succeed in slinging the club in the direction of the target, you will have discovered the feeling that Bobby Jones meant when he described the word "release." It is one of the most important and satisfying feelings you will experience in golf.

"Release" might be defined as *that point in the down-swing, before impact, where all conscious effort ceases.*

Mapping Your Backswing

This works much better with long irons and woods than it does with short irons, although I don't see how it could hurt anyone's short game.

After addressing a ball, place another ball directly behind the center of the clubhead. As you begin the backswing, try to roll the second ball back along the path your clubhead is taking. Once the second ball has rolled away, you can disregard it completely and concentrate on hitting the object ball, as you normally would.

This little drill will reveal three things about your backswing. First, you will find that you cannot lift the club abruptly on the backswing if you are going to roll the second ball away. In other words, learning to roll the second ball away smoothly will widen your swing arc, which is desirable. Second, if the second ball has been rolled a long distance back, you have almost certainly whipped the clubhead away too fast or too forcefully. Practicing until you can roll the second ball about four or five feet away will help you find the ideal takeaway pace. Third, you can read the direction of your backswing by noting where the second ball comes to rest. If the ball has traveled more or less straight back, your backswing path was probably too far outside. On the other hand, its position may indicate that you have swung back along too much of an inside path. The correct position will vary somewhat from player to player. I should add that this is an especially effective drill for curing topped or thin shots.

Lengthening Your Backswing

As I've already mentioned, one of the most common faults is not swinging the club back far enough, whether it be with a driver or a putter. I've seen very few golfers who take the club back too far (and let me tell you that those rare golfers who do could sell that surplus backswing for quite a few dollars per inch). Lengthening the backswing can be hard to do, but it is not an impossibility.

I've tried many techniques to encourage pupils to lengthen their backswings, but the most effective one I've found, by far, is to have them swing back until they think the grip end of the club points up in the air. In a short swing, the grip end of the club will point toward the ground when the player completes the backswing. To lengthen the backswing simply swing back until you think the grip end of the club is pointing at the clouds, and you can be assured that you will have swung back plenty far.

Practice Swings

Practice swings are not worth a damn if you don't visualize and address an imaginary ball on the ground before you swing. Unfortunately, it took me about forty years to learn this.

Leg Action

I know, in my heart of hearts, that no amount of leg action can increase the speed of the clubhead in the downswing. Yet I'm equally confident that improper or insufficient leg action can retard the downswing and thus slow the clubhead through impact. "Leg drive" is a bad term, invented by inexperienced or ill-informed golf instructors who are doing a great disservice to golfers.

In golf, the legs simply support and respond to the swinging of the arms and the rotation of the body. When we study the swings of the great players, we see that proper leg action is a relatively slow and limited action. With a Snead, Nelson, Boros, Palmer, or Faldo, and even Greg Norman, you could read a note pinned to one of their knees while they're swinging.

On the First Tee

Did you ever walk up to a tee and take three or four practice swings with all your might and main? It surprised people when they saw me make furious practice swings with my driver, but it always seemed to give me an aggressive feel for a big tee shot, while also reinforcing the feeling of swinging the clubhead with my arms and hands.

Curing the Spinout

This little jewel, which has helped me more times in pressure situations on tour than anything else I can remember, is chiefly for better players. I discovered that if I envisioned both of my shoulders directly facing the ball at impact, I not only stopped the spinning out but also tended to wind up into a fuller backswing. Thus, when the downswing reached the hitting zone, my body would not be so "unwound" at the ball that I would spin out. If you're a "spinner," I think you'll find this most helpful.

Impact Thoughts

As a general policy, I do not encourage golfers to try to have conscious thoughts during the downswing. In my experience, most downswing thoughts cause something to be left out of the backswing, which will do more harm than good. The only downswing thought that has ever worked very well for me has to do with the relationship of the left shoulder at impact.

If you are pulling the ball, quite obviously your shoulders are pointed left of your target at impact, in which position the shaft has no choice but to swing to the left much too soon. To counteract this, form a mental image of connecting the grip end of the club to the back of your left shoulder as you reach the top of the backswing. Then, keeping that mental image in the downswing, try to hit the *back of the ball* with the back of your left shoulder.

To maintain this feeling through to impact, you will find yourself winding up more in the backswing which will tend to eliminate pulling shots left.

Bizarre as this tip make strike you, it really does work.

From the Top

As I start down from the top of a swing, I like to feel that both arms drop down *behind* me. Further, at my best I always had the feeling that, from the top, I didn't *turn* onto my left foot but merely *leaned* onto it from the waist down.

I make damn sure I don't start down with the shoulders, but rather with some part of me below the shoulders. I believe that a golfer who could hold the left shoulder absolutely still until after he dropped the club down with his hands and arms would play like hell, the reason being that such a move allows the left shoulder to "chase" the arms, as it should.

Overactive Lower Body

My wife Judy has a fine swing, but at times she tends to become overactive in her lower body. Beyond motion necessary to support the arm swing and body rotation, excessive movement in the lower body can actually retard the downswing.

To correct this problem, I've had Judy hit practice shots while addressing the ball with her weight in the middle of her feet and the toes of both feet up in the air. The effect of this is to impose a greater sense of balance, which allows the arms to swing freely and at their ideal speed.

When you try this, you will notice that your toes will react instinctively to maintain proper balance — that is, at the completion of the swing they will no longer be up in the air. I suspect, too, that you will be looking at a pretty good shot.

Proper Wrist/Hand Action

My many years of teaching tell me that one of the most difficult things for average golfers to learn is the feeling of correct arm, wrist and hand action. Eventually I developed a technique for imparting this feeling, which, on occasion, has produced almost miraculous results.

Hit the shot using an iron club and your normal swing, but immediately after impact try to pull the clubhead back behind where the ball rested. Whip the clubhead back as fast as you can.

Should your shoulders be in charge of the downswing, you will find this drill almost impossible to do. However, if you're controlling the club in the impact area with both hands, you'll find pulling the club back a cinch. You'll also love that connected "click" which a two-handed delivery produces, and in the bargain will discover the feel of correct arm, wrist and hand action.

Turn Your Belly Button

For years now, better golfers have been looking for a swing that minimizes or even entirely eliminates hip turn. Thus far nobody has succeeded, and I'll bet they never do.

The idea of retarding the hip turn probably started with Ben Hogan, who felt that by deliberately retarding the hip turn going back, he was building up torque that would accelerate the club coming down.

Well, I may have been privileged to watch Ben hit more balls than almost anyone else, and I can tell you that regardless of what his conscious thoughts were about hip action, his hips *did* turn. With the driver, if Ben was aiming north, his belt buckle almost faced south at the top of his swing.

It has been my observation that a golfer can turn his shoulders quite a bit with a bare minimum of hip turn, but will automatically achieve a bigger shoulder turn by allowing his hips to turn. Furthermore, turning the hips seems to add a certain smoothness to most golf swings.

At times, I've keyed my backswing by turning my left hip *in* toward the ball, and at other times by turning my right hip *away* from the ball, even though I had a hard time focusing mentally on hip action. Finally I found a great substitute for consciously-directed hip action by imagining I was turning either my belt buckle or belly button. When I turn my belly button, *both* hips turn correctly, and I've found over the years that most students also seem to prefer these images.

The Punch Shot

My bread-and-butter shot on tour was a punch shot, that is, a shot in which the follow-through is quickly cut off after impact. I used the technique not only for playing into strong winds, but as my "safe" shot, the one I called on when I

Gardner using the punch shot at Doral Open, 1968.

absolutely *had* to have an accurate shot. Ben Hogan advised me to use this shot regularly, and I finally adopted it as my basic method for iron play.

The punch shot is usually played by gripping down on the shaft, sometimes by as much as three or four inches for extremely low flighting. Obviously, this both shortens and stiffens the shaft the farther down you grip it — indeed, for every inch you choke down, you lighten an iron club by almost eight swingweight points on irons. In my experience, this combination of lighter swingweight and stiffer shaft makes for easier control of both the swing and the ball.

I had two keys when playing my punch shots. First, I took the longest possible backswing so that I could fully cock the club. In doing so, I was particular to set the clubface slightly open. Second, I made sure I turned my left hip out of the way as I swung through. My tendency is to overhook punch shots, so setting the clubface slightly open at the top and turning the hips swiftly out of the way in the downswing were precautions against hooking.

Punch shots can be played with a high trajectory by opening the face at address and moving the ball well forward in the stance. Usually, the lower the trajectory you want, the shorter and lower you make the follow-through.

For the most part, punch shots should be played with more weight on the left foot than the right, at address, and very little weight shifting to the right on the backswing, which helps keep excessive body action out of the swing. In these shots, body actions is not needed, or wanted.

Playing in the Wind

Swing tempo is very important when playing in wind. The best wind players I've seen were Arnold Palmer, Jimmy Demaret, Sam Byrd, Ben Hogan, Doug Sanders and Bob Toski, and I noticed that they all had good tempo. Most golfers tend to get quick, primarily because they shorten the backswing. I had one thought when playing in wind — be sure to swing back far enough; make the longest backswing you ever made.

Wind Shot with Long Iron

One year in Fort Worth, I was paired in the last round with Doug Ford. When we came to the sixteenth hole the wind was blowing so strongly directly into our faces that I considered hitting a three-wood on a par-three hole that normally called for a four- or five-iron. Finally I chose the two-iron, and just buried that shot into the wind, the ball finishing about fifteen feet behind the hole. I'd been outdriving Doug by a considerable margin that day, so I had to chuckle when he drew out an iron. I figured he was planning to lay up short of the pond in front of the green. Well, Doug knocked his ball just over the green about two feet from mine.

As we walked off the tee, I asked him what club he'd used, and he showed me his three-iron. How in the hell, I wondered, could he hit it so far? "There are a few shots you don't know," he smiled, "but I'll show you when we get in."

In the locker room, Doug told me that he had purposely almost bellied the ball by making absolutely no pivot. The resulting lack of backspin, he explained, helped the ball bore into the wind.

You can bet I quickly put that little shot into my bag of tricks.

Turn Slices into Hooks

If you're a chronic slicer and want to change, here's something you can try. Rarely has it failed to teach a slicer how to hook the ball. First, as you take your stance, bend your knees more than you normally would — stick them out toward your toes, while staying in balance. Feel as though your weight remains over the middle of the feet. Then before swinging, thrust your left hipbone as far toward the hole as you can, even to the point where it starts to hurt — and I don't want you to lose that feeling, even as you swing the club back.

During the backswing, the left hip can, and should, turn around, taking care that it does not slide over to the right at all. Once you have the hang of this, I'm confident your shots will draw or hook. Incidentally, this won't work unless the knees, especially the left one, are distinctly bent.

Solid Impact with Irons

To achieve solid impact with the irons, we want the club to contact the ball first, then the turf. We can regulate this, even before we swing, by the way we set up to the shot.

I've noticed that most golfers, when preparing to hit an iron shot, tend to address the ball with the left shoulder too high, and the right shoulder too low, perhaps imagining that this will help the ball in the air. This position is fine for woods, where we want a more sweeping motion, but tilting the shoulders this way for iron shots is more apt to induce a weak, scooping swing.

A slight adjustment in your set-up may be all you need to produce better, more solid contact with your irons. First, position your head so that it is more or less even with the ball. Second, pull the right shoulder up and lower the left one so that the shoulders are more level. You may also want to pull the hands back slightly more than normal. Then swing the club back slightly inside and complete the shot. At impact, if you feel the left shoulder is closer to the ground than the right, you're doing it correctly.

Remember, this is for iron shots, not woods. The set-up I've described above will allow you to hit down on the ball, and contact the ball first and the turf afterwards. The result will be a more solid impact. You won't have to help the ball into the air because, now, you can depend on the loft of the club to do it for you.

Soft, Loose Sand

Before the Buick Open at Warwick Hills, Michigan, one year I played a practice round with a club professional named Billy Markham. I was having a helluva time getting out of the bunkers since they were filled not with real sand but tiny ground pebbles about a foot deep. Billy however, kept knocking them stiff from the bunkers, so I asked him about his technique. He explained that as his clubhead hit the sand, he was trying to bury the back of it — or the part with the name on it — into the sand in back of the ball. It worked like a charm, and thanks to Billy, I played the rest of the tournament with no fear of those loose and slidey pebbles.

Outfoxing a Slice Wind

I don't know many right-handers who don't despise driving into a strong left-to-right wind but have no trouble with a right-to-left wind. What a fascinating mechanism the mind is. Long ago I discovered, quite by accident, that when I came to a hole where the tee shot had to be played into a left-to-right crosswind, there was a way to outfox it. I accomplished this simply by turning around and taking my practice swings with the wind blowing on me from *right-to-left*. Then, by not waiting too long to drive, I found I'd completely lost the usual dread of coming "over the top" that a slice wind induces.

The Mind and Putting

Even as a youngster, I never believed I was a good putter. Of course, I've putted well on occasion, but it was always a surprise to me when I did. The only time in my entire career when I entered a tournament knowing I would putt well was at the Atlanta Open in 1971, and I'll always be grateful to fellow-pro Steve Reid for the suggestion he gave me early in the week.

Noticing my struggling on the putting clock, Steve suggested I try putting *without* taking a practice stroke. When I asked why, he explained that the purpose of a practice stroke is to create a good feel for mechanics and distance. How many times, he asked, had I been dissatisfied with the feeling I got from my practice stroke? I had to admit that I seldom obtained a good feeling, and therefore it followed that when I got ready to putt for real, I was usually filled with uncertainty. Steve reasoned that by not taking a practice stroke, I would be free to anticipate a good stroke. At the very least, he argued, I could stroke the putt and see where it went without anticipating failure.

Well, it worked. I began sinking putts from everywhere. All week, I told my friends I would win the tournament, and win I did, beating Jack Nicklaus in a play-off.

What a pleasant experience that was for a man who never thought he could putt. That week, I got a feeling of how Palmer and Nicklaus felt almost every week.

A Putting System

Someday I would love to have the opportunity to offer the following system of putting to a beginning young golfer who would really stick with it. If he had never putted any other way, including conventionally, before too long I think

Gardner puts out at St. Andrews after driving the 18th green, 1971.

he'd hole so many putts he would start a trend.

Hold onto your orthodoxy, because I am about to suggest that this young golfer learn to putt *cross-handed*, and that he also look at the *target* as he strokes the ball. This is an iconoclastic suggestion, I admit, but let's examine it logically.

Today, the best putters in the world, or at least the majority of them, attempt to keep the left wrist as firm through impact as when they start the stroke. Many of us who use the conventional grip for putting find that preventing the left wrist from breaking down through the ball is extremely difficult. By positioning the left hand on the bottom of the grip, it becomes quite easy to pull the putter through the ball without the wrist breaking down too soon. My observations and experiments indicate that this is especially effective on putts of up to ten feet.

Can you imagine a bowler looking at his ball while bowling it, instead of looking at the pins? Can you name a basketball, football or baseball player who looks at the *ball* while in the act of throwing it? They wouldn't have a chance, but that's precisely what we do when we look at the golf ball as we stroke it toward a target. In effect, we're not trusting our eyes or our instincts to tell us how hard to hit the ball or where to hit it.

Playing in the Philadelphia Open one year, I had the guts to try looking at the hole while putting, and on the final day when I reached the tenth green, I found myself in the lead. Facing a twenty-foot birdie try, I finally did what I'd feared all week—hit behind the ball and moved it only halfway to the hole. Accordingly, I abandoned looking at the hole the rest of the way in—and promptly three-putted four holes to lose by two shots. In other words, I stupidly gave up on the method that had won me the lead.

A Line on Putting

One day when teaching at Frenchman's Creek in Juno Beach, Florida, I did some experimenting with a carpenter's chalk line with a buddy of mine from Birmingham named Linton Selman. Somehow I found a forty-foot putt that rolled absolutely straight. We marked it with a chalk line and then both putted the forty-footer for an hour or so. We were both stunned to find we holed over fifty percent of our putts, which is when I realized the importance of the "line" in sizing up a putt. Also, neither Linton or I had left a single putt short in the entire session.

Fairway Bunkers

Sand shots played with wooden clubs from fairway bunkers have always been the toughest in golf for me. With a tendency to hit the ball out on the toe of the club, I finally began addressing the ball back in the heel, whereupon my abilities improved noticeably.

Another tip for playing a fairway wood from sand: Starting the backswing, the lower you can keep the clubhead to the sand, without touching it, the better your chances.

Long Irons vs. Short Woods

There should be absolutely no contest for the average player when called on to choose between using, say, a one-iron or two-iron or a five-wood or six-wood. With the straight-faced irons, you need a good, flat lie, and trying to hit them from any kind of rough puts you very much against the percentages. With those lofted "utility" woods, on the other hand, you can easily handle almost any kind of lie, including deep grass, while also usually stopping the ball much faster. That's because these clubs allow you to get their leading edges well under the ball at impact. If you're higher than a four or five handicap, I suggest you put that old one-iron beside the fireplace and use it for stirring the coals.

Why Bowlegged?

Some years ago, Jay Hebert was my houseguest in south Florida for about two weeks while we were preparing to play in the Masters. We had taken on a rather heavy load by agreeing to play Ben Hogan and Cary Middlecoff for a few bob each day at the Lost Tree Club. My iron game at that time was pretty good, but my driver was giving me trouble, so I asked Jay to watch me hit a few. After doing so for a few minutes, Jay said, "You're going to think I've flipped my lid, but I'd like to see you stand up to this next ball in a bow-legged stance."

Bowlegged! Well, I did think maybe he'd flipped, but I

tried it on the very next shot. I never hit a prettier drive, nailing it all the way to the end of the range and into a pond that sits out there.

That little tip really solved my driving problem, right quick, and you don't even have to know *why* I think it works to enjoy the same success. Just try it.

Sloping Lies

When you are standing with your feet above the ball, with the ground sloping toward the right rough, you will be inclined to pull your irons and slice your woods. On these sloping, slicey lies, I always tried to make the flattest, hooki-est swing I could. But you'd better practice this action before putting your cash on the line.

When the ground slopes toward the left rough, and your feet are below the ball, you will be inclined to push the woods and hook the irons. I picked up a valuable tip on playing these hooky lies from Paul Hahn, the trick-shot artist, during an outing in North Carolina. Paul had reached the part of his show where he hit drivers from a golf tee that was nearly chest high, and he called me out of the crowd and asked me to try it. I did so reluctantly, and sent the ball nearly ninety degrees off-line to the right, barely missing the heads of the people in the gallery. Paul suggested I hit one more, this time *closing* the face at address. When the ball is at chest-height, he explained, an illusion is created that makes your body move far ahead of the ball, so that you're trying to strike it while your clubhead is still moving right. I did as Paul advised and hit another, which sailed about 250 yards dead center. Even though I'd been on tour for a number of years, this was one I didn't know. You can really learn forever in this game.

If You Can't Muzzle Your Shoulders

No matter how may times I admonish golfers not to put their shoulders in charge of the downswing, they do it anyway. This eventually led to my discovering a mind-picture that seems to work almost immediately in curing the problem.

Imagine that you are attaching the grip end of the club to the outer edge of your left shoulder as you reach the top of the back swing. From there, the trick is to make your only goal smashing the back of the ball with the back of your left shoulder. What this image does is help you avoid using the inside of your right shoulder to force the downswing. Further, by imagining that the butt of the club is attached to the left shoulder, you will more readily sense that when the left shoulder is turned off-line to the left at impact, the club-head must, of necessity, also swing left at impact.

I think you'll find if you use this image regularly that you'll automatically begin to turn your left shoulder around more going back, which will reduce the likelihood that your shoulders will be too open at impact by producing a fuller backswing.

Insights and Instant Cures

What follows are some of the insights and instant corrections I've learned over the years, all of them dug out of the ground with blood, sweat and tears over many hours and after following many false trails. You may find some of them helpful.

Push-Pull

If you are pulling your shots, which means they are starting to the left, move the ball back in your stance and maybe you'll catch it before the club has a chance to swing left. Reverse this if you are pushing your shots.

Turn, Turn, Turn

If you're not turning enough, swing back to the top and stop, then look straight in front of you and ask yourself this question : "How much more would I have to turn in order to start this shot fifty yards right of my intended target?" When you have the answer, that's how far you should turn.

. . . And Turn Again

Here's another tip to help you to turn more on the backswing. Instead of pointing your right foot at the target line in the so-called square position, point it a little away from the target. Ben Hogan popularized the square right foot because he thought he turned his hips too much on the backswing. I'll bet you don't have that problem.

Slice No More

If you positively can't stop slicing, strap a watch on your left wrist and, in the downswing, try to point the face of the watch toward the ground as your swing approaches the ball. Actually do this and you won't have to look to the right for your ball.

Driving

Especially in driving, don't *ever* think that you can eliminate or retard your hip turn.

Soft Wedge Shot

When you're trying to throw a wedge shot straight up in the air and stop the ball quickly, stand much farther away from it than normal. You'll be amazed at just how far away from the ball you can stand, just by bending your knees, and still make solid contact.

Try bending your knees more than you've ever done before, and be certain not to straighten them until the ball is gone.

Short Pitch Shots

In pitching to the green from about forty yards, or less, try pointing your left toe directly at the target at address. You may feel silly, but this adjustment moves the hips almost entirely out of the way, which allows the hands and arms to swing the club unimpeded toward the target. Use this method also if you ever want to slice a short iron.

Great Putters

The Australian tour player Jim Ferrier, who was one of the all-time great putters, told me that most of the world's best putters have the same tempo swinging back as they did swinging through. Jim said to forget about consciously accelerating the putterhead because it leads to jerkiness in the stroke. I've heard that modern putting ace Ben Crenshaw offers similar advice.

Stiff-Wristed Putting

If you desire to putt with a stiff-wristed action, try pulling up on the club with your right hand while pushing down an equal amount with your left hand. Another wrist-deadener is twisting the putter grip to the left with your left hand while simultaneously twisting to the right with your right hand. Both of these techniques tend to firm the wrists during the stroke.

Whatever method you use, remember what Bobby Jones once told me: "Son, a good putter is a match for any man."

Sweet Feel, Sweet Shot

I often noticed in my playing days that if I could make my hands feel great on the club, I would rarely hit a bad shot. This puzzled me somewhat, so I conducted research among my fellow touring pros. I wanted to know how many of them had experienced a similar reaction, and was intrigued when dozens of them responded affirmatively. Even today I'm puzzled by this.

I suppose that after a player has developed a good swing, there really isn't much more to good golf than gripping the club so that the hands feel great on it. I do know that it's extremely difficult to find a grip that feels sweet on each shot, every day. Perhaps if we simply told ourselves, out loud, that the grip feels great, we might somehow produce more sweet-feeling grips—and hit sweeter shots.

Gardner makes a big putt while winning the 1967 Cleveland
Open.

Research and Drill

For me, the practice range is a research and development department, where I seldom tire of searching for better and simpler ways to get the job done. On the practice range, you can hit more six-irons in an hour than you'll face on the course in maybe a year, and can experiment without pressure to maybe find your best way to hit that six-iron.

How very many times have I found a final peg to hang my hat on, so to speak, then asked myself: Is this all there is to playing well? Why did I not discover this sooner? Why hasn't someone else? Although most of these little pegs soon vanish, looking for them constitutes a major part of the real charm of the game of golf. As a result, I've found a million beauties.

I'm an advocate of using drills to learn because they encourage my students to train — or retrain — their bodies to swing a golf club better than before. I think that the main value of drills lies in the fact that they not only provide repetition, but force the golfer to really think about what he or she is doing. Repetition, hopefully, offers a chance to ingrain a better way to swing down below the level of consciousness, so that maybe that better way becomes the *only* way the body and mind know *how* to swing.

Here are some of my favorite drills.

WEIGHT ON LEFT — I've personally found a most useful drill consists of hitting balls with a short iron while jutting my left hip forward and setting and leaving almost all my weight on my left foot. This allows me to play the ball more forward in the stance, which — since I'm already there — practically eliminates the necessity of moving forward in the downswing.

With this drill, you can stop worrying about how much to

shift the weight during the swing. All you need do is to turn as you swing the arms up and think about completing the backswing.

I have no doubt this concept will provoke controversy among fashionable teaching gurus, but how else do they explain the fact that, almost without exception, the masters employ a full backswing with a driver without balancing on the right leg at the top of the swing? Check it out. See how much weight you can shift to the right when both thighs are inclined toward the hole, as you'll see in most top players. Damned little, is the answer.

BALL FORWARD — I have a drill that helps correct my tendency to hit "out" on the ball, but unfortunately it's rather painful. I had been driving poorly prior to a tournament in Florida, so I looked at some film of my driver swing. I discovered that my problem was caused by falling back and hitting out at the ball. I went to the practice range in the early afternoon and beat balls until dark with the ball teed three inches outside, or forward of, my left foot. I can tell you that this was a physically stressful process, and I doubt I hit ten good drives all afternoon.

The next morning, on the first hole, paired with Lee Trevino, I teed the ball just inside my left heel, where I always had played it, and absolutely creamed my first drive well past Lee in the center of the fairway. That day I probably drove as well as I'd ever driven. Reflecting later on why, I figured out that the day before I had hit so many shots with the ball teed far forward that I'd grooved my swing to move on a more inside-to square-to inside arc.

Drills won't always work that well, or that fast, but they will invariably at least start you along the right track — assuming you know which one to try. And, of course, that's what your home pro is for.

THE CHEATING BOARD — Hitting balls from the surface of a plywood board taught me a great deal about a golf swing. If you'd like to try this, get yourself a piece of plywood as straight as an arrow about the length of your driver and about twenty-four inches wide.

If you plan to carry it around in your golf bag, you'll need to reduce the width to about eight inches. Draw a line, lengthwise, straight down the center of the board and make two notches in the plywood, one at the end so that you can tee the ball for wood shots, and a shallow one about twelve inches behind the first notch that will keep the ball from rolling off on iron shots. Then mark a line to indicate the initial correct direction of your backswing.

If the board has been cut straight, it will aid your aim and alignment by indicating the initial target line and allowing you to set your feet parallel to that line at address. You will love the little thump the plywood furnishes each time you strike the ball solidly (no thump = poor contact). With the driver, make certain that you hear a lengthy scraping sound as you start the club back and a shorter scraping sound with a short iron. What's important is that each shot be distinctly heard as you start the club back — no *silent* backswings.

Hitting off the board will not hurt your clubs or your hands and arms, and you'll find that you will spin the ball nicely with each solidly struck iron shot — which will help your understanding of why soft, deep fairways promote "fliers."

The board will also train you to contact the ball at a precise point at the bottom of the swing. I call my chunk of plywood the "Cheating board." I think you'll rapidly fall in love with yours.

GRADUATED SWING-LENGTH TABLE — Some time ago, an outfit came out with a brilliant learning device, a little table with astroturf on its surface that could be adjusted to different heights. Unfortunately, someone at Frenchman's Creek stole mine, and I haven't been able to replace it.

The little table came equipped with several very short six-irons made up in varying lengths and lies. With the table at its *highest* level, the student swung the *shortest* of the six-irons, finding it quite easy to hit acceptable shots. As the student gained confidence, he or she moved to the next stage in which the table height was lowered and shots were played with a six-iron having a little longer shaft. By the time the student reached the ground, where the longest shaft was used, he or she would almost always understand, from both swing feel and results, a great deal more about a golf swing than when starting out. Whoever invented this little table understood a lot about learning golf, and most notably that you should start at a level you can handle, then gradually move to more advanced levels.

Students who used the table quickly realized that a more level backswing is needed to avoid smashing the club under the table, and that there is no need for golfers to turn themselves upside down during the swing.

Sand Shots: Getting the Feel

If you can't seem to get the feel for hitting from sand, you might try a practice tip I learned from Chick Harbert, the former PGA Champion. Chick would tell you to ground the club in the sand behind the ball, exactly where you want to strike into the sand. Once you start the swing, you can see the indentation in the sand and more easily hit the spot you intend to hit. By varying the distance you make your mark behind the ball, you can find the right distance for you. Listening to the sound will help you acquire the feel for proper technique. All good bunker shots produce a distinct "thump" where the flange on the back of the sole hits the sand.

Making Practice Pay Off

As you may have gathered, I have always loved to practice and thus have spent many long hours on the range. I will not say that it was time wasted, but there's no doubt much of it was spent on aimless thoughts and feelings, pursued at random. I wish I had been more disciplined and better organized in my goals and practice routines.

We do learn from experience, although not often enough do we learn from the experience of others. Here are some of the things I've learned over the years about practicing, which I pass along in the fervent hope that they help you to practice more productively.

● I try to practice with an observer knowledgeable enough about golf technique to tell me if I'm doing what I think I'm doing. Instant feedback and correction sure beats long hours of searching on your own.

● I have learned to be more thoughtful in my approach to practice, by deciding ahead of time precisely what I'm going to try to achieve, then focusing strictly on that goal for that particular session.

● I can only pay attention to one swing thought at a time, or, in rare cases, perhaps two thoughts. This takes discipline, but I try not to be distracted by other thoughts.

● If I had it to do again, I wouldn't beat myself up so much. I have been known to hit balls with one club for ten hours, trying to make the damn club part of me. That just won't work.

● There is a limit to everyone's stamina. Sometimes I practiced so much that I was too physically tired to play well, and often I was mentally exhausted as well.

● I would do more physical conditioning at a much earlier age. I would certainly include sit-ups, half-knee bends and chin-ups to strengthen the arms and legs, plus some form of swimming, jogging or biking to build aerobic fitness and stamina. Pull-ups are very effective with the palms facing forward.

● Most golfers, including the pros, devote hours to practicing full shots, but spend little time on the half-shots or three-quarter shots with which we are so often confronted on the golf course. This despite the fact that only thirty-seven percent of the shots played on the tour are full shots. I believe most golfers would reap great benefits from spending appreciable amounts of time on shots that require less than a full swing.

Final Thought

If you think golf is a difficult game to play, you ought to try *writing* about it. I must confess to a sense of futility when I've tried to put into words some of the ideas that I think might help others to play the game better, the biggest problem being that in a book one must deal in generalities instead of the specifics that every individual golfer needs and deserves. I fear I may not have enough years left on this earth to write down every single thing I think I've learned about golf, but, here, at least, I do believe I've covered the most important parts of it.

What was aggravating as hell was to realize all through the writing process that no one can learn how to play this great game well entirely from the written word. All I can hope for, then, is that some of the things you read here will make you more receptive to sound personal instruction from a competent teacher.

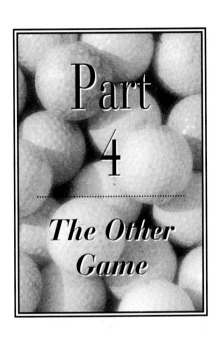

Part 4

The Other Game

Why the Pros Resent Putting

To be perfectly candid, many professionals take an unchar-
itable view toward putting. Most of them, including myself,
either resent it or regard it with suspicion. In fact, I can't
think of one touring pro, past or present, who would want to
be included in this part of the book. It never seemed right to
me that a one-inch putt should count as much as a 300-
yard drive, but it does. It seems unfair, and quite sad, that
putting takes on so much importance in golf, but I suppose
the game isn't fair.

During my years on tour, putting demons like Paul Runyan, Horton Smith, Jerry Barber and Dave Stockton were
considered somewhat mysterious, or at least peculiar. That's
because, as masters of the putting game, they could neutralize the power of an opponent with a stroke of the blade.

It's not that we hated putting, you understand; it's just
that some of us didn't quite understand it. To us, putting
was like the crazy aunt you keep in the closet and bring out
only when you can't avoid it any longer. You just hoped she
wouldn't do anything to embarrass you, but you were afraid
that she might.

We certainly didn't complain when our own putts
dropped, but we never bragged on our putting because it
was considered a sissy part of the game. Manly fellows hit
long drives and rifled two-irons at the hole, we thought,
while the folks who relied on putting, if they were not
downright devious, were clearly playing another game. In
fact, on tour, putting came to be known as just that —
"The Other Game." Of course, I fell right in with this kind

of thinking and developed an attitude toward putting that eventually I came to regret, because when I was younger, I was a demon putter, too.

The Greatest Putter I Ever Saw

Yes, it's true. When I was in high school and college, I was a great putter, although no one knew it because of Wendell Barnes. Wendell was my close friend and teammate on the high school golf team, and later he followed me to Louisiana State University where we played on the college golf team. Even though I was an exceptional putter then, every once in a while I'd miss one. Wendell never did. Fast greens, slow greens, grainy or slick, none of it mattered, because Wendell handled them all the same. My, could he putt! Not only did he make putts from everywhere, he would announce them in advance. Wendell Barnes never played in the pressure cooker of the pro tour, but he was, hands down, the greatest putter I've ever seen.

Wendell was a year ahead of me in school, a good-looking lad with wavy blond hair who was almost as round as he was tall. Because he was chubby, we called him Fat Boy, but he was good-natured and took that in stride. Besides, he was an intense competitor. He had a good swing and played with a controlled hook. Wendell never bothered to learn a fade because, as he said, he wouldn't fool with a shot he didn't know anything about. He just wanted to reach the green any old way, then kill you with his putting.

Wendell had a peculiar grip, holding the putter way up at the end, and he took his little finger off the shaft and rested it on top of the butt. He was a wrist putter, with a stroke like Lloyd Mangrum, Pete Cooper and Billy Casper. I did my damndest to copy his stroke, but there was no way I could. During his preparation, Wendell would waggle the putter and begin tapping his right foot. He'd give about

Putting whiz: Wendell "Fat Boy" Barnes, 1941.

three taps, and then, bap! he'd hit the putt. He stroked down on the ball, almost taking a little turf, and the roll he got was just uncanny. He popped the ball so smartly you could hear it clear across the green. In his mind, no putt was too long to make, none was out of Wendell's range.

Like all of us at that age, he was a little hot-tempered now and then. If a putt or two rimmed out on him, he broke the putter and found another. He showed up with a new putter every two weeks or so, but whether it was a blade, a mallet, a Cash-in, or whatever, made no difference because Wendell could putt with anything. He was just a natural. For a period of five years in high school and three in college, I'm convinced that nobody in the world could have out-putted Wendell. In college, most of us on the golf team could give him two-up a side, from tee to green, but we still had a hard time beating him. One putt on each hole doesn't add up to very many, as he was fond of telling us.

The Games We Played

One day Wendell and his brother Harry, who was also a good golfer, played a match against my dad and me. My dad was a hard-boiled, stubborn competitor from the old school who would rather saw off his arm than concede a putt of six inches. If you had a little kick-away, he'd say, "Go ahead, take your time and tap it in." That day I don't think Wendell missed a single putt, from any length. He ran them in on every hole, and my dad was looking like a dog that just tan-gled with a skunk. When we got to the seventeenth, Wendell missed the green and chipped it up about six feet from the hole. Wendell called my dad "the old bald-headed fossil," and when he was in a hurry he shortened this to "Fozz."

"Hey, Fozz," said Wendell, "you ain't gonna make the Fat Boy stroke this little ole putt, are ya?"

My old man look at Wendell, then looked over at the putt, and finally croaked, "Hell, no, pick it up. I couldn't stand to see another one go in." I was astounded, because I had never seen my dad give anyone a putt, let alone a six-footer. But that's how good Wendell was with the flat stick.

In high school we played nearly every day, and afterwards we would practice. Wendell would go to the putting green and I'd head for the range. Funny, isn't it, how the good putters always seem to practice putting a lot? Most of the time I'd beat balls, or watch our pro Charlie Miller give a lesson.

Eventually Wendell and I started playing a little money game about three times a week. My dad liked to gamble some, and there was a guy in Macon named Pinky Ray who took quite a shine to Wendell; so Pinky Ray would back Barnes and Dad would back me, and we got to playing for quite a bit of money. The matches were pretty intense, because Wendell and I got a piece of it if we won.

After a while Wendell and I started snapping at each other because it had reached the point where we were playing for more than we could afford to lose. It wasn't fun anymore. One day we came to the last hole with something like $800 riding on the last putt. I had a four-footer to win but thought I'd missed it. As I turned around to heave the putter into the creek, I heard the ball drop. As a consequence, we won a bundle.

When we reached the locker room, I turned to my dad. "If you want to play any more gambling games, you'll have to get you another boy," I told him, "because I'm through with it. I've lost the best friend I've got, and it's not worth it." Dad agreed, so we didn't play that game anymore, and Wendell and I became friends again. High school kids have no business playing for that kind of money. Maybe it did teach us how to perform under pressure, but the evil outweighed the good.

Three Hacks Plus One Equals 'Fo'

I'm not sure that Wendell needed the lessons, because he putted the same with or without pressure. He could read greens better than anyone I've seen; he *saw* just where the ball *should* roll, and he knew exactly how hard to hit it.

During college, he and I were paired in the last round of a tournament in Vicksburg, Mississippi, on a course with huge, rolling greens with big shelves. Wendell was holing putts from everywhere, as he usually did. At the seventeenth hole he knocked his approach to the edge of the green about seventy-five to eighty feet from the cup.

Tap, tap, tap went that right foot of his, then over the hills came the ball. As it rolled over the final shelf, Wendell started walking after it with a grin on his face, and before it went in, he said, "You know, I'm getting tired waiting for that baby to get to the hole." Of course, it did.

Wendell was of the school that believes three hacks plus one putt equals "fo." That's a Georgia "fo," as in four. Wendell used to say, "If you never score any more than 'fo,' you'll do just fine." That little saying was familiar to anyone growing up in the South, and later it became the subject of a cute little golf book, written by a character from Sarasota named Old Stoney. If I'd paid more attention, maybe I'd have become a better putter, but in those days that wasn't a lesson I wanted to learn.

How I Rated the Pros

Among the pros, who are the best putters I've seen? Well, I don't know how anyone could have made more putts than Billy Casper. Billy had a wristy "pop" stroke, but he holed so many you wondered why you ever cared what a putting stroke *looked* like. Over the years he was just fantastic, and yet when his putting was mentioned, he'd turn to his caddie, Dell, and whine, "Tell 'em, Dell, I haven't made a putt in two years." Dell would nod and then wink.

Arnold Palmer was certainly one of the three or four best, and don't listen to anyone who says differently — including Arnold. My Lord, the putts that man made would curl your hair, and he griped about it all the time. If I had kept a

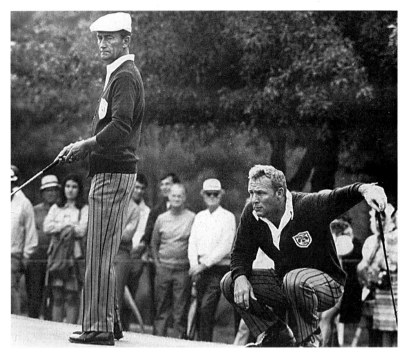

Gardner and Arnold Palmer paired in the 1971 Ryder Cup.

scrapbook of all the articles in which Arnold complained about his putting, the book would be sixteen feet thick. Palmer hunched over the ball, pigeon-toed and knock-kneed, which enabled him to keep his head still. He sort of jabbed at the ball, but he had a visceral feel for the hole and, for nearly a decade, was bold as brass.

Jack Nicklaus, of course, is one of the all-time great putters. Jack probably holed more pressure putts than anyone I can recall, but he, too, always complained that he wasn't that good on the greens. Maybe that's because he practiced putting so little, compared to working on the big shots. His stroke was good, but what was so outstanding about Jack was his calm, almost insistent determination to hole the putt, time after time. I envy him for being able to block out those terrible doubts.

Mangrum Was a Marvel

Lloyd Mangrum is on my list, a marvelous putter and as cool a customer as golf ever saw. He drained more putts in tight spots than anyone I can remember, except Nicklaus. Lloyd wasn't afraid of anyone or anything, and believe me when I tell you that putting was his domain. You never sensed any doubt in him. Lloyd had such confidence because he cut his teeth on making eight-footers in big money matches with professional gamblers like Titanic Thompson.

I always paid attention to anything Lloyd had to say about putting. I remember once at the U.S. Open at Inverness, in Toledo, Ohio, Lloyd came over to watch me on the practice putting clock. He told me I might do better if I used his own practice technique of watching the hands while stroking putts. "If I can make those hands do what I want them to," he explained, "I won't have any trouble with the putter itself." It was good advice, and maybe you ought to try it.

Neither Mangrum nor Casper had what you'd call a beautiful putting stroke, but the ball didn't know that; it kept going in because they did the same thing to it every time. That's the key to good putting, which is the most individualistic of golf strokes. Find a comfortable position where you can be at ease repeating the same action over and over again.

Mangrum wasn't just good, he was smart, and he wasn't a man to mince words. In the 1959 Masters, Lloyd was paired with Bill Hyndman, the fine amateur from Philadelphia. At the eleventh green, the pin was cut in the left rear about six paces from the dangerous pond, and Hyndman's ball lay about forty feet away, across a little shelf that bisects the green. Hyndman started his putt on the wrong side of the shelf, and the ball continued breaking left until finally it rolled over the bank and into the water. After marking down a seven on Hyndman's card, Lloyd said, "That was the dumbest putt I ever saw."

They Called Him Mr. Lloyd

Lloyd Mangrum, 1956

Nobody much fooled with Lloyd Mangrum. Most of the younger players called him "Mr. Lloyd." A native of Texas, Mangrum had served in the Army in World War II, participating in the Normandy invasion and later suffering wounds in action. He won the first postwar U.S. Open in 1946, beating Byron Nelson and Vic Ghezzi. He didn't appear to fear anyone on the golf course. Paired with Sam Snead in the final round of a tournament, the two men stood on the last tee tied for the lead when a loudspeaker on the clubhouse roof blared, "In the event of a play-off. . . ." Mangrum turned to Snead and growled, "There ain't gonna be no play-off, Sambo, because I'm gonna birdie this hole." Snead promptly drove it a foot out-of-bounds on the right.

Lloyd loved to fly, and piloted his single-engine plane everywhere — even after suffering fifty-seven heart attacks. He navigated with a service-station road map. He always said he had to win so he could earn enough money "to get the hell out of Texas." He would tell the story of the eight-foot-seven, 450-pound Texan who went to England and Scotland to play golf, suffered a heart attack and died. They searched all over the British Isles to find a coffin big enough to ship the guy home. Finally someone gave him an enema, and they sent the fellow back to Texas in a matchbox. That was Lloyd's story, not mine.

Stone Face and Other Great Putters

But we were talking about the super putters. I would include Johnny Palmer on my list, too. We called him Stone Face.

"Hey, Stoney," we'd ask, "how the hell do you putt these grainy old greens?"

"What grain?" he'd reply. He paid no attention to grain; he just banged them in. Johnny stood straight up and never moved the top of the putter during the stroke — *all wrists*.

I think the best pure stroke among the top putters I've seen belongs to Dave Stockton. He was, and still is, a superb putter. We didn't particularly admire his swing, nor the way he played golf, but from eight-iron distance in to the green he would beat you to death. If he could have driven anywhere near like he could putt, he would have been really something.

The Fabulous 'Doc' Middlecoff

Cary Middlecoff was a fabulous putter, damn near as good as there was. He sat back on his right side with his head way back over his right foot so that he could look directly down the line, very much like Nicklaus always has. I'm pretty sure that Doc could see the line better than most people. The ordinary golfer might be inclined to hit behind the ball with such a set-up, but Doc never did.

Middlecoff said that he tried to pick out one dimple on the back of the ball, and stare at it. That's hard to do, but Doc would keep looking at that one dimple and try to hit it. Someone said the reason he was such a marvelous putter was that the ball got so tired of waiting to be hit that it gave up and went in on its own. Middlecoff kept the putter quite

Cary Middlecoff and Gardner at the 1961 Memphis Open.

low, broke his wrists slightly going back, and led with the back of his left hand as he stroked the putt. It never broke down, except perhaps on an extremely long putt.

Another marvelous putter was Jackie Burke, who for a few years back in the 1950s holed everything in sight. His great buddy Jimmy Demaret used to say that, at this very minute, a Burke was holing a putt somewhere in the world. We considered Jackie to be an outstanding putting instructor, too, and he helped me often. One day, prior to the Colonial Invitational in Fort Worth, I was practice-putting when out strode Burke. I motioned him over and begged for immediate help because I was due to tee off in five minutes. He watched me stroke a couple putts, then said, "No wonder you can't putt, gripping the club that way. Move your left hand over on top in a strong position, like Tom Watson does."

Well, his tip worked and I had a good tournament. The very next year Jackie again found me on the putting clock at Colonial, and again I asked him for help. I had stayed with his "strong" putting grip for the entire year but recently had been losing confidence

He watched for a moment, then said, "No wonder you can't putt; nobody can putt with such a strong grip. Just move your left hand under the shaft and you'll be fine." That Burke is a beauty, but this incident illustrates how elusive and baffling putting is for some of us.

Putting must seem very easy for Ben Crenshaw. He may be the greatest putter of all time. He won two NCAA tournaments by putting everybody to death, and he's won a goodly number of tour events, including the Masters, primarily with that magic wand of his. As a professional, he's become known as a master putter, but he's been a genius with that wand ever since high school. That's a long time to be a master putter, so I figure he must know something the rest of us don't know.

Many thought that Bob Charles, the great left-hander, had the purest stroke ever, and it would be hard to argue with them. But Bob bitched about his putting, too, which gives you an idea of how high were his standards of excellence. And I would also mention Tom Watson. For five or six years, who could putt better than Watson, with his strong left-hand grip and bold approach? But later, when Tom began to miss those six-foot comebackers, he discarded the bold stroke and his putting prowess began to wane.

Locke's Stroke the One to Copy

But if I were going to copy one player's putting style, it would be Bobby Locke's. It wasn't that this eccentric South African holed so many putts, which he did; it was that he looked so good doing it. It looked to me as though Locke's way was the way you *ought* to putt. You couldn't play a single round with Locke that you didn't wind up trying to putt with a closed stance and taking the club back inside, like he did. You take it back closed, then stroke the thing kind of out and over, and the ball comes rolling toward the hole as though it couldn't go anywhere else.

Locke used to paint dots of Mercurochrome on his ball when he practiced on the putting clock. I asked him one day why he did that, and he replied, "I'm looking for the tumbling action, old boy." He wanted to roll the ball so that the little dots tumbled end-over-end in a perfect roll. If the dots started to wobble, he knew he hadn't rolled the ball end-over-end.

Bobby converted a lot of people to trying his method during his rather brief time on the American Tour. Ben Hogan tried it, as did Gary Player, and certainly Gary's been a great putter over the years. Locke once told Gary that, as he finished, he should put the putterhead on the ground just *after* he hit the ball. "If you try that for thirty days," he said, "you'll always be a good putter."

Ordinarily if you asked Locke about putting, he wouldn't tell you a thing. All he would say is, "Look in Bobby Jones's book, it's all in there." Jones felt that the putting stroke was just a miniature golf swing, which is kind of hard to buy, but it obviously worked for him. Jones is certainly on my list of great putters. Dow Finsterwald was a great one, too.

Doug Ford and Jerry Barber would make the list, too. Barber would have weeks where nobody could putt as well as he could. He always putted with a super-heavy putter, and it was so upright that no one but Jerry could use it. He's still a wonderful putter at the age of seventy-eight.

Another great putter, whom I admired in college, was Dale Morey. Dale wasn't particularly long off the tee, but he could fell Goliath with his old Tommy Armour putter, on any kind of green. Dale was one of the most positive men I ever met.

As a group, the current generation of players is head and shoulders above mine in putting skills, although few, in my opinion, would be ranked among the truly great putters. Yet, understand that the fellows I've mentioned were gifted beyond the norm and displayed a mastery of "The Other Game" that would be noticed in any era; they were, in a word, peculiar — or at least peculiarly gifted.

Money Games with Sam Snead

In my day, we used to engage in little contests on the putting clock. Once in a while I would be dumb enough to try Sam Snead. Usually I got whipped, but I got old Sambo good one year during the Citrus Open at Rio Pinar in Orlando, putting for a dollar a hole and double on aces. I was on a streak and I had him down about forty-five dollars when Sam announced he wanted to double the bet.

"Oh no," said I, "you get out of this the same way you came in, a dollar a hole."

Finally Sam was called to the tee. "I got to go; I'll pay you when I get in," he growled. "No sir," said I, "you can go right *after* you pay me."

Well, he reached in his pocket and counted out all that nice green money into my hand, and that's the only time I can remember beating him on the putting clock.

Not many could stay with Sam on the practice green; he would beat most of the guys to death. I think he was the best I've seen in those betting games. Eventually nobody would try him anymore. Why? Because he may have been the best gamesman who ever lived, and he would always find a way to beat you. His stroke wasn't pretty — he sort of broke his wrists coming through — but obviously you don't win as many tournaments as Sam did without being a pretty good putter.

Snead was an exceptional long putter, with his great touch, but what people forget about Sam is that he hit the ball so close to the hole so often, he was just bound to miss some of those short putts. Of course, those are the putts people remember, but believe me, Sam Snead holed more than his fair share.

Hogan probably wouldn't be included in this list if you counted his entire career, but he was a phenomenal putter during the 1940s. I think most of the fellows on tour during that era felt that Ben was the deadliest putter of all from ten or twelve feet in. I didn't know him then, but I have no reason to doubt it. A number of his peers have told me that if they had to hole a sidehill eight-footer for their lives, and they could have chosen anyone to putt for them, they'd have picked Hogan.

I never heard anyone say that Byron Nelson wasn't a good putter. He would put both thumb nails on the shaft, and if he made one on the first hole, look out, because he'd run the table on you.

The Pros' Putting Teacher

When I worked for Hogan at Tamarisk Country Club in Palm Springs, it was a toss-up as to which of us was the worst putter. We practiced unfailingly, yet neither of us seemed to improve very much. It was pathetic, really. Then, over a period of several weeks, my putting showed dramatic signs of improvement. Naturally, Ben was curious, and finally asked me if I could account for the sudden turnaround. "George Low has been helping me each morning," I replied.

Among the players, George Low was known as perhaps the best money putter in the world. He had spent most of his life "teaching" well-heeled friends and acquaintances the finer points of the putting game. His teaching method was to throw a wad of bills on the grass, raise his eyebrows, and inquire, "Would you care to putt?" Make no mistake, George Low could putt, and I imagine that he's still a great putter at the age of eighty-something.

What we liked best about George was that he knew exactly *how* he did it, and even better, he could show others how to do it. During the course of his "lessons," George would quietly slip your cash into his pocket, murmuring words of encouragement, but nobody minded because George never failed to make you a better putter.

Years ago, Demaret had annointed George with the title of "America's Guest," a role that just naturally suited his temperament. George traveled around the country visiting wealthy, well-connected friends in golf, living out of the trunk of his Cadillac, and stopping wherever the pasture was greenest and the welcome mat widest. His visits lasted for months. George was a marvelous companion and storyteller, and as long as he didn't find your credit card, a wonderful fellow to have around.

George Low's Method

George Low's method for putting was simple. He advocated holding the putter firmly, with both thumbnails pinched into the grip, and insisted on addressing the ball well into the heel of the putterhead. This forced you to address each putt the same way, he said, and encouraged you to swing the putterhead immediately inside. He strongly believed in hinging the wrists on the backswing, which opened the blade slightly as he took it back. From there, he merely held that slight wrist-cock, and gave the ball an aggressive crack. George was so positive about putting that invariably some of his confidence rubbed off on you.

After I had finished teaching in the morning, I'd head for the putting clock where George was waiting to continue my "lessons." Later we'd putt to see who would buy lunch. When

George used his putter, it wasn't a contest, not even close, so he switched to my twenty-two-ounce training driver and beat me with that. Then he beat me using his wedge, and after that, with one of the pins from the cups in the putting green. Finally he announced that he'd show up with his kicking shoes the next day, and damned if he didn't beat me kicking the ball. George didn't buy any lunches that winter.

Palmer's Lessons

Rarely did I see money part from George Low's hands anywhere near the putting clock. He followed the tour almost every week, preferring to remain close to such a ready supply of cash and customers. He loved the game of golf. George did not always pluck basket cases like me. He spent a great deal of time with Palmer, before he became Arnie, and not long after that Palmer became recognized as the best putter in the world. Many of us credited George Low, which just added to George's reputation, although it always puzzled me that Arnold never gave him any of the credit — or anything else, according to George.

In the fifties, George made a deal to represent Cuttysark Scotch whiskey, which he was known to sample rather freely. He was furnished with a new Cadillac painted a brilliant Cuttysark yellow, with decals all over it, and George never looked so pleased as when he wheeled that baby up to the players' entrance and skidded to a halt.

Back in my day, we didn't dream that you could putt as well as the fellows of today. I don't think our standards were high enough. We never imagined that you could make them all, like the players today, as a group, seem to do. Back then you were admired for being a great shotmaker or a long driver, rarely for putting. As I've mentioned, I fell right in with that crowd, and so did Arnold Palmer, as great a putter as he was. Arnold would have everyone believe he drove all the greens, then three-putted every one for pars. Well, that's baloney; it was just the reverse.

Palmer was leading money winner from the trees; he robbed more people with a putter than Robin Hood did with his bow and arrow. Later, of course, Arnold became one of the greatest drivers in the game, but during the years he was leading money winner, if all I had to do was play him from tee to green, conceding all putts, I think I'd have done okay. People forget how many Arnold holed, from all over. Believe me, I was envious.

Advice from Horton Smith

Looking back on it all, I realize that I just *talked* myself out of the putting game. One Monday morning I was at the Detroit Golf Club to qualify for the U.S. Open, and while eating breakfast in the grill room, Horton Smith, the most famous putter in the world and Detroit's head pro, sat down and asked about my game. "It's very good," I said, "except for the putter." Smith proceded to tell me how he had become a good putter.

The long and short of it was that Horton had convinced himself that he *would* putt well, even when he couldn't. He told me that he wouldn't even stay in a room where anyone was talking about poor putting. Of course, we all know what a great putter he became. When we finished breakfast, Horton accompanied me to the putting clock, and as he talked, I began to think positively. I went out and shot 67-66 to lead the nation in qualifying.

Why I didn't follow his mental advice forever, I'll never know. I would rather talk about bad putting than good putting, so I never gave myself a chance. I would dwell on it until, literally, I had no idea how I should putt. As a consequence, I couldn't putt worth a damn. And of all the dumb things you can do in golf, that's the dumbest.

Part
5

The
Tournament
Game

Tournament Golf Is Not a Game

On the surface, professional tournament golf looks like a game. Dozens of good players meet in a tournament which appears very festive with all the tents and logos, large enthusiastic galleries, colorful personalities, and all the contenders, both favorites and dark horses. The word *tournament* derives from an old French word *torneur*, meaning to turn, and was applied to a series of contests presented as an entertainment, or a competition to declare a champion. In the Middle Ages, the term became associated with jousting and other knockout sports, along with competitive games like archery and swordplay. In those days, all the valiant men competed until one was left standing.

The term has survived, but the original purpose has not. Professional tournament golf is not a game, it's not even a contest; it's a business — in every sense of the word. Money has changed everything, including the attitudes of the players. Today all you need is two or three good weeks to have a big year on the pro tour. That wasn't true during the tour's formative years, when the pros competed for only twenty paying places. Now they play for seventy places. Today these fellows spill more money than we played for.

We're approaching the point where we're making a science of competitive golf, and maybe too much so, because I think it's taken some of the fun out of the game. I can remember in high school that I couldn't wait to get out there on Saturday morning in the cool air and smell that freshly mown grass. I wanted to see what I could do. I haven't felt like that in so many years I've almost forgotten what it was like, but I know it was wonderful. Once I made a business of golf, it was never the same again. It took the charm from the game. To show you how jaded I had become, toward the end of my career I scored a hole-in-one and didn't even get excited about it. Yet I can remember when scoring an ace was an occasion for great joy.

Champions: A Vanishing Breed

When I started on tour, I wasn't good enough to win. I'm not sure I realized it at the time, but I guess I did. So my goal was to make a check. Today we have fields full of players with that attitude. That's probably why we don't have more great champions. They're a vanishing breed. The prevailing attitude on the tour is too passive. You don't find many out there today with the hell-bent-for-damnation attitude that produces a winner. The watchword seems to be, "If I don't win, it doesn't matter. As long as I finish in the top twenty or thirty, I'll still make piles of money." This attitude didn't start with today's generation. It's been around for a while. Frank Beard was a perfect example. He said titles didn't mean anything; only money counted. He was a good player and led the money list one year, but I never thought he played as well as he *should* have.

In psychology, when we studied the theories of learning, we discovered that when you reach a learning plateau, your performance goes downhill unless you change something. What was needed to reach a higher plateau was a change of method or attitude. In golf, you must be willing to make changes if your performance indicates that you should. Ben Hogan did, changing his method when he knew he must. If you're a player like Sam Snead, there's probably no need to make mechanical changes, but perhaps attitudinal ones might have helped.

No game in the world is quite like professional tournament golf, nor do I think it can it be understood by outsiders. Nerves play a role in all competitive sports, but in other games players aren't affected as much because they have an opportunity to "run it off" and rid themselves of that tension. In professional golf, it all goes inside. In that respect, it's unique. Ben Hogan once asked, rhetorically, "Why in the world would a player be nervous on the first tee? You've just proved, or *should* have, over and over again that your swing works (on the practice range)." Yet even the greatest players — Jones, Hogan, Snead, and Nicklaus — are affected sooner or later by nerves, and some, like Nelson, sooner than others.

So much of the game is played between the ears. I've heard people say that golf is anywhere from fifty to seventy percent mental. Years ago I agreed with that, but I've changed my mind. Once you acquire a reasonable golf swing, golf is ninety percent mental. History teaches us that certain moves in a golf swing will work better and more often than others, and if you disregard that knowledge, you're crazy. Yet I've seen some of the darndest swings you can imagine work because the golfers *think* they will. How can you explain that? I spent about seven years studying human nature, but don't ask me to define it for you.

As you may have seen, there are successful players on tour with no more technical ability than the average weekend golfer, but they're winning golf tournaments and lots of money. Some of them don't look pretty doing it, but they know how to make a number. If Miller Barber really knew how bad he looks, how many pars do you think he'd make? But Miller *thinks* he can play, so he can. We all saw Raymond Floyd at age fifty-one in the 1993 Ryder Cup matches when, on the last day, he played his best golf of the week in beating the Spaniard, Jose Maria Olazabal, to win a crucial match for the American side. Raymond *believes* he can do it; he *wants* to do it; and he *imagines* himself doing it.

Choking and the Fear
of Success

A fellow doesn't have to be blessed with natural ability or be a mental giant to succeed at golf, so long as his thoughts are positive. If you focus only on positive thoughts, you don't give negative thoughts much chance to influence the swing. We might put this another way: To win, you must treat a pressure situation as an *opportunity to succeed*, rather than an opportunity to fail. Why? Because, invariably, your attitude will govern the action. Show me the fellow who steps on the tee with an air that says, "Step aside boys, this is my tee," and I'll show you a winner. Gene Sarazen is the best example I can remember. He might not perform every single time, but I don't think he ever thought about failure, and I guarantee you his Adam's apple was not jumping up and down.

Choking is a word we don't hear much anymore. Now we call it "lack of concentration." We hear television announcers say, "He lost his concentration," instead of, "He choked like a dog." Frankly, I don't think choking has anything to do with guts. It has to do with your brains. What does your brain imagine? If it imagines that you can't do something, the odds are you can't, and you won't. In some people, it's the fear of failure; in others, it's the fear of success. Some people are afraid to succeed in the same sense that they're reluctant to show off. Once I had matured, I think I might have been a much better player if I had bragged more. Most of the great winners have been show-offs, or at least had a strong streak of brag in them. Gene Sarazen, Walter Hagen, and Sam Snead come to mind. Arnold Palmer loved showing off, and Jack Nicklaus, too, though in a different way. Jack liked to assert his superiority, and, of course, he could back it up. Some personalities never quite get used to

One that didn't get away: 1968 Doral Open victory.

dealing with the fear of success. This was brought home to me in a most unexpected way.

Sometime in the 1960s, we were playing the PGA Four-Ball Championship in Palm Beach Gardens, not far from my home. On Sunday night after the tournament was over, we ended up at a party with all sorts of people. Later a bunch of us, including John McArthur, the billionaire who owned the golf course we played, Arnold Palmer, and businessman Lewis Keller piled into cars and found our way back to my house in North Palm Beach. There was no shortage of drink, and neither Arnold nor I was missing any rounds. Eventually we found ourselves sitting on the living room floor solving the world's problems in a semi-stupor. The conversation turned to tournament golf and how ephemeral was the habit of winning. I advanced a theory that when Arnold won his first Masters by holing a bunch of putts on the final round, it affected the way he played Augusta National from that moment on. "You figured if you could hang on until that last nine on Sunday, this miracle might happen again, and damned if it didn't. You got to waiting for it to happen."

"Yeah, you might be right," said Arnold.

I grew pensive and wondered aloud, "Why don't I play better on Sunday? Lord knows, I've had chances to win at least fifty tournaments, yet I've won only eight. I just don't understand it."

"You don't? Well, anybody could tell you why," said Arnold.

I blinked at him. "Then be kind enough to do so."

Arnold stared at me, "It's too important to you. And you need the money too bad." And you know something? He was right. Winning meant too much to me, and I reached the point where I was afraid of it.

For some people, treating pressure as an opportunity to succeed rather than fail is very hard to do. It was for me, especially when it came to putting. The mind, we learn in psychology, tends to forget unpleasant things, but not in my case. How very difficult it was for me to come up with positive thoughts and to keep them firmly in mind. Perhaps that's the secret to concentration.

Hogan's Concentration

Ben Hogan was famous for his concentration and his silence while playing. The "Wee Ice Mon," they called him, because he didn't talk to anybody. In the 1965 PGA Championship at Laurel Valley, I was paired with Hogan and George Knudson the first two rounds, during the course of which Knudson scored a hole-in-one. A grim "nice shot," was all he got from Hogan. But paired with George Fazio in another tournament, Hogan demonstrated just how intense was his concentration. At the fifth hole, when Fazio holed a six-iron from the fairway for eagle, Hogan uttered not a word. At the end of the round, Ben handed Fazio his card, all filled out, which included a four at the fifth hole. "Ben, you've marked me for a four at the fifth; I made two there," said Fazio.

Hogan looked at George, thought a minute, and said, "Are you crazy? That's a par-four."

"But Ben, don't you remember I holed a six-iron?" Fazio protested.

Hogan looked blank. "No, I don't remember that."

Before Ben would sign the card, Fazio had to get the third member of the group to attest that he had, indeed, witnessed the stroke. George had a wonderful golf swing. He was poetry in motion. He turned his hips more than anyone I've seen, but he was smooth as silk. He could land the ball very softly, just like Snead. George had great imagination, some said too much, although I've always felt that imagination plays a role in concentration. Let me give you an example.

Greatest Golf Shots - III

Bob Toski and Bo Wininger used to travel together quite a bit, and my buddy, Fred Wampler, and I would frequently caravan with them the first few years we were on tour, so we became pals. Toski was so skinny that we called him the "Mouse," but he was one of the all-time wizard shotmakers. There was little the Mouse couldn't do with a wedge, or any other club. In 1954 at the Havana Open, Fred and I had finished the last round when we got word that Toski was on the seventeenth hole with a chance to tie Porky Oliver and two others for the tournament if he could par the last two holes. We hiked out to seventeen in time to catch Bob on the green, which he two-putted for par. On the eighteenth, Toski pushed his drive over behind a row of Royal Palm trees. We followed him over to his ball, and when I saw his predicament, frankly I couldn't see any way he could make four on the hole. Toski just grinned as he looked at us. "Watch this, Blue," he exclaimed.

Aiming straight across the fairway at the clubhouse, which was out-of-bounds, Bob launched his ball between the trees and curved it around that entire row of Royal Palms. It landed just short of the green, bounded up on the putting surface and finished cold stiff. He tapped it in for birdie to win the event, and Old Pork Chops, who was standing near the green, threw him a salute. It was the most fabulous shot you've ever seen, and an example of how imagination can influence a player's concentration. Toski's great imagination allowed him to visualize the shot, and certainly this was a big help in focusing his concentration. I don't recall ever witnessing a more fabulous shot, but I shouldn't have been surprised because Bob had that kind of talent.

The Wizards

The finest shotmakers are not necessarily golf's greatest scorers, though many of them are. The wizard shotmakers are those who, using a combination of imagination and talent, could fit a golf ball into, out of, or around just about any obstacle and circumstance. I wouldn't care to rank these players in order of proficiency, but I can name a few, all of whom shared a single attribute — they all had great hands. Walter Hagen, Paul Runyan, Lloyd Mangrum, and Jimmy Demaret were players who had this special gift. One of the best I've ever seen was Arnold Palmer. His fabulous recoveries are still vivid in my memory. It seemed that no matter how wild his long game, Arnold could find a way to get up and down from just about any place. To me, this indicated a sharp mind, great hands (ever watch his waggle?), and a vivid imagination.

Another was Tom Watson. The first or second year we played at Harbour Town on Hilton Head Island, South Carolina, I was paired with Watson, who was then a fledgling tour player. In those days, the Harbour Town tournament was played at Thanksgiving and we brought our families along so that we could celebrate Turkey Day together. My youngsters followed us around, and, that night they were referring to Tom as "Jungle Jim" because, it seemed to them, he had driven into the trees on many of the holes, yet still managed to play fantastic recoveries through the branches for pars and birdies. It was no accident. Tom knew just what he was doing, although I admit it puzzled me how he could thread a long iron through a narrow opening between the trees and yet couldn't seem to drive the ball into a fairway that was forty yards wide. Later, of course, when Tom became the tour's premier player, his inventive shots around the green became legendary.

This category certainly includes but is not limited to scramblers. The "wizards" I refer to here simply had more ability than most to play the proper shot at the proper time. In many cases, they had the ability to pull off golf shots most of the other players didn't even *know* about. Chi Chi Rodriguez was one of these. He played consistently marvelous recovery shots, thanks to one of the greatest pairs of hands in the game. He could really spin the ball, hit it high or low, and move it either way. Chi Chi might have developed these skills of necessity, since he often drove into some pretty unusual spots. Those of you who have been fortunate enough to see Chi Chi Rodriguez in person or on television will know what I'm talking about.

This may surprise you, but I don't think I've ever seen anyone who could do more things with a golf ball than Gary Player. Almost daily he did things with a golf ball not many others knew how to do nor, indeed, even imagined doing. I don't think Gary was dealt all the physical talent in the world, but he never let it bother him. At Greenbrier one year, I was practicing alongside Ben Hogan and remarked that I didn't think the recently arrived Mr. Player would be able to "cut the mustard" with that slicey swing of his. Ben disagreed, and what a prophet he turned out to be. "Oh, yes he will," said Hogan. "You see, when all those other players have gone to their rooms or to the bar, Mr. Player will be out there practicing. He'll *outwork* everybody."

Bob Rosburg was a certified wizard. He was a superb chipper, a fine putter, and a much better player than anyone ever acknowledged. I remember that he won the long driving contest in the NCAA Championship at Stanford. What confidence he had. Rossie had a little short chipping stroke; he popped the ball in the back, just the way he putted. He didn't take the club back very far, he said, reasoning that "if you don't take it back very far, you can't get very far off-line." His method was quite wristy, just the opposite of what most pros advocate, but when it came to chipping, I've never seen a more deadly stroke and I certainly wouldn't bet against him.

In a Class by Himself

When discussing wizards, though, one fellow stands out above the others. For twenty-five years, Doug Ford was in a class by himself with the wedge. Doug was a wonderful player, the winner of two majors — the Masters and the

Doug Ford and Gardner at the Seniors Championship.

PGA Championship — as well as twenty PGA Tour events, and had an absolutely marvelous short game. You hear about players who can get up and down from a manhole; well, Doug Ford could. And from anywhere else — deep grass, bare ground, caliche, cuppy lies, sand, pine needles, hardpan, or mud. Doug could run the ball, pitch it, back it up, flop it, whatever the situation called for.

Ford was a marvelous bunker player, too, although he didn't look like it because he didn't hit his bunker shots very high, but I've seen him hole a lot of sand shots. He holed one on me at Thunderbird that I still remember. His ball was up under the lip of the bunker, and the pin was clear across the green. He pitched the ball out on that low trajectory of his and it rolled into the cup. At the time I thought he was kind of lucky, but I changed my mind after watching him over the years. Most golf fans remember that he holed a shot from the deep bunker beside the eighteenth hole at Augusta National to win the Masters tournament in 1957. During a senior tournament in Hilton Head, Doug and I were paired, and I told my wife, Judy, to watch Ford when he played wedge shots. About halfway through the round, he played a nearly impossible shot between the trees, bouncing it up about four feet from the flagstick.

"Magnificent shot," said Judy.

Doug looks at her, and snorts, "Magnificent, huh?"

Judy figured she'd talked out of turn, so she decided not to say anything more. Five holes later, Doug had a shot that God couldn't play, and he curled the ball up to within inches of the hole. He turns to Judy and says, "Now, you could say that was magnificent, Judy." And then laughed like hell.

Ford's technique with a wedge was different from most other players. He used a very strong grip, particularly with his left hand, and during the stroke he would let his right hand pass under his left, a move that some people might describe as a "breakdown" of the left wrist. But the face was always looking at you; it *never* turned over. The effect was that it imparted true backspin, with very little sidespin. Doug obviously felt this gave him greater control and accuracy. It didn't matter if you put him on concrete or marshmallow, he could play the shot. He just had a feel for it, and he knew what he was doing. We had some other great wedge players, like Julius Boros and Sam Snead, but they played soft shots. Doug could hit the soft shots, too, but he could also hit all those other shots. Jerry Barber was another great wedge player, but in the final analysis, if they had a wedge contest, Ford would win.

A Solid Putting Stroke

Doug Ford was a great putter, too. He was gutsy. He rapped his putts, hard, like Palmer did, except Ford's misses didn't go quite as far by as Arnold's did. Doug would practice hitting balls against the baseboard in his hotel room at night. Pow! Pow! He would smack balls up against the wall for hours. He wasn't trying to hit the ball straight; he was trying to hit it solidly. Guys used to argue over who would room with Doug, because they thought his attitude would rub off on them. Dow Finsterwald usually won, and he learned a lot from Ford. If you roomed next to Ford and Finsterwald, you didn't get much sleep. They beat that baseboard to death all night long.

Finsterwald had a fantastic short game, too. He was a magnificent wedge player, chipper and putter, and always worked very hard at these departments of his game. Dow had great success, winning the PGA Championship in 1958, the first year it was played at stroke play, and had a long stretch when he finished high in tournaments. He was nearly the leading money-winner one year. Finsty insisted on playing with a left-to-right flight pattern, which, I thought, cost him distance and quite a few tournaments. If he had learned to draw the ball, I'm sure he would have driven the ball farther, hit shorter irons into the greens, and finished closer to the hole. With his putting stroke, you have to believe he would have made many more birdies.

Whether deliberate or not, Finsterwald placed his hands behind the ball at address, particularly with the driver. It's pretty hard to start the ball down the right side of the fairway when your hands are three or four inches behind the ball at address. To draw the ball, you ought to hold them at least even with the ball. Still, Dow was a fine player who had a good head on his shoulders and managed his game well. He was in a class with Billy Casper, Ford, and Bobby Locke with the wedge and putter. They all gave you the impression they owned those clubs. Of this group, though, Ford was the most aggressive.

People talk about Arnold Palmer being a charger. Doug Ford was even more of a charger on the greens. He was a wrist putter, a "crack" putter, if you will, which means he hit right down on the ball and gave it a terrific crack. You could hear it clear across the green. It would make your mouth water. Ford hit his putts as hard as anyone I've seen, yet the ball never rolled very far past the hole. I don't know how he did it, but he rolled it beautifully.

Ford's attitude was always positive. If you hit the ball off in the trash, he believed, then go find it and hit it again. That's the way he played all the time. Ben Hogan told me once that Doug Ford was just a hair away from being the best player he ever saw.

Ford had a flattish swing, the kind Ben liked, and he cocked his hands as far as they'd go. To watch Doug today, you'd never know he had a long swing, but he did; he hit a lot of greens and won lots of money. As was the case with Cary Middlecoff, if you could finish ahead of Doug Ford, you'd win a big check.

In those days, Doug and I were not very close because I was a slow player and Doug was an extremely fast player, indeed, one of the fastest in history. He wouldn't come anywhere near a slow player. Can you imagine the tour's fastest player, Ford, and the tour's slowest player, Middlecoff, playing the 36-hole finals of the PGA Championship? It happened, though, at Meadowbrook Country Club in Northville, Michigan, in 1955. Some people believed that Middlecoff's slow pace would drive Ford crazy, but Doug never let anything drive him crazy — he was above it. He just played his game, and beat Doc, 4 and 3.

Baiting a Giant

While Doug Ford never let anything bother him, there were times that his fast pace bothered others, and Doug was not above baiting a slower player. Paired with George Bayer and me in the last round of the Insurance City Open in Hartford, Doug had the honor at eighteen. After hitting his drive, he immediately took off down the left side of the hole. Bayer got ready to drive but you could tell that Doug's movement had distracted him. He paused and waited for Doug to stop walking, then finally hit his drive but pushed it straight over the fence and out-of-bounds. You could see the purple creep up that big old neck of George's. He teed up another, but Doug kept on walking, his white shoes flashing as he strode down the left rough. Bayer put another ball out-of-bounds. This time George hollered at Ford, who stopped and watched as George nearly hit another one out, but, fortunately, this one stayed in the right rough. Bayer went on to make a nine on the hole.

Afterwards in the locker room, Doug was sitting on the bench changing his shoes while chatting with his little red-haired son. Soon Bayer walked up, still hot, and slapped his huge, meaty hand on Doug's shoulder. George is over six-foot-five and must weigh in the neighborhood of 240 pounds. He looked down at Doug and growled, "Damn you, Ford, if you ever do that again, if you move so much as one inch past me while I'm driving, I'll flatten you."

Ford looked up at Bayer, and said, "Go f—k yourself, George."

With that, George picked up Ford, who was close to six feet tall and strongly built, and stuffed him in the open locker. Now, Doug is pretty hefty, and he wouldn't really fit in that locker, but George made him fit anyway, slammed the door, and held it closed.

Little Doug was screaming by this time and beating on big old George's leg. "Let my daddy go," he howled.

That was Doug Ford. He didn't care who you were, or how big you were; he wasn't intimidated. Doug was very athletic and very strong, and besides, he was Italian. He wasn't afraid of anything. I watched him go after a drunk in the gallery in Detroit one year. We were playing the Motor City Open at Red Run Country Club, and a contingent of Detroit's blue-collar population had come out to see what this "golf stuff" was all about. Ford was then one of the leading lights on the tour and, consequently, had attracted a large gallery. Some of them evidently had consumed quite a few beers because they began heckling the third member of our pairing. They made snide remarks, clapped when he missed a shot, and finally tossed beer cans onto the fairway as he was preparing to hit a shot. Ford had seen enough. He dashed across the fairway, jumped over the gallery ropes and grabbed one of the hecklers by the throat. "You miserable S.O.B. If I hear one more word from you or your pals, I'll mop up this fairway with you." I think the fellow understood that Doug was not just passing the time of day, because there was no more heckling.

The Longest Hitter

When George Bayer appeared on the tour, he kind of rearranged our concept of how far you can hit a golf ball. George was a huge man who briefly had played tackle with the Washington Redskins, but unlike many football players he was very supple and flexible. George was the longest driver I've ever seen, and he quickly made the rest of us obsolete in driving contests. Someone asked me recently if John Daly wasn't as long as Bayer, but I don't think so. People who were around in those days may have forgotten how far Bayer hit the ball, but I haven't. He didn't look to me as if he exerted himself as much as Daly does. If I had to bet $100,000 on George Bayer or John Daly, in their absolute primes, I'd have to put my hundred-thou on big George.

Bayer could hit it in the neck farther than anybody else could flush it. He hit a ball at Whitemarsh Valley in Philadelphia that I'll never forget. We were paired in the Philadelphia Open and had reached the third hole, a long par-five that played from a high tee. With the honor, I hit one of my best drives, but George outdrove me by a hundred yards. Those lush fairways at Whitemarsh didn't give much roll, but George must have driven the ball at least 375 yards. It went out on a line, not real high, and kept going forever. I laid up short of the water in front of the green with a two-iron, and then walked for quite a ways before reaching Bayer's ball.

I turned to my caddie, Mitch. "Can you believe this?"

Mitch shook his head. "Nossir."

I don't think I've ever seen a ball driven that far. No one ever went for that green in two, but I think most of us could have reached it with an eight-iron from where George hit his drive. What happened next astounded me. Bayer pulled out a heavy sand wedge, and I told Mitch he must be crazy because even George Bayer couldn't reach the green with such a lofted club. George hit a gentle pitch up near my ball, far short of the water. I couldn't believe it and asked George why he had laid up. "I've put my last ball in the water on this damned hole," he said. He then pitched his ball to the back of the green and three-putted for a bogey. He got just what he deserved.

Fellows like Greg Norman and Fred Couples are certainly long, and Daly is probably the longest hitter today. Before Bayer came along, I suppose Jimmy Thompson was the longest driver, although Sam Snead and Ben Hogan were both very long. Snead and Thompson probably won more driving contests, but Hogan was extremely long when he wanted to be. When Ben was hooking the ball back in the early forties, before he changed his swing, his drives went so far you wouldn't believe it. They say that Ben is the first man to knock it green high in two at the long, par-five tenth hole at Pinehurst No. 2, and I saw him hit the eleventh green at Colonial, another long par-five, in two shots, and hole the putt for a three.

Today the players are routinely flying it on the greens from 260 to 270 yards with fairway woods. The longest hitters in my day couldn't do that. I don't think the fellows today are any stronger than the players were in my day. There may be more of them, but certainly none is any stronger than Sam Snead, or any faster through the ball than Ben Hogan. It makes you wonder what Bob Jones might have done with the equipment they're using today.

People tend to think the players in their own eras were bigger, better, and stronger than any others, but I've seen all these players and frankly I don't care who was the longest. I'm not talking about driving contests, now, but rather what I've personally seen these players do in competition — when they're trying to hit it as far as they can and catch their dead level best. Personally, I've not seen anyone who could hit the ball as far as George Bayer.

The Strong and the Quick

Distance, to a great extent, comes from the Almighty. Those blessed with natural strength and quickness of muscle tend to be the longest hitters. George Bayer, Mike Souchak, Sam Snead, Jack Nicklaus, and Arnold Palmer were examples of players who were very strong physically, while fellows like Bob Toski, Ben Hogan, Chi Chi Rodriguez, and perhaps myself were not as physically strong but possessed great quickness. Clubhead speed is what produces distance, provided it is correctly applied, so hand-eye coordination and sound technique come into the equation.

Mike Souchak was a marvel. Mike joined the tour in the early fifties out of Duke University, where he had also been a football player. He had huge forearms, thighs, and neck, and his paws were enormous. He was a very powerful man yet had beautiful tempo. And, my, what a world of ability. He played the best four rounds of golf I ever saw when he won the Motor City Open in 1959. The tournament was played at Meadow Brook, a fine course where Chick Harbert was the pro. Mike drove it about 310 yards down the middle of every fairway, knocked all the flags down with his approach shots, and holed whatever putts he had left. It was awesome.

Souchak had easy power. He swung a driver that weighed about fifteen ounces, but in his hands it looked like a feather. Nobody in those days was longer, except George Bayer, and George was longer than everybody. Mike had a solid all-around game, and he could putt, too. He won about sixteen tournaments in his career, but I always wondered why he didn't win more. He gained financial success too early, I think. After his early success, he laid off for a long time, but when he came back he didn't putt as well. Mike still holds the all-time scoring record for seventy-two holes, which he set in the 1955 Texas Open at Brackenridge Park. His mark of 257 wiped out Byron Nelson's old record of 259, and I believe Mike also shares the nine-hole record of 27, which he set in the same tournament. Mike's raw power, combined with his great bursts of scoring, made him a crowd favorite for many years.

The world loves long hitters; it always has and always will. Who packs the baseball stadiums, a fine hitter like Wade Boggs or sluggers like Ted Williams and Mickey Mantle? The bombers fill the stadiums. The fans instinctively love violence and feats of strength, and always have since the days of the Romans. You rarely hear people talking about beautiful players like Paul Runyan, Chip Beck, or Larry Mize. They're too busy "oohing" and "ahing" bombers like Jack Nicklaus, Arnold Palmer and John Daly, or even a mighty mite like Ian Woosnam, who may be the longest hitter of his height in history.

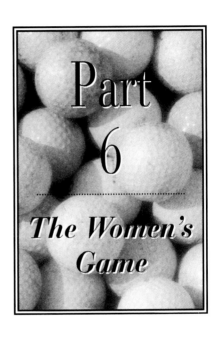

Part 6

The Women's Game

The $10,000 Wager

One of my favorite tournaments was the Mixed-Team Invitational in which the men and women pros paired up in teams. The first such event that I can recall was sponsored by Haig & Haig Scotch and was played at the Harder Hall and Pinecrest Lakes courses in Central Florida. One of the charms of the rickety, old Harder Hall Hotel in Sebring, which served as players' headquarters, was the huge, wooden, circular bar off the lobby. Each night after

(L-R) Sonny Renfield presents winners' check to Ruth Jessen and Gardner at Haig & Haig Mixed Team event.

play had ended, all the guys and gals would gather here and, over a drink or two, would get to know one another better.

One such evening, Marlene Bauer Hagge began extolling the virtues of the LPGA's marvelous player, Mickey Wright. Marlene, never a shrinking violet, claimed that Mickey Wright was so good she could win on the men's tour, as well. In fact, said Marlene, if Wright were allowed to compete on the PGA Tour, she'd probably be the leading money winner there, too, as she was on the Ladies Tour. Well, I had listened to about enough of Marlene's claims. I made the statement that Mickey wouldn't even make a cut on the PGA Tour because she couldn't drive far enough, long as she may have been in comparison with the rest of the girls.

Marlene exploded, just as I thought she would, sputtering that Mickey could outdrive almost all the men pros. I replied that, even though I was one of the shortest hitters on the men's tour (I wasn't), I believed that I could outhit Mickey Wright with my four-wood! That did it. Marlene offered to bet me $10,000 that I couldn't, and I told her, "You're on." That night, I made one telephone call and covered my end of the bet. The next couple of days, I heard that Marlene was scrambling around trying to raise her $10,000.

Finally Dow Finsterwald, who was her partner in the team event, chided me about trying to rob the girls. I informed him that the whole thing was Marlene's idea and that if she wanted out, it would be okay with me. Dow persuaded her that she had made a bad bet, and she called it off.

The next day I saw Mickey Wright hitting balls on the range. I waited until she had worked through the shorter clubs and began hitting the driver. I motioned my caddie out beyond hers and hit my four-wood past her longest drive. But I didn't tell Marlene. I was very fond of her.

Fear of Embarrassment

I began this section on women's golf with the story of the wager to illustrate a point. It's obvious that Nature has given men a physical advantage in playing sports, including golf. It's obvious, too, that men score better than do women, but not all of that can be attributed to physical superiority. Those of us familiar with both tours know, for example, that the men chip and putt much better than do the women, even though these skills require no particular strength. If there is any department of the game in which women should be equal to men, it's putting, but they're not. Chipping, too.

Why is this so? Since physical strength is obviously not the answer, perhaps it lies more in the emotional or psychological differences. In my opinion, women seem to have more fear than men. Fear of what, I'm not sure, but it seems to express itself most often in the fear of embarrassment. Women, in general, tend to be more circumspect than men and less inclined to disrupt social conventions. Even today, women are less apt to show off or flaunt their egos in public. In men's golf, the great players have strong egos and have no fear of displaying it. Men like Gene Sarazen and Sam Snead would walk to the tee with an air that the place belonged to them. They loved to show off, and they could back it up.

Maybe it's sexual. Men are biologically the more aggressive sex, so perhaps they're just flaunting their masculine genes. There are exceptions, of course. Not all women exhibit the fear I'm talking about. It's been my observation, though, that most women don't *really* like to compete. Confrontation, especially head-to-head with an opponent, bothers them because they've been taught most of their lives that it's not nice to beat somebody else. Men love it, of course, although I can name a few women who weren't bothered by it at all: Babe Zaharias, Joanne Carner, Louise Suggs and Sandra Palmer come to mind.

Babe Zaharias presents 1952 Florida Open trophy to Gardner.

There's something else, too, that separates the boys from the girls. Recently I paid a visit to Ben Hogan in Fort Worth, accompanied by Mike Donald, the touring pro. After lunch, Mike said he thought he'd wander out to the practice range to hit some balls. Hogan looked up and said, "I wondered what you were doing in here so long. It's still daylight, you know." It was that attitude that defined Ben Hogan and players like him. There do not seem to be many with Hogan's attitudes on the LPGA Tour.

Teaching Joanne Carner

In the early 1970s, a close friend of mine, Dr. Art Seitz, called and asked if I would mind looking at the swing of a friend of his. He informed me that his friend was Joanne Carner, who, as Joanne Gunderson, had won five U. S. Amateur Championships. In those days she was known as The Great Gundy. Joanne had married Don Carner, and, at age 31, turned pro. I agreed to see her, and the next morning Don and Joanne pulled up to my golf shop at the Riverbend Club in Tequesta, Florida, on two motorcycles.

For several minutes I watched her hit shots with her little "Patty Berg"-type ladies' sticks; in her hands, they looked like toys. She had won an LPGA event prior to our meeting, but I was astounded she had done as well as she had with those tiny clubs. These, combined with a very short, upright backswing which carried the club practically over her face, would have been near-fatal impediments for anyone with less talent than hers. I began to flatten her swing a bit and suggested she try hitting my clubs. I found she could carry the ball farther with my *four-wood* than she could with her own *driver*.

I began working with Joanne fairly regularly and suggested she slim down a bit, which she did. Eventually I flattened her swing to some degree on all shots, added three or four feet to her backswing, and taught her the wedge and sand game. I even gave her my Toney Penna sand-wedge. She was easy and fun to teach, for she could do damn near anything I suggested — immediately. She is truly one of the *great* woman athletes. During the time I worked with her, Joanne won twenty-two tournaments, and, if memory serves, she never finished worse than second on the LPGA money list.

Since I was not in the business of giving lessons at the time, I refused to charge Joanne for her lessons. One Christmas morning, she showed up at my house with a

Gardner and Joanne Carner, mid 1970s.

new Plymouth sports car and presented me with the keys. When I declined the car, with thanks, Joanne began to cry. That'll get me almost every time, and it did then. But that car was very much a Joanne Carner gesture. Joanne is a great gal, now in her fifties. She hasn't won for several years, but I think she *could* have continued to win, even into her sixties, if she had not chosen to shorten her back-swing again and discard all our hard work together. But that comes under the very large heading of "none of my business," and I wish her nothing but the best.

Judy Dickinson

Nothing gives me a bigger kick than seeing a golfer make a dramatic improvement and watching the sparkle in his or her eyes. The knowledge that I've made a contribution to this golfer's enjoyment of the game is enormously satisfying. Teaching has brought many rewards, including personal ones, for it was through teaching that I met my wife, Judy Clark Dickinson. A friend named Larry Dornish, a club pro from Philadelphia, introduced us on the veranda of the clubhouse at Sawgrass in Ponte Vedra, Florida, during the first Tournament Players Championship.

She asked if I would consent to help her with her game, and I agreed to do so. Shortly thereafter, she came to see me at Frenchman's Creek, a course I designed in North Palm Beach. She made amazing progress. Judy could do immediately almost anything I suggested. After about ten lessons, she returned to her home in southern New Jersey where she won every amateur tournament in which she played. In addition, she qualified for the U.S. Women's Amateur and U.S. Women's Open tournaments. That summer of 1978, she cut her handicap from eight to nearly scratch.

In the fall she called again, requesting more lessons. After five sessions, she mentioned, "I'm going to try for my card pretty soon."

And I said, "What kind of card?"

She replied, "My LPGA card."

And off she went to Sarasota, and, by God, she qualified. She's been playing the LPGA Tour ever since. It's been fun, I can tell you, watching Judy's progress over the years, and being a part of it. She's a gifted athlete, while also being thoroughly feminine. Obviously, I couldn't (nor did I) ignore that.

We were married in 1985, and four years later we were blessed with the birth of twin boys, whom we named Barron and Spencer. They've turned out to be marvelous kids, and,

Judy Dickinson, 1985.

The Dickinson twins, Spencer and Barron, 1992.

indeed, are a blessing. All the while, Judy managed to keep her career going. Our buddy, Joanne Carner, said that the only reason I married Judy was to get my name up on the leader board again. Well, she's right; that probably is the only way it'll get there. Given Judy's talent, her name *should* be up there every week.

Judy has one of the finest golf swings I've ever been privileged to see, man or woman. I confess it's puzzling to me — and many of my peers — why she ever finishes out of the top three. The answers can be found in her inherited personality traits and in her short game. In her work from ten yards off the green alone, Judy spots her rivals on the LPGA Tour at least two shots a side. That's too many. I'm not sure she's mean enough on the course, nor as competitive as some of her rivals, like Dottie Mochrie or Joanne Carner. Judy *cares* how others fare; she never challenges anyone, or says an unkind word. So everybody likes Judy, but they also think they can beat her in the "cool of the evening." I wish I could be her caddie, for then she'd win many tournaments — either that or I'd end up with a wedge sticking out of my skull.

With her natural popularity, Judy was elected president of the LPGA and served for three years. During her tenure, the LPGA Constitution was re-crafted to put the policy-making power in the players' hands, where it belongs, and the incumbent commissioner, Bill Blue, was fired. Blue clearly appeared incompetent, and irritated most of the LPGA's sponsors. A new commissioner, Charles Mechem, was hired. Mecham headed up Taft Broadcasting for nearly twenty-five years, and since he took over, the LPGA's sponsor-relations and business health have improved measurably. The girls also fired their legal counsel, Rogers and Wells, and replaced it with the very capable Leonard Decof.

With these responsibilities behind her now, those of motherhood have taken over, and they're increasing. Still I don't think Judy has yet reached her peak as a player. Even in her early forties, if she'll work and stay in shape, the best is still ahead for her. After all, I made the Ryder Cup team when I was almost forty-five. I don't think there's a shot I know that Judy can't play, perhaps even better than I could. And should you have the opportunity to watch Judy perform in coming months and years, you'll see a beautiful, powerful golf swing exhibited by a wonderful, beautiful woman who, quite literally, exudes class. Prejudiced? You bet, but I wouldn't brag on her unless she deserved it.

What Women Don't Learn

Before leaving the subject of teaching golf to women, let me make a few comments on how they're taught. The end results of the kind of golf instruction women receive in our country can be seen very clearly in those who show up on the LPGA Tour. They're supposed to be the best in America, and I guess they are. Unfortunately, many show up on tour hoping, even needing to learn *how* to play. They've come as far as they have with competitive guts and a fine short game; in other words, they have the ability to scramble.

Why don't they play more consistently? What's wrong with their swings? Well, let's start with their divots — or lack of them. You heard me correctly, divots. You could collect all the divots taken all week on the golf course during any LPGA tournament, and they wouldn't fill my little white cap. I've never seen a golfer whose iron game I admired who didn't hit the ground with an iron club. When you make a swing with an iron club, you want the lowest point in the swing to occur just past the ball. This produces backspin, which gives the ball lift and allows the player to control the ball in the air. When this is done consistently, the wind affects the ball flight less, and the golfer can better judge where the ball will stop. That's the way it works.

Certainly, one can sometimes hit acceptable iron shots without taking a divot; Macdonald Smith used to play this way, and he was a fine player back in the 1920s. But in modern times, no great iron players would dream of hitting an iron — unless he were playing a specialty shot — without taking a divot. Yet most of the girls appearing on the LPGA Tour leave this out, and at least ninety percent of them have been taught to play by a golf professional somewhere. These teaching pros obviously don't think it's important enough to emphasize to their prize pupils. It's important, because it changes the shape of a person's golf swing. I have always contended that if it is correct for male golfers to hit down on irons and take a divot, then it follows that this method is correct for females, as well.

As an example, let me describe the problems I've had with one of my own students. Lynn Connelly is a lovely girl who, one must admit, has done quite well with what she has. Lynn seldom, in actual play, takes a divot with her irons. Over the years, I admit, this has driven me up the wall. I've racked my brain in search of ways to coax Lynn to take a divot. Many times I've succeeded while we were on the practice range, but when we moved to the golf course, *not one divot* could she make. I take that personally, for logic tells me that any instructor worth a damn can teach anyone to hit the ground with a golf club.

I know the following: (1) If the clubhead arrives ahead of the hands in the hitting area, a divot is unlikely; (2) Most golfers who take a divot have the preponderance of their weight leaning left; (3) If a golfer's head is leaning too far toward the right foot, a divot is unnecessary and unlikely. I also know many other moves to encourage or avoid taking divots, and I've tried them all on Lynn, to no avail. So be it! I guess I'm a lousy instructor.

Tour Dress

Can you remember when the women on the LPGA wore women's, not men's, golf shoes and didn't go everywhere else in those ugly sneakers they now wear? Why doesn't someone tell them how unattractive they look in high-top anklets instead of low peds? The same goes for visors, which don't enhance a pretty girl's looks.

The guys on tour today are no better. If they're paying more than $8.99 a pair for the shabby-looking, wrinkled slacks they wear, they're being ripped off. You seldom see players wearing a tie anymore. If you collected all the ties and all the jackets these players carry with them on tour, you could carry them in one hand.

The young people of today are the worst-dressed generation in the history of America, but do the members of both tours have to look like all the rest? I'd tell them to dress presentably or get off the tour.

Length and Course Set-up

Length is not the only reason women pros don't score as low as men pros. The fact is, I can't think of one phase of golf in which women are better than men, though I can assure you that the women play wonderful and skillful golf. Yet the LPGA players — and *only they* — are constantly comparing their scores with the men. The girls mistakenly believe that the public constantly makes this comparison. They're wrong.

The girls have no rivals, save themselves. Nobody else cares, because they recognize the fact that women do, indeed, play excellent golf. Yet the LPGA persists in trying to dupe the public by playing "little old ladies' tees." I can't tell you how many times I've followed Judy on tour, seen 365 yards marked on the hole sign, stepped it off and found the hole to be 335 yards instead. I can't tell you, either, how many times I've seen the field staff take the driver out of Judy's hands, and out of the hands of other long hitters.

I've always believed that the set-up of a tournament course should be done in such a manner that the best all-round player in the field will win. Not the best putter, not the best scrambler, not the best long- or short-iron player, not the best wedge player, not the best driver, but the best of *all* these categories should prevail. I don't think the LPGA field staff has in mind determining the best player each week, because they set up the courses too short, an obvious tilt to low scoring. Their dubious policy seems to be that if any of the players in the field can reach a par-five in two shots, then the tee-markers should be placed far enough forward so that *all* the players can reach the green in two.

The short hitters love this, of course, but is it fair to the longer hitters? What, then, is ever done to help the poorer putters? Putting, after all, is half the game. Historically, on any tour you care to mention, the game has been dominated by some of the longest hitters. They didn't shorten the courses when Mickey Wright was in her prime, and Mickey outdrove the gals by enormous distances. Even then Mickey didn't win every week, by any means. Why, then, shorten the courses now?

In my opinon, an ideal course set-up would disregard the shortest hitters and set the yardage long enough that nobody could win with only wedges and putters. Short hitters, like lousy putters, are damn lucky to be out there. They should keep their mouths shut and strive to get longer, as Paul Runyan, Gary Player, Mike Reid, and others have done. The field staff should set up the course so that most of the players can reach the holes in regulation with some club in their bag. What are those fairway woods and long irons for, anyway? You might be surprised how far some of today's women can drive a golf ball; I'm sure the LPGA field staff would be, too.

In the 1993 U.S. Women's Open at Crooked Stick in Indianapolis, Judy hit wedges on twelve of the fourteen long holes (par-fours and par-fives) during the first round. That's a test of golf?

Check out the winners of the women's major championships the past few years. How many would be considered the best all-around player in the field? The shorter hitters and lesser players prevail by their numbers and seem to be dictating LPGA Tour policy. By comparison, the men play almost every *foot* of the courses on the PGA Tour, and we don't hear the short hitters complaining about it. They wouldn't dare, because they'd be laughed out of town. But the women aren't like that; they don't much care for ridicule.

The LPGA Hall of Fame

The time has arrived, I believe, for the LPGA to review the eligibility rules for its Hall of Fame. As of this writing, thirteen women have been inducted, the most recent being

Patty Sheehan in 1993. When one examines these thirteen members, one has to wonder at the peculiar qualifications for membership.

We notice that some of the present members have scoring averages of 76 or 77. On the other hand, the founders of the Hall of Fame, several of whom were among the early members, established the requirement that members must earn either thirty career victories, including two different majors, or forty victories, including one major. How, then, did Betty Jameson gain her spot in the Hall? Jameson owns a career scoring average of 77.77 and only ten victories. Betty was a fine player and a wonderful girl, but you wonder if maybe she just wasn't present at the first meeting in 1951 when the Hall of Fame was voted in. And why no Betty Hicks or Helen Detweiler, despite their fine records?

The point is, it's much more difficult to win on the LPGA Tour today than it was thirty or forty years ago. Sheer numbers tell you so. Some of the tournaments then were little more than "get-togethers" and players had to worry about beating maybe ten to twelve players. Today's tournament fields mostly consist of 144 players, and the number of players capable of winning runs to as many as forty.

The thirty or forty victory rule leaves out many former and current players who have won close to thirty events. Marlene Bauer Hagge comes to mind immediately, having been the LPGA's leading money winner at one time and having won, I believe, twenty-five tournaments. Judy Rankin has won twenty-six, and was the tour's leading money winner twice — in 1976 and 1977. Jane Blalock captured twenty-nine victories. What about little Sandra Palmer with twenty-one victories, leading money winner in 1975 and winner of the U. S. Women's Open and the Dinah Shore — before they decided to call it a major championship? Susie Berning's eleven wins, which include three U.S. Opens, won't get her in the Hall of Fame. Neither will Donna Caponi's twenty-four wins, nor Marilynn Smith's twenty-two.

Current players who have not yet won thirty events but are getting close enough to consider include Amy Alcott, Betsy King and Beth Daniel. I wonder if some of the original Hall of Famers, in their heyday, would like to play these gals. Times have changed, ladies, and situations are different. Isn't it time to take the bull by the horns and change those requirements? Patty Berg, an original Hall of Famer, urged the gals last year to modernize the rules. Crank up those engines of change, ladies.

The Ladies' Sponsors

For the past eight to ten years, I've been quite closely associated with the Ladies Professional Golf Association, principally through my wife, Judy, who, until recently, led the LPGA as its president for several years. I have watched with some interest their little show grow from some $1.2 million in purses in the early 1970s to over $21 million now.

The LPGA is a band of personable young women, some of whom are determined to close the gap between the men's and women's tours. In my opinion, their potential is almost unlimited and relatively untapped. The LPGA has never marketed itself very well, and I don't presently see any improvement in their marketing approach. There is no reason on God's green earth for the vast differences in marketing of men's and women's golf, though I admit that, in a thousand years, the girls will never be able to play golf as well as the men. They don't need to, because they play damn good golf — better than ninety percent of the men amateurs — and most of the gals are a damn sight prettier and nicer than the men.

Ross Johnson, the former CEO of RJR-Nabisco, told me that the girls can have anything they want — if they stand *together* and ask for it. I believe him. Cadillac spends about $40 million each year on seventy-eight old men on the PGA

Senior Tour, for example, and not one red cent on the LPGA Tour. How many women drive Cadillacs, or tell the old man what make of car to buy? I don't think American women would take kindly to the notion that Cadillac is discriminating against women, do you?

What about RJR-Nabisco? It spends millions on the Senior Tour yet funds its own Nabisco-Dinah Shore event — one of the LPGA's four major championships — with a purse of $700,000. One can scarcely think of a Nabisco product that isn't directed toward women, so wouldn't it make sense to show greater support for women's golf? Perhaps someone should remind Nabisco that women do most of the supermarket buying, and they do have a choice. Incidentally, RJR-Nabisco just gave the PGA Tour $21 million to buy out its contract to sponsor the PGA Tour Championship, for which Nabisco received exactly nothing.

Buick, which is a division of General Motors, sponsors four tournaments on the PGA Tour but none on the LPGA. Several regional food chains, including Ralph's in California and Kroger in Cincinnati, currently sponsor events on the PGA Senior Tour, but their logos are missing from the Ladies Tour. Why did Jim Kemper and his Kemper Insurance group drop an LPGA tournament and retain one on the PGA Tour? The same would hold true for New York Life, who, at Deane Beman's urging, dropped the ladies from a tournament that was sponsored in Jamaica and moved it to Puerto Rico for the senior men. I guess women don't buy insurance or influence anyone who does.

The equipment manufacturers also seem to be abandoning women's golf. Foot Joy dropped its sponsorship of the LPGA, and its representatives are hard to find on the girls' tour (but they show up for *all* the men's events). Very seldom, in fact, do any of the equipment manufacturers send a representative to the LPGA events. Many of them have even abandoned the four majors. No longer does Acushnet send its white-coated reps to the LPGA events to pass out Titleist golf balls and gloves, but they appear weekly on the PGA and Senior Tours. I've been told that a rookie on the PGA Tour is paid up to $15,000 a year to play Titleist balls, but LPGA rookies are offered nothing. If I'm not mistaken, there are now as many, if not more, active women as men golfers in America. I wonder what they think about these inequities?

How about K Mart, who puts on a million-dollar tournament in Greensboro for the men, but no tournaments for the women. Do women buy anything in K Mart? AT&T sponsors the old Bing Crosby Tournament at Pebble Beach, while Southwestern Bell and G.T.E. sponsor big events in Texas, all for the men, but I fail to see any companion events for the ladies. But, then, women hardly ever use telephones, do they? The list goes on: United Air Lines, Nestle, Federal Express, Hardee's, Anheuser-Busch, Honda, Shell Oil and Ford.

This is a big subject and it needs to be treated by someone. If I were the sort to fly off the handle, I might raise a few questions, say, in this book; but I won't! Like hell I won't. I suppose it is a man's world, and I'm not certain that I don't agree with that. But I've come to realize that if the women of this country, including the women of the LPGA, are waiting for men to serve them with equality, they'd better try an hallucinogenic drug. Apparently someone will have to do the job for the ladies of the LPGA, for I've found from experience that the girls probably won't make any demands for themselves.

Women play more golf than men, they have more money than men, and they seem to control all the sex in this world. So why shouldn't they assert themselves more? In my opinion, if they band strongly together, they can insist on a better deal and more equitable treatment from the men who run and control the corporate sponsors.

Part
7

The
Political
Game

Deane Beman and the Ping Case

Let me state right off that I have been concerned for some time over the direction of the PGA tour. Because I was closely involved in the formation of the tour in its present structure, I am sure that my personal feelings about this run deeper than many of the younger generation of players on tour today. What follows, if you choose to read it, will undoubtedly seem blunt, critical and, to some, controversial.

It would not surprise me, nor any of my peers, if I were accused of being at times hardheaded, opinionated, curmudgeonly, prejudiced and just plain angry, and I have no doubt that at one time or another I've been guilty of all the above. But I think my fellow pros would concede that when it comes to the business of the tour, I am fair and have the best interest of the players at heart.

In the event that some of the current young tour players actually read this, I feel obliged to set down my personal views on the recent history of the PGA Tour. It took quite a few fellows a number of years to found and popularize the tour. This may astound some of the younger generation, but Arnold Palmer did *not* found either the PGA Tour or the Senior PGA Tour. Many, many players over the better part of this century have had a hand in turning us from a little hand-to-mouth road show into one of the world's top sporting entertainments. From Walter Hagen, Gene Sarazen and Horton Smith to Ben Hogan, Byron Nelson and Sam Snead — to say nothing of the enormous contributions of Bing

Crosby, Bob Hope and Jimmy Demaret in keeping golf in the public eye during and after World War II — all played an important part in building the professional tour.

Tradition Be Damned

Each generation has an obligation to itself to prosper and grow, but each generation also has an obligation to history and to the fellows who have gone before who helped to build something. What they built is called tradition. Judging by some of the actions taken by Deane Beman, the former long-term commissioner of the PGA Tour (1973-94), we've wandered a long way from tradition. Should the PGA Tour be in the business of owning golf courses? Should the PGA Tour become its own rulesmaker, thus usurping the United States Golf Association? Should we be spending millions of dollars in chasing frivolous legal points down a blind hole? I refer to the recent lawsuit involving Ping and its owner, Karsten Solheim.

This case was settled out of court in April, 1993, after four years of legal wrangling. The PGA Tour ended up conceding the main issue to Ping and paid court costs and lawyer fees for both sides. As *Golf Digest* reported, "Deane blinked, and Karsten winked." Although details of the settlement were kept secret, the cost to the PGA Tour and its insurance company was estimated to exceed $15 million. In reviewing the case here, my purpose is to expose the flawed process in the way the PGA Tour business was conducted by Deane Beman and his associates. The consequences for the players, in my opinion, have been unfortunate and serious.

About four years ago, Beman authorized an expenditure of several hundred thousand dollars to conduct tests on whether or not square grooves provided an advantage over the traditional V-shaped grooves used on iron clubs. Square grooves were first authorized by the United States Golf

Association in 1984, to accommodate the investment casting process of manufacture, and shortly thereafter the Karsten Manufacturing Company of Phoenix, Arizona, incorporated square grooves in its Ping Eye-II line of irons.

Perhaps bowing to pressure from such prominent players as Jack Nicklaus, Tom Watson and Greg Norman, Beman let it be known that he, too, suspected that the square grooves gave the user a significant advantage in spinning, and thus stopping a golf ball.

Beman hired Dave Pelz and Joe Braly, a veterinarian and Deane's former business partner, to conduct these tests for a fee that is purported to have been $250,000.

Pelz & Co. conducted the field tests in Palm Springs in the off season and reported the results to the policy board the following spring and to the membership that summer.

The testing included four main different groove ratios. The different ratios were a 2.6:1 U groove, a 3:1 V, a 3:1 U and a 4:1 U groove. The amazing thing about the Pelz test results was that every player performed best under all the different conditions with the 2.6:1 U groove. The 3:1 U groove performed next best for every single player, followed by the 3:1 V and the 4:1 U, respectively. After seeing this presentation at the Western Open in Chicago, the players were even more convinced about the positive effects of square grooves.

The interesting thing about the actual test, however, is that under certain conditions only two of the players actually hit the shots with the 3:1 U and 3:1 V grooves, the grooves at the center of the dispute. All of the other results were fitted in using a statistical method. However, the players were never told about this method of fitting in data involving shots that were never hit.

Another interesting fact about the best-performing 2.6:1 groove, which was to represent the Ping 2.6:1 groove, is that Pelz admitted that the measurement of that groove was in fact only 2.1:1 in spacing. Of course a 2.1:1 groove is going to outperform the 3:1 grooves.

Questionable Tactics

What happened to the other test players? We never found out. Neither Beman nor Pelz ever told us.

Frank Thomas, the director of testing and research for the USGA, and Frank Hannigan, the USGA's executive director at the time, testified under oath that the Pelz tests were designed to achieve a predetermined outcome. They also testified that, based on all the testing ever done and all the available knowledge, there is no significant difference in performance between V-shaped and U-shaped grooves.

This might lead you to wonder if Pelz and Braly set out to "prove" Deane's theory on square grooves, rather than to report objectively on their findings. If there was a whiff of funny business to these tests, they nevertheless provided Beman with some data that supported his theory that square grooves provide an unfair advantage.

Can anyone name me one player who, in the last four or five years, has won a tournament he shouldn't have won because he used square grooves? If Beman's theory were valid, why wouldn't every player on tour have square-grooved irons in his bag? The players are not so pure that they wouldn't try graphite shafts, feather-lite irons, or metal woods, all of which, in some way, might provide a measurable advantage. At a meeting of the Senior Tour Advisory Board, I told Deane that this matter should be left up to the USGA rulesmakers and informed him and the Board that I opposed further action. So did Miller Barber, as I recall.

Most of the players, however, were swayed by Beman's argument, and square grooves were promptly banned by the PGA Tour. With millions of dollars in club sales at stake, with his reputation and pride in his products on the line, Karsten Solheim, the inventor of Ping clubs and principal owner of Karsten Manufacturing Company, which makes the clubs, reacted by hiring one of the country's most prominent attorneys, Leonard Decof, to fight Beman's ruling.

Karsten may well have felt compelled to act because of the potential liability if the approximately million and a half sets already on the market were returned by disappointed customers. Anyone who had purchased a set of the Ping Eye-II clubs would presumably be well within their rights to demand a refund, or receive a free set in exchange.

A precedent for this dates back to the 1947 U.S. Open at the St. Louis Country Club, when an official discovered that the grooves on the Wilson Top-Notch gooseneck irons were too close together, and thus illegal. So many players were using the clubs that Wilson sent a cargo plane to St. Louis to exchange all the illegal sets for new ones, and for several years after this incident, golfers who wanted a new set of Wilson irons had little trouble obtaining a free set in exchange for a set of the illegal clubs.

The Formidable Mr. Decof

Leonard Decof, the attorney Karsten chose to represent him, runs an international law practice in Providence, Rhode Island, and is the chief counsel for the Ladies' PGA. A graduate of Yale University and the Harvard Law School, he's a former president of the International Academy of Trial Lawyers and has lectured all over the world.

I met Decof about ten years ago at Frenchman's Creek, where I was giving lessons at the time. Lenny is a golf nut, and I'm a closet lawyer, which made us double-first cousins, and we soon became great pals. I never imagined that I'd become friends with a staunch liberal, which Lenny is, because I'm generally about forty miles to the right of the John Birch Society. But Lenny's intelligence has forced me to take a different view of some things, and it's just possible that I've caused a small change in the way he views certain things.

In thirty-odd years of practicing law, Decof's trial record has earned him a formidable reputation in the business world. Ross Johnson, former chairman of Nabisco, once told me, only partially in jest, that if he were opposed by Decof in court, he'd plea bargain the case — even if he were innocent. The reason is an impressive string of victories in courts across the country, including precedent-setting cases in the U. S. Supreme Court. Among his legal peers, Lenny is known as "a hitter."

With Decof in charge of the legal case, Karsten promptly filed suit for an injunction against the ban on square grooves, which the court granted, and then Decof prevailed in a subsequent appeal before the Ninth Circuit Court of Appeals in San Francisco, which upheld the injunction. Through early 1993, Decof had prevailed at every turn. The PGA Tour was represented by the law firm of Rogers and Wells, in Washington, D.C., which itself, several years ago, was sued and ultimately settled the case, paying some $40 million. Rogers and Wells were the PGA Tour's attorneys in the loss of an antitrust suit brought by Art Silvestrone in Orlando regarding certain players' access to the Senior Tour. After that loss, Beman told me that Silvestrone's lawyer was superior to the Rogers and Wells attorney who represented us, lending some credence to Deane's claim that he has lost cases only because he has been out-lawyered.

Lawsuits like this one are a field day for the lawyers, who, as we all know, get paid no matter who wins. In his fear of being out-lawyered, Beman discharged one law firm and hired another, which, totally unfamiliar with the case, then charged the players a fortune to acquaint themselves with the intricacies of the case. And all of it, in my opinion, to no avail. As the case progressed to its ultimate conclusion in court, and with each succeeding legal maneuver, it became clearer to me that we would lose.

Players Risked $600 Million

Since damages are tripled in antitrust lawsuits, as this one was, the PGA Tour faced a potential judgment of as much as $600 million, plus reasonable attorney's fees. The pension plan is in fact a deferred compensation plan. Under the plan, the monies put aside for the players future is in reality an asset of the tour. This could make these funds subject to any judgment against the tour. A hard-boiled corporation might conclude that taking even the slightest chance on that scenario developing would be folly.

The irony of this battle of the lawyers is that Leonard Decof is a players' man who, long before the Ping lawsuit erupted, was asked to serve as a member of the Senior Tour policy board. Decof's nomination was supported by the players, including Miller Barber, then a member of the players' committee, but evidently Beman persuaded Barber to change his vote, and so Decof was not elected.

When Beman first presented the results of his tests to us at a meeting in Ponte Vedra, Florida, I was astounded at his contention that square grooves made so much difference in play. He claimed that the grooves on the Ping Eye-II wedges stopped a ball played from the rough much faster than wedges with V-grooves. When asked how much faster, there was considerable hemming and hawing, but finally Beman & Co. said that the ball stopped three to five feet shorter. So all of the hullaballoo was over a claimed difference of three to five feet with a wedge shot, when struck out of wet rough from forty yards.

Shortly thereafter, Beman proposed to the regular tour's policy board that square grooves be banned, and it was suggested that the four player members should abstain from voting because all had contracts with competing golf equipment companies, and this might raise questions about conflicts of interest. On Beman's recommendation they complied, and the PGA club pro members abstained on advice from Beman's attorney, leaving the three businessmen directors — Hugh Culverhouse, Del DeWindt and Roger Birk — to vote Beman's way. However, the PGA Tour bylaws clearly state that three of the four *player* directors must vote for any measure brought before its policy board concerning equipment or rules changes. I know, because I helped to write that provision.

Players Surrender Their Rights

Karsten realized that the policy board's action was illegal without the player directors' votes, and he charged that the ban could not be enforced. When Beman realized he had goofed, he called all the policy board members to inform them there would be an executive session at the next policy board meeting, scheduled for the following week, to address this problem by changing the by-laws. This change would make it so that any directors with a conflict of interest could not vote and would not count toward the total number of votes, thus eliminating the players and allowing the three businessmen directors to constitute a majority. This change of the by-laws occurred at the same time that lawyers from both sides were appearing in Federal Court in Phoenix, Arizona, to argue over Karsten's demand for a restraining order.

I have often wondered why our lawyers had not thought to change the by-laws well in advance of the first vote, considering that the square-groove issue had been around for two years.

By this action, the players were robbed of their right to make their own rules and run their own business, something for which so many of us had fought so hard, often at the risk of our livelihoods.

This blanket grant of power is something we never had in mind for the businessmen directors. I very much doubt that any of the three had much of an idea what a square groove was, or could have identified one under oath. Shortly thereafter, Beman also tried to persuade the Senior Tour players to grant such power to its businessmen advisors, but that attempt was shot down the minute it was brought up.

Beman's insistence — some might say arrogance — in defending himself to the death against the Ping lawsuit was a tragic example of egomania leading to excess and waste. The record is replete with examples of Beman's making critical decisions on the lawsuit without informing either the players or the full board, of seeking board approval to obtain power in advance to make decisions involving millions of dollars (attended by a small cabal of attorneys, free from the inconvenience of explaining his actions to the players, or even the full board) until after the fact.

For example, Deane granted full indemnity to any players who would agree to join the countersuit filed against Karsten, even though such legal indemnity was not covered by the PGA Tour's insurance, and thus he obligated the tour for all damages that might arise from any legal actions.

By February of 1993, it was rumored that the PGA Tour had spent an estimated ten million dollars on attorneys and had yet to appear in court. That ten million might have been put in the players' pension fund, but instead that very retirement fund was being placed at risk, largely to protect Beman's personal power and his ego as the czar of golf. Even in winning, what indeed would we have won?

The lawsuit was not about Beman's and the tour's right to pass rules and regulations by which to govern themselves. It was about square grooves, which the USGA has declined to ban, and by that action has declared perfectly legal. In fact, the USGA never made an issue of square grooves, *per se*, but rather over the *spacing* of the grooves, and when the USGA decided to settle its dispute with Karsten, the issue of square grooves appeared to be safely resolved.

The Integrity of the Game

If Deane really felt so strongly about preserving the integrity of the game, he might have gone after metal woods and their super-light shafts. Or perhaps he should have started by banning the present-day golf ball from the tour, which even the USGA admits goes eight yards farther than in the 1960s. From personal observation, I would estimate that the ball today travels from twenty to thirty yards farther, when hit solidly by top professional golfers, although I have no tests to prove it.

Recently we even heard that Beman considered requiring all players on tour to play the same *brand* of ball during tournaments. He said this would provide a level playing field by eliminating any "hidden advantages," as far as the ball is concerned. But this would also give the commissioner unprecedented leverage over the ball manufacturers.

The Case Cracks

As the Ping Case wended its way towards a trial, an interesting legal development occurred. The Tour had filed a series of motions for summary judgment, seeking to have the case thrown out without a trial. The judge denied virtually all of these motions across the board and, in a sweeping decision, stated that Karsten had the right to proceed to trial and prove his case. The judge also denied the Tour's motion to dismiss Karsten's claim for punitive damages, whereupon Decof moved to produce income tax returns and financial records of Beman and the businessmen directors on the grounds that the personal finances of these defendants would be relevant evidence in proving punitive damages. The court granted Decof's motion and ordered the records be produced. Shortly after these events, the PGA Tour settled the case out of court.

The problem then facing Beman was just how to save face

in public and somehow reassure the players that they, not Karsten, had won the case. Give Beman credit; he seems to have accomplished those objectives. He issued a notice to the players stating that the legal case had not been financed by the players' money but, rather, had been covered completely by our insurance. This was disingenuous, because insurance covered only $10 million, leaving approximately $4 million in cost to the tour. Karsten Solheim chose not to press for financial damages, only legal costs, so we may never know the true cost of the lawsuit.

Beman Makes the Rules

Does the PGA Tour have the right to pass rules that unfairly harm legitimate businesses or individuals? History and legal precedent tell us that no one has that right, but apparently in the Ping case Beman simply could not bring himself to back down because his power and "face" were on the line. Apparently, he didn't mind if he busted the tour in the process. Our commissioner appeared willing to make his own laws; our own lawyers have been reported as saying that Deane simply did not listen to them when they opposed his views. Yet one of the oldest canons of the law states that, "He who represents himself has a fool for a client."

Deane Beman ruled the PGA Tour for nearly twenty years, almost autonomously and without supervision, or at best the token supervision of a policy board whose membership and attitudes he was always able to heavily influence, if not dominate. He thus was able to conduct much of the tour's business in secret. His ability to select, manipulate and stroke the businessmen directors is legendary within the inner circles of golf.

To illustrate, until the Karsten lawsuit none of the players on tour had any idea of how much money Deane was paid. Further, he had arranged things so that not one player director sat on the committee that determined his salary. The players learned about Beman's salary only after pressure was applied because of an article in *Golf Digest*. His salary was $1.4 million, plus an expense account and the unlimited use of the tour's jet. In addition, he was receiving over $700,000 in bonuses based on the tour's performance.

When, as president of the LPGA, my wife, Judy, was reworking its constitution, she asked Deane for suggestions in writing rules that could be clearly understood and followed. Deane told her, "We don't go by the PGA constitution; we make our own rules." This would have been news to our players. When the PGA Tour and the PGA of America were reunited after the split in 1968, they issued a joint statement of principles which, though giving the PGA Tour far more power to govern itself, did so only under and subject to the constitution of the PGA of America.

How the Monkeys Escaped

Lest I be labeled a turncoat by one of the cadre of loyalists who worked in Beman's office, let me tell you something of my background and involvement with the PGA Tour. In the late 1960s, I was elected to the PGA Tournament Committee, the policy-making group set up by the players themselves, and eventually I became its chairman and chief spokesman, a position I did not seek.

As it happened, I was chairman during much of the players' fight for power with the parent PGA of America, then headed by president Max Elbin, with labor lawyer Bob Creasy hired as executive director to "put the monkeys" in their places. The monkeys, of course, were us — the tour players. Creasy had held some sort of labor position under President Truman.

We consulted lawyer friends all over the country and were advised to hire a good labor attorney ourselves. With help from Dan Bernheim, a good friend and prominent New York advertising executive, we secured the services of Jimmy Hoffa's man, William Buffalino, who proved to be more than a match for Creasy. At the U.S. Open at Baltusrol in 1967, the PGA Executive Committee posted a notice on all the players' lockers informing us that we had been kicked out of the PGA. I immediately contacted Buffalino and set up a meeting with the PGA officers and Creasy.

That evening, as we entered the dining room at the hotel where all the players were staying, I passed a table where Arnold Palmer and his agent, Mark McCormick, were seated.

"Nice going," Arnold said, looking up. "I understand you hired a hood lawyer to represent us."

I stopped, and replied, "Really? Well, he's Jimmy Hoffa's attorney, if that's what you mean, but why don't you ask your own lawyer about it, since he's sitting right there?" McCormick glanced up, as I continued. "We offered the job to your attorney first, but he turned us down."

Arnold turned to Mark. "Is that true?" McCormick looked a little flustered and mumbled something unintelligible, and that's the last we heard about Buffalino from Palmer.

The next day, Buffalino began the meeting by stating to "Mr. Creasom" that he didn't know just how much money the PGA had, but that if, by the following morning, all the tour players had not been restored to their full memberships, the players would soon own all of the PGA's assets. End of meeting.

The following morning, a notice appeared on our lockers restoring our full membership. Buffalino had served our purposes well and had done so with no pay. He refused to take a fee, so I took up a collection among the players and we gave Bill Buffalino an engraved watch from "The Boys."

The PGA's next move was to take after me personally with veiled threats of retribution, so once again Dan Bernheim delivered for us by arranging an appointment with Samuel Gates of the prestigious Park Avenue law firm of Debevoise, Plimpton, Lyons and Gates. Jack Nicklaus, then a tournament committee member, also was feeling some personal heat and wanted to accompany me to New York, so Jack and I held the initial meeting with Sam Gates.

The Players Gain Their Independence

The subsequent liaison with Gates turned out to be a happy one for the players. Acting on our behalf, Gates won three straight legal skirmishes against the PGA's well-oiled Washington lawfirm of Arnold, Fortas and Porter, one of whose partners, Abe Fortas, was a former Supreme Court Justice. Out of all this legal fighting with the PGA came the players' right to run their own business.

With few exceptions, the players backed our Player Committee completely and, for the first time in the existence of the tour, we presented a united front to the PGA. I spent so much time with Sam Gates that I almost began to feel like a member of his law firm. Sam and I conceived the idea of today's PGA Tour Policy Board. Together with other player members of the Tournament Committee, we worked long and hard on its conception and structure, and we spent many hours working out the details and job descriptions of the commissioner we would hire and the prospective board members who would oversee his activities.

One day Sam suggested to me that, in order to offset any public apprehension, it might be a good idea to appoint three members of the policy board from the business world. I wasn't crazy about the idea, but we finally agreed that it was a good public relations move, and to minimize "politics," we also decided that the businessmen members would name their own successors. Their role was to serve solely as financial advisors, or, if necessary, as referees in any disputes with the club pros.

Neither Sam nor I envisioned any long-term need for the businessmen, nor did we envision their assuming any role other than *advising* us. What's more, the players who framed the original statement of principles never intended that the businessmen directors would, or should, be retained permanently.

The Political Games

I first came to know Deane Beman well when he served on the Tournament Committee as a "young player" advisor. Deane, although a small man, was a pretty damn good player — sort of a good field, no-hit type. He had a short, flattish backswing, and was therefore quite a short hitter. But he was fabulous around and on the green.

Even then, he was very vocal and outspoken. We had received some criticism from the younger players who thought that the governing players were looking out only for themselves, which was untrue. But a young players' advisory committee seemed a good idea, so we formed one consisting of two young players, appointed by us, who would serve a term of three or four months. They were urged to report back to all the younger players and advise them how their business was being conducted. I remember one of the early members was Dick Lotz, who was a fine representative of this group. Beman came along soon thereafter, and thus began his political career on the PGA Tour.

After my term on the newly-formed Tournament Policy Board was up, Deane was elected to the board with, I believe, the encouragement of Joe Dey, who had been appointed our first commissioner. Joe served us well and with his customary dignity. He also became quite friendly with Deane. When Joe announced his intention to retire in 1973, the board began to search for a new commissioner.

Deane tossed his hat into the ring almost immediately but refused to surrender his position on the policy board, as many felt he should. We were told later that Dey and board chairman J. Paul Austin, the chairman of Coca-Cola, huddled privately with Beman in March and offered him the commissioner's job. However, the board continued the subterfuge of interviewing candidates until as late as August, and when Jay Hebert found out about this, he was livid, for he had gone through a long interview for the job and, in my opinion, would have made a wonderful commissioner.

A Secret, Illegal Ballot

It is not generally known, but Deane was elected commissioner by a secret ballot. Sam Gates would have been appalled. I remember sitting with Sam in his Park Avenue office far into the night grinding out the new rules and regulations, and I remember as if it were yesterday Sam's insistent voice urging me to be sure that the players retained control of the commissioner's office.

In order for any candidate to be elected commissioner, Sam advised, we should fix it so that he must receive the votes of all four players who sit on the board. I happen to know that Lionel Hebert, who was one of the four player members, did not cast *his* vote for Beman. Therefore, the vote was illegal, by definition, and, as I've mentioned, it was conducted by secret ballot.

Our principal intention in the beginning was that the players would make the policy, and the policy would be administered by the commissioner and his staff. It took Beman twenty years, but he managed to usurp virtually all of the policy board's power.

The first thing he did, after Joe Dey retired and Dan Sikes and I had left the board, was to get rid of Sam Gates as legal counsel and replace him with his own hometown law firm. At that point, the players began to lose governing power and began digging their own graves. Later, after Beman had been serving as commissioner a while, Dey told me that recommending Deane for the job was the biggest mistake he'd ever made, and he apologized for having done so. Other periods of Beman's tenure deserve scrutiny.

Some years ago, Deane spearheaded an attempt to take away the permanent exemptions granted to all previous winners of major championships. When it appeared that he might be successful, a group of the former champions hired an attorney and, with Jackie Burke as their leader, told Beman that they would sue both him and the PGA Tour for "some large green" if he so acted. They had reasoned, and I think correctly, that if Beman could have revoked their exemptions, then he could also have required them to return their prize money. Burke pointed out that every player who teed it up knew full well that he was playing for a lifetime exemption, as well as the monetary prize. Soon thereafter, Beman's zest for reclaiming all those permanent exemptions turned out to be, after all, not so dear to his heart.

Another project that Deane pursued aggressively was the all-exempt tour, an idea of Gary McCord's initially that, unfortunately, the commissioner latched onto and was able to push through. This brilliant stroke eliminated the most democratic idea in sports, the Monday qualifier, in which any golf professional or aspiring pro in the nation could earn a spot in the current week's official tour event. If the player qualified successfully, he could continue playing each week until he missed a cut or decided to take a week off. That's a tough road to go but a pretty fair deal.

Deane brought the idea of the all-exempt tour to the Board and was turned down immediately. He then began showing up at many of the tournaments, where he would invite small groups of players to dinner to sell them on the all-exempt idea. Clearly, if the all-exempt tour were adopted and resulted in more secure and higher weekly income for the "also-rans" — as it has — their support for Deane would increase. It took quite a while, but eventually Deane got his way, and now the all-exempt tour is tour policy. Should the commissioner make the tour's policies, or should he execute the players' policies?

The Senior Tour

When a group of us over-50 guys got together and formed what is now the highly successful PGA Senior Tour, I was one of the original policy board members and several years later I served another three-year term as Player Director. After Beman's failure to get the seniors on television, a group of us met with Ohlmeyer Communications in New York and secured a television deal. Beman had resisted our earlier efforts, but he was quick to jump on the senior bandwagon, and I understand that now he takes credit for developing the Senior Tour.

Ever wonder how the Senior Tour got started? Here's the straight of it. The dramatic finishes of the first two "Legends of Golf," which were televised in 1978 and 1979, whetted the public's appetite for seeing the old, familiar stars in action once again. That fall, at the PGA Senior Championship in Miami, a group of the seniors called a meeting of the more famous over-fifty players. We decided to organize ourselves, and right away Leo Fraser — the former PGA of America president — jumped up and offered to put on the first "official" senior event at his venerable Atlanta City Country Club. The Suntree Country Club of Melbourne, Florida, also came aboard, and we were off and running.

We passed a few ground rules which we felt would make the senior events appealing for both the players and the public. There would be no cut, which meant that some of the older legends would be on view the entire tournament. Competitors would receive a guarantee of $1,000 and be able to ride in a golf cart, if they so desired. We also agreed to play in two pro-ams and attend two sponsor parties each week. The public ate it up. From a marketing point of view, the most important single factor was that Sam Snead promised to play in all the events we could schedule. I don't think he knew just how many events we could book, but Sam kept his word!

Some of us on the original Senior Policy Board realized

that our chances for big success would depend on television exposure, so we asked Beman to explore this for us. In a meeting at the Charlotte tournament in 1981, Beman reported that he had canvassed all the networks and found that we, the seniors, were not the least bit saleable. I then suggested that, if he didn't mind, we'd try to sell the seniors to television ourselves. A group of five or six of us, at our own expense, flew to New York City and met with Ray Volpe of Ohlmeyer Communications. When we adjourned that afternoon, we had the basis for a televison deal. The players, not Beman, accomplished this, just as the Ladies PGA had shown Beman how to establish a players' pension fund.

Rules are Killing Nostalgia

During this period, I had signed on to represent Nabisco, a major sponsor of the Senior Tour. One night at dinner, Nabisco's chief executive, Ross Johnson, suggested that a "Super Seniors" division be added to the Senior Tour. Nabisco would put up a small purse for the event, which would feature famous tournament winners over the age of sixty. Beman was opposed to this concept, too, and subsequently made misrepresentations to the players concerning antitrust liability. He changed the original Super Seniors concept from a tour of achievement to a chronological one by admitting all players over sixty, regardless of past performance.

Because of the formats required on the Senior Tour, the seniors and super seniors compete in the same groups and over the same course. Beman decided, however, that super seniors should not be eligible to win money in the regular seniors division if they also competed in the super seniors. He also proposed that the super seniors' money be declared unofficial, and thus it would not count towards eligibility. Under this rule, players who chose to compete in the super seniors would shortly not have enough official

Gardner on the Senior Tour.

money to remain eligible to play the Senior Tour.

Now, unfortunately, the players on the Senior Tour have forgotten the one basic principle on which the Senior Tour rests: They're not selling competition, as such, but nostalgia. They've forgotten that they're seventy-eight old men who are not offering the world's best golf, but damn good second-best golf. They seem to forget the public is paying to see the Sneads, the Nicklauses, the Trevinos, the Boroses, the Januarys, and not the "Johnny Appleseeds" who are riding their backs. It's almost as if the public were allowed to see Ted Williams and Mickey Mantle smashing home runs, or Johnny Unitas throwing touchdown passes once again. That's nostalgia.

Unfortunately, Deane Beman was the principal agent in turning the Senior Tour into a watered-down version of the regular tour, one that features dozens of journeymen and no-names. He seemed determined to eliminate the game's legends as fast as he could.

'Conduct Unbecoming'

Players like Doug Ford and Jerry Barber, realizing what Beman was trying to do, protested in the strongest terms and proposed that the players over sixty no longer participate in super seniors events. This angered Beman; the monkeys were getting out of line.

Shortly thereafter, Beman arrived at the Vintage Seniors event in Indian Wells, California, and while the tournament was in progress, he went out on the golf course and threatened Ford with large fines and suspension unless he ceased advising his fellow players. Doug and his amateur partners were distracted and somewhat embarrassed by the incident, which later came to be known as "conduct unbecoming a Commissioner of the PGA Tour." A letter from Ford to Beman, via Leonard Decof, promised strong legal action, and that ended the matter.

In 1992 a respected investigative reporter, Marcia Chambers, published a three-part series in *Golf Digest* on Beman and the PGA Tour's methods of doing business. Beman, apparently apprehensive about the Chambers story, traveled to New York with some of his entourage to meet with *Golf Digest* executives.

If this was an attempt to persuade *Golf Digest* not to publish the Chambers series, or at least soften some of her findings, it fell on deaf ears. The first installment was entitled, "Can Beman Survive?" When Deane saw the headline, it was reported that he remarked that it wasn't a question of whether he, Beman, could survive, but could *Golf Digest* survive.

The Feds Investigate

Among the problems reported in the *Golf Digest* series was the fact that the Federal Trade Commission had been investigating Beman and his programs for some time, although I don't think many of the players were aware of the government's interest in their affairs. The probe seems to have focused on possible violations of antitrust laws, and possibly tax-exemption issues. Beman dismissed this investigation as meaningless and routine. In my inexpert opinion, it would seem his policies have left us open to several antitrust questions.

Internally, there are also problems at the PGA Tour. During the formation of the Tournament Players Division, the forerunner of today's PGA Tour that I've already discussed, the players decided to give the soon-to-be-named commissioner the sole power to grant releases from regular tour events (when tour members want to play in conflicting events, they must obtain a release to do so). It seemed to me there was considerable risk in vesting this kind of power in the commissioner's office, but our first commissioner, Joe Dey, handled these cases with fairness and impartiality. Unfortunately, the same cannot be said of Beman. In my opinion, and that of many others, Deane abused this power either to keep players in line or to curry favor.

In one instance, Mark Calcavecchia asked Beman for clearance to play in the winner-take-all Million Dollar Challenge in South Africa. I'm told that Mark had received permission to do so from the U.S. tournament sponsor that same week, but that Beman denied the release. If Calcavecchia still insisted on playing in South Africa, Beman said he would fine Mark more than he could earn in the Million Dollar event, and suspend him to boot.

Needless to say, Calcavecchia did not go to South Africa. This is not an isolated incident, only an example. It surprises me that no player has challenged this kind of action in court, since the U.S. government protects its citizens' rights to make a living almost more than it protects their lives.

Another example of what I regard as Beman's abuse of power occurred during the Seiko Match Play tournament some years ago. It had to do with Deane's readiness to muzzle comment and dissent. We have rules that are supposed to discourage players from making rude remarks or voicing public criticism while at tournaments. In this case, the tournament officials had seeded some of the players in hopes that some big names would reach the finals, to enhance television.

This practice, in effect, amounts to paying appearance money, since the farther you advance, the more money you receive. Our rules strictly forbid appearance money, and this event was co-sponsored by the PGA Tour. Bob Gilder griped to the press because he was unseeded. Beman called Gilder on the carpet and reportedly said, "You may think you have free speech, but you do not." Gilder was fined and meekly paid up.

Clearing the Air

Prior to Deane Beman's resignation as commissioner earlier this year, a move was underway by players to institute an independent audit of the tour's finances. The PGA Tour never underwent an outside audit during the nearly twenty years that Beman held office.

Our audits were done annually by Ernst and Young, the giant accounting firm that was much in the news during the S&L scandals and has since paid huge sums to settle cases brought against it for irregularities in accounting procedures.

Before resigning, however, Beman managed to push his handpicked successor, former assistant Timothy Finchem, into the commissioner's job. (Finchem led Walter Mondale's unsuccessful campaign for President before joining the PGA.) As Finchem begins his term, he should clear the air of all doubts, rumors and innuendos by ordering an independent outside audit of the PGA Tour. It's common practice in business for a new administration to start with a clean, clear slate, and that's exactly what Finchem should do. In my opinion, any resistance to ordering an audit could only be considered as trying to cover up some sins of the past. And if no improprieties are found, at the very least an audit would quiet Beman's critics, including me.

The 'Winter White House'

Meanwhile, Beman can keep working on his golf game, which he did frequently while occupying the commissioner's office and supposedly representing the players.

For three to four months every winter (such as it is in Jacksonville, Florida, home of the PGA Tour offices), Beman and company would move the tour's main functions to La Quinta, one of the California desert's fanciest winter retreats. There's no telling how many thousands of dollars were spent shuffling staff and sycophants back and forth across the country. I also understand that two executives of the now-defunct Landmark Land Company deeded two beautifully decorated condominiums to the PGA Tour, and that Beman either owned or occupied them rent free. Did Landmark get anything in return?

Why did Beman migrate to sunny Southern California during the winter? It is reported that he practiced almost daily; one fellow suggested that Beman hit as many balls as Hogan in his prime, but I'm certain that's an exaggeraton. And the players of the PGA Tour, many of whom Beman will now compete against on the Senior Tour, paid for his hours of practice.

But that's nothing new. Several years ago Beman sought and received permission from the PGA Policy Board to participate in the Legends of Golf with partner Al Geiberger. How can a commissioner make rulings or decisions on fellow tournament players if he, too, is a contestant?

This same board was silent when Beman vacationed in Great Britain and participated in several senior tournaments while he was commissioner of the PGA Tour. He was leading the British Senior Championship entering the final round but shot a high score in a roaring gale to lose to Gary Player.

Irregularity and Beman are old friends. When Deane left his insurance business in Washington, D.C., to join the tour in 1967, he routinely contacted sponsors and pleaded for sponsor's exemptions instead of having to qualify on Monday like everyone else. He continued this practice for several years until he finally played well enough to earn his exemptions. As a result of this abuse, the Tournament Committee passed the unofficially named "Beman Rule," which limited the number of sponsor exemptions to three for a first-year player.

Regaining Control

Deane Beman has always seemed anxious to persuade the world that he alone has been responsible for the remarkable success and growth of the tour during his tenure. He certainly deserves some credit, perhaps a great deal of credit, for the current financial success, but he didn't invent television —

the largest source of cash — nor did he invent Arnold Palmer, Ben Hogan, Sam Snead, Bryon Nelson, Bing Crosby and Bob Hope, and Dwight David Eisenhower, all of whom made tremendous contributions to golf's popularity. Neither did Beman conceive "stadium golf" or "stadium courses"; those ideas originated in the 1960s from a Long Island golf architect named William F. Mitchell.

As Beman exercised his personal control over the tour in recent years, he entered into several areas that never were properly and openly discussed. For example, why is the PGA in the business of building and owning golf courses, with their attendant thousands of employees and benefits? And why is the tour in the business of endorsing anything? That should be the prerogative of our individual players.

I felt very strongly in the late 1960s and early 1970s that the tournament players should have the right to run their own business and not be governed by club professionals, who were often unqualified to run professional tournament affairs. I feel a great fidelity to the tour and have devoted an enormous amount of time and thought to the cause of the players. Let me assure the current tour players, and those yet to come, that neither I nor my peers ever had in mind turning over the ultimate authority for our tour to any individual. Those of us who conceived the Tour Policy Board had in mind placing the policy power in the hands of the players, not its commissioner or compliant businessmen advisors. Despite our warnings, most of the rank-and-file players, and even some of the stars, don't want to rock the boat; they are content with their almost "guaranteed" high incomes. But the current structure is flawed, and sooner or later we'll all pay the price for fixing it.

As Timothy Finchem begins his term as commissioner, I hope he will try to learn from the past and, with an eye on the future, return control of the PGA Tour to the players. They're the ones who make it all possible; without them, the PGA Tour is a Broadway play without actors.

Part

8

·············· ··

Living on
Tour and
with Yourself

Inspiration

Playing tournament golf for a living, which I've done most of my adult life, is a game of constant emotional ups and downs. They say that golf is like life, but don't you believe it; to golfers, it seems much more complicated than life. Any serious golfer will know what I mean. A poor stretch of golf tends to plunge you into the depths of despair, a good streak to raise you to the heights of elation. In golf, these ups and downs seem to occur more often than they do in life, and for less reason. I think that anyone who wants to play golf for a living would do well to fortify himself, or herself, against these sudden changes by whatever means can be found. In my case, the answer has come partially from poetry.

I was introduced to poetry by Miss Emma Wilkerson, my sixth grade teacher at Monte Sano grammar school in Augusta, Georgia. "Miss Emma" was a wonderful person and an inspirational teacher who opened our minds to the importance and beauty of our language. To this day, I can still remember most of the poems she had us memorize. When my childhood buddy, Carl Sanders, became governor of Georgia, he proclaimed a statewide "Miss Emma Wilkerson Day." Because of her, many students, including this one, subsequently made all "A"s in English, and I have continued a lifelong interest in reading.

My appetite for poetry was further whetted by my mother, Fredericke Pilcha Dickinson, who gave me her little leather-bound book entitled *Poems of Inspiration*, collected by Joseph Morris and St. Clair Adams. That little book was an inspiration to me for many years. On more than one occasion its poems were a boost to my head, my heart and my wallet. I can still recite many of the poems, and get a lift whenever I leaf through it.

On the following pages, I want to share a few of these favorite poems with you. If you don't like poetry, you can skip the next few pages, but I think you'll be doing yourself a disservice. I warn you that they have nothing to do with hitting a golf ball, at least not directly, but they do say something about holding the soul together.

IT COULDN'T BE DONE

Somebody said that it couldn't be done,
But he with a chuckle replied
That "maybe it couldn't," but he would be one
Who wouldn't say so till he'd tried.
So he buckled right in with a trace of a grin
On his face. If he worried he hid it.
He started to sing as he tackled the thing
That couldn't be done, and he *did* it!

Somebody scoffed: "Oh, you'll never do that;
At least no one ever has done it";
But he took off his coat, and he took off his hat,
And the first thing we knew he'd begun it.
With a lift of his chin and a bit of a grin,
Without any doubting or quiddit,
He started to sing as he tackled the thing
That couldn't be done, and he *did* it.

There are thousands to tell you it cannot be done,
There are thousands to prophesy failure;
There are thousands to point out to you one by one,
The dangers that wait to assail you.
But just buckle in with a bit of a grin,
Just take off your coat and go to it;
Just start to sing as you tackle the thing
That "cannot be done," and you'll *do* it!

Edgar A. Guest

THE QUITTER

When you're lost in the wild, and you're scared as a child,
And death looks you bang in the eye;
And you're sore as a boil, it's according to Hoyle
To cock your revolver and die.
But the code of a man says fight all you can,
And self-dissolution is barred;
In hunger and woe, oh it's easy to blow;
It's the hell served for breakfast that's hard!

You're sick of the game? Well, now, that's a shame!
But you're young, and you're brave, and you're bright.
You've had a raw deal, I know, but don't squeal.
Buck up, do your damnedest and fight!
It's the plugging away that will win you the day,
So don't be a piker, old pard;
Just draw on your grit; it's so easy to quit,
It's the keeping your chin up that's hard.

It's easy to cry that you're beaten and die,
It's easy to crawfish and crawl,
But to fight, and to fight when all hope's out of sight,
Why, that's the best game of them all.
And tho' you come out of each gruelling bout
All broken and beaten and scarred —
Just have one more try. It's dead easy to die.
It's the keeping on *living* that's hard!

Robert W. Service

Whether in golf or in life, any man needs what Everard
Jack Appleton described, in a nautical vein, as:

THE WOMAN WHO UNDERSTANDS

Somewhere she waits to make you win,
Your soul in her firm white hands —
Somewhere the gods have made for you,
The Woman Who Understands!

As the tide went out she found him

lashed to a spar of Despair,
The wreck of his Ship around him —
The wreck of his Dreams in the air;
Found him and loved him and gathered
The soul of him close to her heart —
The soul that had sailed an uncharted Sea,
The soul that had sought to win and be free —
The soul of which she was part!
And there in the dusk she cried to the man,
"Win your battle — you can, you can!"

Broken by Fate, unrelenting
Scarred by the lashings of Chance;
Bitter his heart — unrepenting —
Hardened by Circumstance;
Shadowed by Failure ever,
Cursing, he would have died,
But the touch of her hand, her strong warm hand,
And her love of his soul, took full command,
Just at the turn of the Tide!
Standing beside him, filled with trust,
"Win!" she whispered, "you must, you must!"

Helping and loving and guiding,
Urging when that was best,
Holding her fears in hiding,
Deep in her quiet breast;
This is the woman who kept him
True to his standards lost,
When, tossed in the storm and stress and stife
He thought himself through with the game of Life
And ready to pay the cost.
Watching and guarding, whispering still,
"Win you can — and win, you will!"

This is the story of Ages
This is the Woman's way;
Wiser than seers or sages,

Lifting us day by day;
Facing all things with a courage
Nothing can daunt or dim,
Treading Life's path, wherever it leads —
Lined with flowers, or choked with weeds,
But ever with him — with him!

Guider - comrade - golden spur —
The men who win are helped by her!

Somewhere she waits, strong in belief,
Your soul in her firm, white hands,
Thank well the gods, then she comes to you —
Your Woman Who Understands!

And how truly did Ella Wheeler Wilcox write in her poem entitled:

SOLITUDE

Laugh, and the world laughs with you,
Weep, and you weep alone;
For the sad old earth
Must borrow its mirth,
It has trouble enough of its own.

Sing, and the hills will answer,
Sigh, it is lost on the air;
The echoes bound
To a joyful sound,
But shrink from voicing care.

Rejoice, and men will seek you,
Grieve, and they turn and go;
They want full measure
Of all your pleasure,
But they do not want your woe.

Be glad, and your friends are many,
Be sad, and you lose them all,
There are none to decline

Your nectared wine,
But *alone* you must drink Life's gall.

Feast, and your halls are crowded;
Fast, and the world goes by;
Succeed and give,
And it helps you live,
But it cannot help you die.

There is room in the Halls of Pleasure
For a long and lordly train;
But one by one
We must all file on
Through the narrow aisles of Pain!

S. E. Kiser might have written this just for me:

UNSUBDUED

I have hoped, I have planned, I have striven,
To the will I have added the deed;
The best that was in me, I've given,
I have prayed, but the gods would not heed.

I have dared and reached only disaster,
I have battled and broken my lance;
I am bruised by a pitiless master
That the weak and the timid call Chance.

I am old, I am bent, I am cheated
Of all that youth urged me to win;
But name me not with the Defeated,
For tomorrow, again, I begin!

The following poem, by the famous sportswriter, Grantland
Rice, is one of my all-time favorites:

MIGHT HAVE BEEN

Here's to "The days that might have been";
Here's to the "Life I might have led";

The fame I might have gathered in —
The glory ways I might have sped.
Great "Might Have Been," I drink to you
Upon a throne where thousands hail —
And then — there looms another view —
I also "might have been" in jail!

O "Land of Might Have Been" we turn
With aching hearts to where you wait;
Where crimson fires of glory burn
And laurel crowns the guarding gate;
We may not see across your fields
The sightless skulls that know their woe —
The broken spears, — the shattered shields —
That "might have been" as truly so.

"Of all sad words of tongue or pen" —
So wails the poet in his pain —
The saddest are "It might have been"
And world-wide runs the dull refrain.
The saddest? Yes — but in the jar
This thought brings to me with its curse,
I sometimes think the gladdest are
"It might have been a damned sight worse!"

How many times have I told myself that I was going to
camp on that practice green until I could out-putt Ben
Crenshaw? And then I never do it. I think St. Clair Adams
had people like me in mind when writing:

GOOD INTENTIONS

The road to hell, they assure me,
With good intentions is paved;
And I know my desires are noble,
But my deeds might brand me depraved.
It's the warped grain in our nature,
And St. Paul has written it true,
"The good that I would I do not;

But the evil I would not I do!'"

I've met few men who are monsters
When I came to know them inside;
Yet their bearing and dealings external
Are crusted with cruelty, pride,
Scam, selfishness, envy, indifference,
Greed — why the long list pursue?
The good that they would they do not,
But the evil they would not they do.

Intentions may still leave us beast-like;
With unchangeable purpose, we're men,
We must drive the nail home — and then clinch it
Or storms shake it loose again.
In things of great import, or in trifles,
We our recreant souls must subdue
Till the evil we would not we *do* not
And the good that we would we *do*!

In life, many things seem impossible to accomplish, at
least on the surface. In golf, the same is true, as anyone
would know who has watched Hogan, or Snead, or Nicklaus
perform. Yet Napoleon was quoted as saying that the word
impossible is found only in the dictionary of fools. I'm
certain that the word "can't" belongs in there, too.

CAN'T

Can't is the worst word that's written or spoken;
Doing more harm here than slander or lies;
On it is many a strong spirit broken,
And with it many a good purpose dies.
It springs from the lips of the thoughtless each morning
And robs us of courage we need through the day;
It rings in our ears like a timely-sent warning
And laughs when we falter and fall by the way.

Can't is the father of feeble endeavor,

The parent of terror and half-hearted work;
It weakens the efforts of artisans clever,
And makes of the toiler an indolent shirk.
It poisons the soul of a man with a vision.
It stifles in infancy many a plan;
It greets honest toiling with open derision
And mocks at the hopes and the dreams of a man.

Can't is a word none should speak without blushing;
To utter it should be a symbol of shame;
Ambition and courage it daily is crushing;
It blights a man's purpose, and shortens his aim.
Despise it with all of your hatred of error;
Refuse it the lodgement it seeks in your brain,
Arm against it as a creature of terror,
And all that you dream of, you someday shall gain.

Can't is the word that is foe to ambition,
An enemy ambushed to shatter your will;
Its prey is forever the man with a mission
And bows but to patience, and courage and skill.
Hate it with hatred that's deep and undying,
For once it is welcomed 'twill break any man;
Whatever the goal you are seeking, keep trying,
And answer this demon by saying, "I can!"

Edgar A. Guest

Studying People

My roommate in graduate school at the University of Alabama was a fellow named Bob Lokey. He was an upright, religious person, and a very good golfer, as well. One afternoon when studying in our room, Bob startled me by smashing a book into the wall above the wastebasket with the heated exclamation, "What a bunch of trash!"

Anyone who could elicit such a violent response from Bob

Lokey, I thought to myself, must be quite an author, so I retrieved the book. It was *Opus 21* by Philip Wylie. Thus, with Bob's flash of anger, was I introduced to one of America's most interesting intellects and authors. I devoured *Opus 21* and then set out to read everything I could find by Philip Wylie, including *Finley Wren, An Essay On Morals, Innocent Ambassadors, Crunch and Des, The Disappearance*, and, my favorite, *Generation of Vipers. Vipers* was the sort of book you could pick up and start reading anywhere. I kept it with me for years, and each time I read it, I learned something. I didn't always agree with Wylie's ideas but am constantly impressed and stimulated by his intellect.

Some of Wylie's writing was pretty deep and heavy, but, just when I was convinced he was a dark cynic, Wylie would come back with an encouraging idea that might solve society's problems. In *Vipers*, written in 1940, his foresight as to what might happen in this world during and after World War II was quite uncanny, almost clairvoyant. President Franklin Roosevelt, I'm told, recognized the brilliance of Wylie's mind and appointed him to some sort of presidential advisory council.

What I suppose I'm getting at is that Philip Wylie's provocative ideas made me examine many things more deeply. His writing helped me to appreciate the heritage my family had passed down to me, and to understand that intelligence — which can be defined as the native capacity for knowledge — is largely inherited. Wylie made me realize that studying people is one of the world's finest games.

Essentially, that's what I do when I teach golf. Before trying to improve a golfer's game, I try very hard to place myself inside that person's head and look out through his or her eyes, to *see* and *feel* what that golfer sees and feels. If a teacher can't do that, at least to some degree, I feel that he'll be a teaching failure — even if he possesses all the right information.

In my teaching, when I see the slightest doubt or apprehension creeping into my students' demeanor, I just tell them to hit the ball and see where it goes. Don't presuppose failure, I tell them, because if you do, you'll seldom be able to make anything new and unfamiliar work. Sometimes my students will complain that "this new stuff" feels very uncomfortable. Damn right, I'll say; if what *feels* good to you was working, you wouldn't be here, would you? I never promised it would *feel* good, but next week, it probably will. With diligence, I'm quite confident it'll work. If I let a student leave with all the same old feelings instead of new ones, then I've cheated him.

With most golfers, some reinforcement and a couple week's diligent practice is necessary for visible improvement. I don't see why it should take longer than that, although I've been told that some of these wonder-teachers like David Leadbetter have convinced more than a few unsuspecting young pros to stay with them for at least five years. They must be able to talk better than I can, but quite frankly, I believe I could teach a left-handed orangutan to play golf cross-handed if I had that much time to spend with him.

'Esse Quam Videri'

In my sixty-five years on this Earth, I've always tried to live by the Dickinson family motto: *Esse Quam Videri*, which, translated from the Latin, means, "To Be, Rather Than to Seem." That's seldom a very popular cause, for the "seemers" so often seem to get ahead, even though their methods are based on B.S. In much of the golf instruction we see today, teachers and their methods are not always what they seem. The Good Lord knows I don't always live up to my own motto; but imagine how much better would be our politics and our nation, not to mention our golf instruction, if more of us strived "to be" rather than "to seem."

The Louisville Loudmouth

In my opinon, the greatest sports column of all time was the piece Jim Murray wrote for the *Los Angeles Times* on April 27, 1967, entitled, "Louisville Loudmouth Secedes from the Union." Although Jim Murray is probably the finest golf writer among American newspapermen, this column is not about golf. When I read it, I could scarcely believe how beautifully he expressed what we should feel for our country. When I saw Jim shortly thereafter, I congratulated him for composing such an outstanding piece and asked how long it had taken to write it. "No longer than it took to type it; you see, in college I majored in American History."

Several years later, Jim recanted and endorsed Muhammed Ali, as the "Louisville Loudmouth" now calls himself. I asked Jim why the change? "I figured the United States Supreme Court knew more about history and what constitutes a 'preacher' than I did," Murray replied. Even so, and with Jim's kind permission, I want to reprint it here.

"LOUISVILLE LOUDMOUTH SECEDES FROM THE UNION"

There is a stillness at Appomattox, all right. The bugles of Shiloh lie mute.

The campfires on the Potomac have all burned out. The blood in the Rappahannock has all gone to sea.

The caissons no longer rot in the sun at Gettysburg. The trumpets in the dust of Bull Run are silted over.

Muffle the drums of Vicksburg. Battle the Fleets of Farragut. Call the roll of Chancellorsville, Fredericksburg, the Wilderness, Antietam.

Spike the guns of Sumpter. Hobble the horses of

Sheridan. Listen no more to the ghostly treads of Sherman's marchers to the sea.

Dismantle the gallows at Harper's Ferry. Burn the banners of the noblest cause man ever fought for. Scuttle the ironclads. Drop no flowers in the watery resting place of the Monitor off Cape Hatteras.

Put the torch to Uncle Tom's Cabin. Flog old Uncle Tom — it's okay! No one likes him anymore. Set the bloodhounds on Little Liza — who cares?

Forget the Gettysburg Address. It's just another piece of Fourth of July oratory, campaign promises, high-blown histrionics. Hang it up, Abe. Nobody's listening. Tell it to John Wilkes Booth.

"The world will little note, nor long remember what we say here." Right, Abe! "But it can never forget what they did here." Oh, yes it can, Abe!

You see Cassius Marcellus Clay, one of the greatest heroes in the history of his people, has decided to secede from the Union. He will not disgrace himself by wearing the uniform of the Army of the United States. He will never fight "a white man's war."

Not for all the gangrene in Andersonville will he march. From the safety of 103 years, he waves his fist at dead slave owners. Down to his last four Cadillacs, the thud of Communist jack boots hold no dread for him. He is in this country, but not *of* it. The devil is a white man, and vice versa.

After 100 years of freedom he sulks, "We don't own no railroads." The attar of truth perfumes his charges. But only the scent. You buy railroads at the stock exchange the same way you buy silk shirts at the store. Clay has preferred to buy a religion, not the New York Central — But — don't give us freedom, give us railroads!

So, turn off the watchfires of the night. Send our sword to Bobby Lee. Tell Jubal Early there's been a terrible mistake. Apologize for the 70,000 dead along the Rapidan. Cover the trenches of Petersburg. Tell those who fell in the "gloomy thickets of Chickamauga" we're sorry. Come back, General Rosecrans. You've been outflanked by a Louisville loudmouth. The Bill of Rights has been mugged! Wave no poppies for Soldier Clay. John Brown's body may be a-mouldering in his grave, but Cassius won't! Strip the laurel from the graves of the Blue. Let the willow wave over the GAR and the Gray alike.

When lilacs last in the door-yard bloomed, and the great star early dropped in the western sky in the night, this legatee of Lincoln picked up his sword — and ran it through his country's breast. The last full measure of his devotion! Twenty-five million of his people watched silently. He has posed a dreadful moral dilemma for them. Uncle Toms? Or rend the Union again? Serve or smite?

You were right, Abe, "We cannot consecrate — we cannot hallow." It is "far above our poor power." This point needs your wisdom, Abe. Is it our fault? Or his? Has he dishonored the dead? Or have we? Were we all listening when you said "that from these honored dead we take increased devotion to that cause for which they gave the last full measure of their devotion — that we here highly resolve that these dead shall not have died in vain — that this nation — under God — shall have a new birth of freedom"?

One of us wasn't listening, Abe. Which is why no leaves stir at Appomattox — but the blood still caulks the rocks at Shiloh.

Humor: The Three Sows

Humor is a wonderful thing. Sometimes I think it's nature's way of helping us deal with our frustrations and our intelligence, or lack of it. Have you noticed that the smarter we are, the more we seem to need it? You've probably noticed that golf is a frustrating game at times, and that, consequently, it's a rich storehouse of humor. Believe me, we golfers need it. Golfers are inveterate storytellers. Many of their stories are about golf, some are not.

Among the best of golf's storytellers, at least in my lifetime, is Sam Snead. Many's the time that one of Sam's stories has lightened the burdens of a day. This one, which has nothing to do with golf, is one of his favorites, and mine too, so I thought I'd share it with you.

The story concerns a West Virginia farmer named Jake, who owned three old female hogs who had "come into season." The farmer says to his neighbor, "I'd surely like to get some piglets out of these three old sows." His friend suggests he take them over the mountain to see a man named Luke, who owned a $5,000 stud. So Jake loads the three sows in his truck, and over the mountain he drives. Luke tells him the stud can take care of the three sows, but it'll cost twenty dollars apiece. Reluctantly, Jake agrees, and, after the deeds are done, he asks Luke, "How do I know if this took?"

"Do you have a pond on your farm with some mud and clover at one end?" Luke asks.

"Sure do," says Jake.

"Well, when you wake up at daybreak, first thing you do is go look at your sows. If they're out in the clover, then it surely took. But if they're wallowing in the mud, it didn't — in which case you'll have to come back."

Next morning at sunup, Jake jumps up, looks out the window and sees all three sows wallowing in the mud. So, not too happy, he reloads the hogs in the truck, drives over the mountain and pays another sixty bucks. Bright and early the following morning, Jake looks out his window, only to find the three sows back wallowing in the mud. Well, over the mountain he goes again, and pays another sixty bucks.

When Jake arises the next morning, he shakes his wife awake. "Maw, see can you spy those three old sows. Could be I'm a jinx." Up she gets, looks out the window, and says, "Yup, I see 'em."

"Are they in the mud?" Jake asks.

"Nope," says the wife.

"Are they in the clover?"

"No, they ain't," she replies.

"Dammit, then, where the hell do they be?"

"Well," says the wife, "two of 'em be in the back of the truck, and one of 'em be up front blowing the horn!"

The Sarge Picks Up

Some of the humor about golf, of course, is true. Clayton Haefner was a huge, redheaded boy who came out of North Carolina with a big, walrus mustache and a wide-brimmed, white straw hat. We called him "Sarge." Haefner had a temper, could be quite intimidating, and could play like hell, despite using a swing that appeared to "come over the top." After playing with a golfer once, he could imitate his swing and mannerisms to a tee.

The tour that week was at a narrow little course in Beaumont, Texas, that didn't exactly suit Clayton's style — he preferred a wider field of vision. A little old lady bought Sarge in the Calcutta pool, then proceeded to follow him every step of the way. On a particularly narrow hole, Sarge knocked his tee shot into the woods, and, in trying to play back to the fairway, hit a large pine and bounced farther into the forest. Haefner hit another tree, then another, and finally told his caddie to "pick the son of a bitch up."

At this point, the little old lady came running up and pleaded, "Please, Mr. Haefner, don't pick up. I own you in the Calcutta!"

Sarge glared at the lady, handed her his club, and growled, "Here, lady, you hit the son of a bitch. I'm going to the clubhouse." And off he marched, leaving the little lady holding his club.

A Lesson for His Wife

Gibby Sellers was an old-time tour player and sometime golf hustler from Arkansas who knew his way around the betting arenas as well as the golf course. He had a fabulous pair of hands, and I loved to watch him "zing" those iron shots. After Gibby's playing days were over, he took a club job at the Hot Springs Country Club.

One day his wife of some forty years announced that she wanted to take up golf, now that Gibby was retired from the tour. Gib groaned, for this was the last thing he wanted his wife to do. He decided to cure her itch for the game. The next morning he told his wife to come out to the range, where he threw down a bucket of balls in the light rough — on a downslope. Gib handed his wife a two-iron. "You just hit those balls, honey, and when you can get them to where they all go up in the air, come see me, and I'll show you the rest of the game." After struggling for thirty minutes, she threw down the club in despair and never returned for another "lesson." Gibby just chuckled.

Friendship and Friends

Rather early in my career, after I had gotten to know Ben Hogan, I told him what a nice bunch of guys I'd met on the tour. Hogan looked at me. "How much are you making?" he inquired, rhetorically. "On your way up, you'll have lots of friends — as long as you're not winning lots of money. You start winning some big checks, you'll notice how fast those friends will evaporate."

His eyes narrowed, as he continued. "Don't worry about being friends with these guys. You don't actually need their friendship; you want their respect." You don't demand respect, said Hogan, "you *command* it."

Ben was right about this, when it came to the competitive aspect of life on tour, but even though I didn't get to the very top, I'm thankful for all the wonderful people golf has allowed me to know and the great friendships I've made in the game.

Not many readers will know Freddie Guest, and I feel sorry for them because he is one of the best. Freddie taught me to fish for speckled trout in Panama City, Florida, where I sometimes spent the fall, and I taught Freddie how to play wedge shots, to the point where he's now known as "Mr. Wedge." These were my lean years, and Freddie often provided my wife and me with a room at the beach in a motel he owned. Once, when I was low on funds, he handed me a check and later wouldn't accept repayment. I've always been grateful for the friendship of Marie and Freddie Guest, and don't know where I'd be today had it not been for them.

Della Dickinson

No writing about my life in golf would be complete without paying tribute to my former wife of twenty-eight years, Della Dickinson, the mother of my three older children, Dickie, Randy and Sherry. Della and I were almost constant companions for about twenty of those twenty-eight years, and Della had a large role in any success I might have had during that time. There were, of course, some lean years, and times

Sherry Dickinson Fredrickson with her father, 1986.

that Della went beyond the call of duty. Many times she
picked up my bag of practice balls, went out on the range
and shagged balls for hours. Della was a woman of many talents; there was little she couldn't do, from carpentry to cook-
ing and sewing to dancing. She had a smile for almost everyone and always went out of her way to help people. I hope

Gardner Dickinson IV and Randall Ben Dickinson.

Sherry Dickinson.

that she will enjoy these stories of my experiences in golf and life, for she was very much a part of them.

Della and I used to spend New Year's with Al and Barbara Zimmerman at Paradise Valley in Scottsdale, Arizona, on our way to the Los Angeles Open each year. Al was one of the finest wedge players alive, and always worked with me on my wedge play. Al used an old yellow-shafted Spalding "P.D.N." and, from about 120 yards in, I promise you he could eat with that club. Al introduced me to one of his members, Nelson Davis, of Toronto, a Canadian billionaire, who became one of my closest friends. I have very fond memories of the times we spent with the Davis and Zimmerman families.

'Wingy' Furgol

Ed and Helen Furgol were two of the most courageous people I've known. As almost everyone knows, Ed broke his arm in a playground accident as a youngster. It set improperly, and, as a result, withered. When he took up golf, Ed merely held the club in his left hand and lashed the ball with his right arm and wrist. And could he lash it! We all came out to watch "Wingy" hit those sky-high 250-yard one-irons during the pro clinics. He was a "tough dude," and a somewhat violent man, and, as a consequence, was a lousy putter. Even though he did win the U.S. Open, had he putted better, no telling how well he might have done. After Ed seriously injured his right arm, which was abnormally strong, it was all over for him competitively. He made relatively few lasting friends, although I hope I'm one of them; and I hope he'll revel in the knowledge of just how good a player he was.

Lionel Hebert

If a man had two or three friends like Lionel Hebert, he wouldn't need any more during his entire life. We've been so close over the years, and continue to be, although we don't get to see each other as much as we once did. We met at Louisiana State University, as mentioned earlier. Lionel would take off at noon on Fridays to get back to his hometown, Lafayette, Louisiana, where he had his own dance band. Lionel was the band's trumpet player deluxe; he could play!

One night Lionel and I and our wives were standing in a long line on Bourbon Street in New Orleans to hear the great trumpet player Al Hirt. Al found out we were standing in line and whisked us inside to a table beside the bandstand.

Lionel Hebert on trumpet.

Hirt introduced us, then handed his trumpet to Lionel and invited him to play a number. Lionel declined, saying he couldn't get a decent sound out of Big Al's huge mouthpiece. Al borrowed another horn from the band so Lionel couldn't decline. Up he went, and after a couple of nervous "boo-boos," he smoothed out and wowed the crowd. Hirt stopped the band and told Lionel, "Hey, you Coon-ass, if I'd known you were *that* good, I'd never have invitied you up here." Lionel beamed, and we all had a blast.

Lionel cares about people. Harry James became a pal and loved to play drums while Lionel tooted. He called Lionel the "greatest untapped trumpet in the world." Lionel does, indeed, seem to have a "feel" for that horn, as did Harry. When James died in Las Vegas, Lionel flew out to the funeral, which was held in a little chapel there. He told me that our pals, Frank Sinatra and Phil Harris, were the only celebrities there. And when I married Judy, Lionel stood right beside me at the altar — as my best man. He's always been my best man!

Gardner E. Dickinson, Sr.

I scarcely know where to begin this tribute to my Dad. He was, to me, a wonderful man, highly intelligent and educated, and God had given him many other skills, not the least of which was athletic ability. It's true that Dad never accomplished very much in this world monetarily, having spent much of his life during the Great Depression. Because of this, he became ultraconservative, and, consequently, would never really take a chance on anything new and unknown in order to better himself financially. He possessed great organizational ability and a vocabulary second to none. He was also a fine writer and a member of the Golf Writers' Association of America.

Gardner and his Dad, 1968.

Dad won all-state honors in Georgia as a 137-pound scatback at Riverside Military Academy, and he held the Georgia state high school broad-jumping record, a record that stood until the late 1950s. He captained the baseball team at Vanderbilt University and sang lead in the Vanderbilt glee club. Sometime after college, Dad took up golf, and *nobody* loved the game more. He became proficient enough to win the Augusta City championship, the Golf Writers' championship, and the Southern Senior championship. He certainly encouraged me to play, and he and

Gardner Dickinson II, circa 1965.

my mother were very supportive of me my whole career.

He and I met three times in amateur events, and I was lucky enough to "eek" him out each time, and, consequently, there was little conversation between us for about a week after my wins — he was competitive! Dad died at age 68, which is pretty young; I only wish he could have stayed longer to have counseled his five grandchildren, as he did me.

Part 9

Potpourri

Masters Memories

For many years, I looked forward to playing in the Masters in my old home town of Augusta, Georgia, for it meant an enjoyable week staying in the home of my old Fort Jackson Army buddy, John Fleming. I met Lt. Fleming when we were both infantry shavetails living next door to one another in a Bachelor Officers' Quarters. The phone was outside my door, and when no one else would answer it, I did. It was always some sweet little lady who'd say, "May I please speak to Lt. Fleming?" John was the post football coach, a fine athlete, and a handsome young man. He had more good-looking gals after him than he could handle, so I did him a favor occasionally and took care of one.

John was shipped to Korea during the war, and I thought I'd be on the boat right behind him but got lucky. John got shot in the Achilles tendon his first week or so of combat, and his rehabilitation was long and slow.

John is an avid golfer and a fine defense attorney in Augusta. He knew practically everyone in town, it seemed, so one year I asked him to contact Freddy, the Augusta National caddiemaster, to see if Freddy couldn't get me a good caddie who could read those damn greens during the Masters. John did so, and when I checked with Freddy, he told me he'd given me the best reader of greens at the club. I told him to be ready the next morning for a practice round.

The next day, Freddy introduced me to a tall black guy called "Reindeer" by his fellow caddies. Reindeer was huge, with hands the size of a catcher's mitt. When we reached the first green, I began to study my putt. I'd left myself

Gardner on the Augusta National putting green, 1956.

about a twenty-five footer with a pretty obvious break of twelve inches to the left. I was astonished when Reindeer read the path and said it would break thirteen inches to the *right.* I said to him, "You mean it's going to break to the left, don't you?"

"No sir," he replied, "it's going to break to the right." An alarm went off in my head, and when Reindeer called my path on the next three holes dead backwards, I knew I'd been had.

But Reindeer was a rather pleasant fellow and something

of a character, so I kept him for the rest of the tournament. When I went to practice at the range, he would entertain the gallery by catching in his catcher's-mitt hands all of my practice shots he could reach *on the fly*. One-irons and drivers, too, in his bare hands!

Bob Goalby

One of the few guys I've missed since I've cut way back on my participation in tournament golf is my old buddy Bob Goalby. Bob and I have had many good times together over the years, and I've always found him to be a stand-up guy and a real friend who'll do what he says he'll do. We both served two full terms on the PGA Tour Senior Policy Board, and I've found Bob to be an intelligent and articulate representative of the players.

Bob was a helluva player, too, despite the temper tantrums he previously displayed on the golf course. He

(L-R) **Fab Foursome: Bob Goalby, Sam Snead, Lionel Hebert, Gardner Dickinson, 1989.**

had, like me, a great chance to win the U.S. Open at Oakland Hills the year Gene Littler won. He did later win the Masters, and it's a damned shame his victory had to be tarnished at the time by the Roberto de Vicenzo disqualification. But, we all must play by the rules, and Bob didn't write that "5" on Roberto's card. Tommy Aaron did, inadvertently. If the USGA would give the scorer *some* kind of responsibility in keeping a competitor's card, we might eliminate most such unpleasant incidents. Often the fellow keeping my card has little idea of what I made on the last hole, for often he didn't even see me play every shot.

Bob played wonderful golf that year at Augusta, and I know I wish I could tell people that I was a former Masters Champion.

Bob's got that temper in check now, but I can remember when at times he was a holy terror. Once in a tournament, they sent us back out on the course after a violent rainstorm. There were hundreds of rather deep mud puddles all over the course, and it took most of us quite a bit of extra time to detour around them. Well, Bob didn't bother to miss any of the puddles, but rather stomped right through them. After emerging from one particularly deep and muddy puddle, Bob looked down at his once-white golf shoes, and exclaimed "There, you white S.O.B.s, try shining in my eyes now!"

I've had lots of fun with "putting Bob on" about that one, but Bob is really the champion agitator of all time. I accuse him of agitating himself in the bathroom mirror after he gets up, just to get ready for the day.

Best Golf Announcers

As perhaps I've mentioned, the PGA Tour lost two of its best player announcers when, at different times, they sought small salary raises. The first I remember was the case of Cary Middlecoff with CBS. Cary had been hired as an expert commentator and was a regular for several years on the CBS telecasts. One year, he decided to request a small raise in salary, perhaps to bring his paycheck more in line with the professional announcers.

Much to Doc's surprise and consternation, he not only didn't receive more money but was informed that CBS was terminating him. Shortly thereafter, I believe, CBS's great director, Frank Chirkinian (known as the Ayatollah), hired Ken Venturi, who had a problem with stuttering, as Doc's replacement. Television somehow cured Venturi's stuttering, and I think he's done an outstanding job for CBS over the years. Still, I miss Doc Middlecoff. He was, in my opinion, one of our best golf commentators.

Bob Goalby, formerly with NBC, suffered a similar fate with that network. At the end of the season a few years ago, Bob asked NBC for a rather modest salary increase. He got the same treatment Middlecoff did: he was fired. Why? I don't know to this day, for Bob Goalby was, in my opinion, head and shoulders above any other expert commentators who worked for NBC.

If I were putting together an announcing team, both Middlecoff and Goalby would be joined by Bob Toski. As I remember, Toski was formerly the lead golf commentator on Dick Bailey's Sports Network, and we thought his performance was outstanding; he was informative, entertaining, and innovative. I think he could still do it. Of the current crop, Jim Nance of CBS is so much the best professional golf announcer on television, it's no contest. He will reign supreme a long time, in my opinion.

I was dismayed at the treatment ABC gave to its best golf announcers when it terminated Byron Nelson, Chris Schenkel, and Dave Marr. None of them felt that they should publicly "knock" any of the players, even though a "knock" might have been news, or even appropriate. Chris Schenkel is one of the nicest men I've ever known and possesses a beautiful speaking voice. It did not surprise me that he would not put the knock on players, even when urged to do so by the network. He's rock solid.

Could I assemble my own all-time announcing crew, it would include Doc Middlecoff, Bob Goalby, Jim Nance, Bob Toski, Dave Marr, Ken Venturi, and Chris Schenkel as anchor. If I could have a little talk with Peter Allis, I'm sure he'd be a great addition, too. I'd want to tone Peter down a bit (ask him not to be quite so sarcastic), but he's a real talent — if you can get through all his B.S. Finally, if he promised not to make predictions, I'd include the intelligent, articulate Bob Rosburg.

Jack Tuthill and Bill Booe

I'd be remiss if I didn't mention two of my good friends who have now retired from the PGA Tour but who played a tremendous role in the way that the tour was shaped. They constitute a big part of the tour's history — not that any of the present-day players give a damn about history; they could care less with their "What have you done for me lately" attitude.

Bill Booe, who kicked extra points for Yale, is a former tour player. We played a few practice rounds together. When he retired from playing, he was hired to help run the Tournament Bureau and did a helluva job for us. When we split with the parent PGA of America, Bill moved to New York City and ran our American Professional Golfers' business, and did an outstanding job. Bill is a man of great principle, and I have nothing but respect for him and his contributions.

Jack Tuthill, recently retired after many tour years, is a former FBI agent. Jack started under Tour Supervisor Joe Black and took over after Joe left. And what a beautiful change it was. Should you call for a ruling and Joe Black came out and told you "no drop," you'd be furious. But if Tuthill told you the same thing, you'd just go on about your business and play.

Jack is an extremely intelligent man with a "way" with people, and I never knew of a player who didn't like Jack.

Gardner and Jack Tuthill.

And since Jack could play well enough at times to beat some of the tour players, we felt like he could understand us and our problems. Jack's shoes were huge ones to fill, and I hope he knows how very much we appreciate his contributions.

Louis Wanniger

Louie and I have been close friends some fifty-five years, beginning in Augusta, Georgia, where we attended the same Baptist Sunday School and participated in the same YMCA class. I remember watching Louie's dad "Pee Wee" Wanniger play at least one summer for the Augusta Tigers Class A baseball team. Louie, like his dad, was relatively short in stature, so for a while I called Louie "Pee Wee," too, after his dad. But one summer his dad went on a streak of popping out to the infield about every other time at bat, and the Augusta fans dubbed him, "Pop Up Pee Wee." It was a shame to acquire such a demeaning nickname, since Paul Wanniger was a professional ballplayer in every way, having played a few years for the great New York Yankees. So, I didn't call Louie "Pee Wee" much after that.

In 1940, Louie's family moved to Macon, Georgia, and so did mine, and as freshmen at Lanier High we played Police Cadet sandlot football together. Later we played varsity football at Lanier. Louie was one hell of a high school athlete, starring in football, basketball and track. If he'd been four inches taller and thirty pounds heavier, he'd have been truly awesome, for he was very talented.

Louie, like our buddy George Wright, was really a fun-loving guy, always seeming to be involved in pranks at school. I can vividly remember Louis in Professor "Pistol Pete" Brake's algebra class one high school day. "Pete" seldom tied his shoes while lecturing, and one day he got so exasperated with Louie in class that he screamed at him and kicked his shoe off up into the air. Louie caught the shoe on the fly, jumped across a couple of rows of desks, and flew out of the ground floor window. Pistol Pete went right out screaming behind Louie, and the sight of a cackling Louie and a wailing Pistol Pete flying around the campus left the rest of the class in stitches. But Pete didn't catch Louie — nobody in school could have.

At Lanier High, we had an aged teacher named Professor Coates, whom two thousand had nicknamed "Speedy." Ol' Speedy, being a stern disciplinarian in his English literature class, became a natural target for pranks by his boys.

One day Louie came into Speedy's English class with a pocketful of air-rifle BBs, and all during class he flipped the BBs against the blackboard and windows, much to Speedy's consternation. Though he strongly suspected Louie as the culprit, try as he might he could not actually see Louie flipping those tiny BBs that made such a racket when they bounced off the windows. Naturally, the next day most of the class came in loaded with BBs and it was an hour of chaos with Ol' Speedy half out of his mind.

Speedy was certain Louie was at least one of the culprits, so he had him come to the front of the class with his literature book and recite to the class. This was right up Louie's alley, and he continued to pepper the windows so hard that I feared they would break. Somehow, Louie never laughed, even when Speedy proclaimed that the lowest yellow cur dog in Bibb County would not be guilty of such conduct. But he could never catch little Louie, and the following class had a helluva time walking to their desks what with all the BBs covering the floor.

Athlete that he is, Louie took up golf after college and lamented the fact that he had declined my invitation to play golf in high school. Later, between our fishing trips in the coves of the Savannah River, Louie and I had some really fun golf games.

Clayton Heafner

Joe Wehrle was an old-time equipment salesman for the MacGregor Golf Company, and his territory encompassed both the Carolinas. Joe was devoted to MacGregor, but he absolutely worshipped Ol' Sarge, Clayton Heafner, who was on the MacGregor advisory staff. When ever Ol' Sarge was not on tour, he and Joe Wehrle played daily at Clayton's hometown Charlotte course, which Clayton owned.

Joe and Clayton did almost everything together, including attending yearly the giant Duke-Carolina football game. It was, and is, really some rivalry. This one particular year, they had great seats to the game, up high on about the forty-five yard line. Snow and frigid weather was predicted, so the two buddies armed themselves with warm lap robes and a quart each of bourbon whiskey. Sure enough, as predicted, the weather was frigid, and the two went at their bourbon bottles with vigor. Right before halftime, Clayton finished his quart and put it down under his seat.

Shortly thereafter, Ol' Sarge felt the need to get rid of some of that bourbon, and glancing down at all of the jammed aisles on the way to the men's room, he knew he'd never make it back without missing a great deal of the game. Sarge then decided that he'd take his empty bourbon bottle, and, under the concealing lap robe, he'd relieve himself. He did so and then placed his now almost filled whiskey bottle back on the concrete under him.

Joe, having just polished off the last of his quart, lifted up the lap robe and spied Clayton's almost filled bottle, and said, "Hey, Sarge, gimme a slug of your booze!" Sarge promptly replied, "I ain't got no more, it's all gone." Joe did not accept Sarge's explanation, and for fifteen minutes or so bombarded Heafner with, "You tight S.O.B., c'mon and give Joe a little drink!"

Sarge, finally tired of arguing with Joe, picked up his bottle and handed it to him and said, "Have it your way, you stupid S.O.B. Help yourself!" Joe took a giant swig, abruptly jumped up, and blew the stuff out over about eight rows, shouting, "Hey, Sarge, you bastard — that's piss!"

Shortly after Joe told me this incredible tale, I checked with Clayton, and he confirmed it with, "Sure as hell, it's true. I got tired of Joe pestering me!"

Great Harbour Cay — Bahamas

My great, late golfing buddy in the Palm Beaches, Truman Connell (a former world-record-holder of a speed-skating title), had secured for me a deal to be golf director at a new resort in the north end of the Berry Island chain of the Bahamas, Great Harbour Cay.

This was a most beautiful island, eight miles long and about one-half mile wide; one coast had high cliffs down to the beautiful, clear, green ocean, and the other side had eight miles of snow-white beaches. It was spectacular! The first tee of our Joe Lee designed course sat some seventy-five feet in the air, where nature had long ago piled great dunes of sand.

Great Harbour was a paradise which never quite worked out. The development was financed by the Canadian gambler and high-roller, Lou Chesler, who loved all the touring golf pros. I think Lou dropped about $12 million at Great Harbour before he finally threw in the towel. We had a helluva golf course, of which I was in charge, with the finest, fastest set of greens a man ever stepped on.

For opening day, I got about two dozen of the tour pros over for a fabulous one-day pro-am, which cost Lou Chesler about six million dollars (and included my buddy Perry Como, and Sam Snead). The island owned several airplanes, including Bing Crosby's old DC-3, and one of my jobs was to fly some of the wealthy golfers I knew over to the island.

One day Jack Nicklaus went over with me in his Lear jet; we played golf and Jack lost six balls on the first six holes. (The fairways were fairly narrow, and surrounded by impenetrable, junglelike rough). We also went bone fishing and caught eleven beauties and lost one monster. Jack fell in love with the island, bought a ridge-top lot overlooking the entire island, and built himself a beautiful island home.

My association with Great Harbour began in 1968 during the week I won the Doral Open, and afterwards I headed up many golf sorties to the island. Several years later, five of us flew over to the island in the company's Aero Commander for a round of golf and a tour. We were late getting back to the plane, and our pilot (who had 33,000 hours in the air) was mad, and had both engines going as we were boarding. (He must have had a hot date in Miami that night.) After we had boarded, the pilot tore down the runway at breakneck speed downwind; then he spun around and headed down the runway into the wind. At eighty miles per hour, he got us slightly airborne (which was pretty slow for such a full load), and in a couple of seconds we descended again, and I heard a loud *crack*.

Truman Connell, a bomber pilot in WW II, was riding copilot and screamed to the pilot, "Pour the coals to it!" just as it seemed we would end up in a heap on the fourth fairway. We did get airborne and began to circle while gaining altitude. Truman then told us that they were afraid the resettlement on the runway had broken the right wheel strut, and sure enough, it would not come down and lock. I knew a belly-landing was now inevitable, so I suggested to Truman that we head to Miami where they could foam the runway. But the pilot elected Nassau in order to land in daylight, and away we went.

I was sitting by the door; Truman instructed me to unlock it but to hold it shut 'til we had stopped after landing. Well, I can tell you that it's true that your entire life suffers a fast review in front of your eyes, but the pilot kept our nose up beautifully after he landed it on the grass, and it seemed we stopped in no time. I *flew* out of that door with five grown men right on my tail. As soon as the little bit of smoke on the bottom stopped, to the amusement of the others, I dashed over to the plane and retrieved my golf clubs. It was kinda tough boarding another plane a couple of hours later.

Foreign Players

I have nothing whatsoever against foreign players coming over to America to play the PGA Tour, though I do think they should conduct themselves as guests, which they are. The nice, regular guys never seem to have a problem, and are liked and treated beautifully. Only hard cases like Tony Jacklin, Bruce Crampton, and Nick Faldo have any problems. I never met nicer men than Gary Player, Kel Nagle,

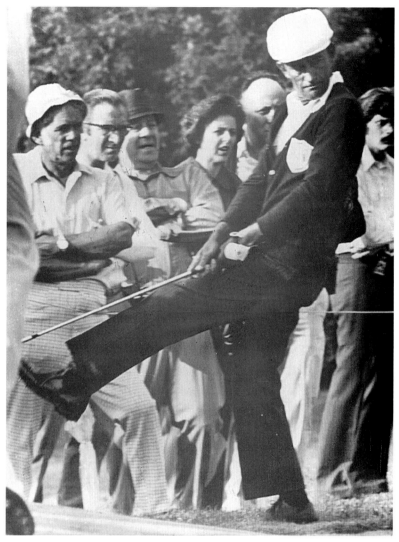

Gardner beating Tony Jacklin in their 1967 Ryder Cup match.

and Roberto de Vicenzio — ask them about how they've been treated.

I recently read with a little interest and considerable amusement in the newspaper where Tony Jacklin might be visiting America again. My buddy, Tony Jacklin, coming back to the good ol' U.S.A.! I can hardly wait.

First of all, let me tell Tony that in his absence, nobody missed him. When Tony first arrived here, he was an attractive kid of Italian heritage who looked as if he had come over on a banana boat and not on an airplane from Great Britain. He could drive the ball a long ways, though we were never sure what country it would come down in, and he could putt like a wizard, and little else. His dress on the golf course was atrocious; sometimes he wore slacks with one white pantleg and one black. He might as well have worn a big sign on his head imploring people to "Look at me!"

He despised Bob Goalby and me, and I do take pride in that. When Jacklin first came to the U.S.A., he acted as if he were the great grandson of George Washington instead of a guest, and, for the most part, he seemed to think he was doing our tour a favor by playing it. Well, I've got news for Tony. Most of the players on our Tour shared Bob Goalby's and my opinion of him, and nobody shed any tears when he went back home. And I never heard of even Nick Faldo (another Jacklin type) moving out of his native land to the Isle of Jersey to avoid paying income taxes. I still consider one of the highlights of my career my thumping of Jacklin in the Ryder Cup matches in Houston, after Jacklin birdied the first two holes. (I put seven-under on him from there on in!)

But while I would welcome foreign players, I don't think they should be given a damn thing. They should earn their way in here. But we don't pay much appearance money in this country, and I don't think we'll see much of the very best European players competing over here as long as they can demand the huge appearance fees paid over there. (We hear they're stopping the practice, but I am confident they'll find a way to get around it!)

I think probably that the commissioner, the press, and the foreign players should remember this: I've never heard of a potential golf fan approaching the admission gate on our Tour and asking if Faldo, Woosnam, and Jacklin are playing — or they won't buy a ticket!

Bob Hamilton

Bob Hamilton, my man! What a helluva player and a helluva man. I played the last round at Fort Wayne with Bob; I played well but putted horribly. Afterwards, Bob said to me, "Let's play a practice round next week at Tom O'Shanter in Chicago, and I'll straighten out that putting." I then told Bob I wasn't playing Tam. He exclaimed as he reached in his pocket, "You must be tapped out!" (Broke!) Well, I was but told him I wasn't. Bob stuck six one-hundred bills in my pocket, and said, "You *be* there!"

There was no arguing with Bob. We played Tuesday, he fixed my putting and I won several thousand dollars. I wrote Bob a check for twelve hundred dollars; he looked at it and lit his cigar with it. After several months and attempts to repay Bob, he finally said , "Okay, you can give me back my six hundred." So I finally (almost) got even. Imagine a player doing that today!

Jimmy Thompson

Hard-swinging, hard-drinking, barrel-chested, curly-haired, handsome Jimmy Thompson was golf's longest "bomber" off the tee during the thirties and forties. Jimmy won quite a number of tour events, but he swung damn near as hard at his wedge as he did his driver. He had a beautiful golf swing — when you could see it.

The first time I can remember seeing Jimmy was at the New Orleans Open in 1947 at Metairie Country Club. Bud Timbrook and I had walked back out to the eighteenth tee to see if Thompson could reach the long eighteenth (par-five) in two. He pushed his tee shot far off to the right, and the gallery moaned. Jimmy remarked, "It's okay! It's *over* everything." Sure enough, he had carried all of the swamp and had an iron to the green.

Years later, having finished the ninth hole during the Doral Open, as I walked toward the tenth tee I said to my caddie, Mitch, "I think I know that old fellow there in the wheelchair." After I hit my tee shot, I went down to him and said, "Mr. Thompson? Gardner Dickinson, and I remember you very well." Those lifeless eyes (for he had had several strokes) lit right up, and he said "Thank you so much for coming over to say 'hi,' Gardner. You know, you're the only one who has recognized me." Indeed, Father Time is cruel, and fame is fleeting. I glowed a little on that back nine.

Christopher J. Dunphy

Anyone who knew Chris Dunphy will never forget him, and I feel very sorry for those who didn't have that privilege. My first encounter with Chris occurred in 1952, just minutes after Fred Wampler and I had checked into an oceanfront (four dollars per night!) hotel room on Miami Beach. We were in town for the La Gorce Pro-Am and the Miami Open in December. I answered the phone when it rang, and a voice said, "Gardner, this is Chris Dunphy. I've drawn you as a partner in the La Gorce Pro-Am, and I'd like you to come out and play a practice round with me." When I asked how he had located me, he replied "I know where you are at all times."

I went out to La Gorce, and Chris had arranged a game for us with a moving company magnate, and he made all the bets for me on the first tee. In the middle of the front nine, Chris remarked that in his lifetime he had won more than a million dollars from "Tommy," the moving company owner. I said, "Sure, Chris," but on the back nine Tommy sidled over and confided to me that the little white-haired guy, Dunphy, over the years had beat him out of more than a million dollars. That's when I realized that Chris was the "hustler supreme."

Until his death, Chris ran the Seminole Golf Club in North Palm Beach *completely*, making up every member's game for him each day. And, at least once a year, each member was expected to make his little "donation" to Chris on the golf course.

Don't think Chris couldn't play. He was a beautiful, if not long, driver, but he was really better known for his proficiency with a one-iron. There was *none* better out of the sand, and he taught me a great deal about bunker play. I played maybe a hundred rounds with Chris, and since he always insisted on me as a partner, I did okay.

In the winter of 1960, Chris brought his buddy, the Duke of Windsor, down to my club at The Breakers, and we had a game. In the course of the round, I offered the Duke a few suggestions that really helped his game that day. When we finished, the Duke dug down into his little leather snap-purse and offered me an old, wrinkled twenty-dollar bill. I tried to decline it, but Chris whispered to me, "Take it, for God's sake! You're the first man the Duke has tipped in forty years!"

One day I was a little short on cash at Seminole, and Chris personally cashed a hundred-dollar check for me. The next week I won my first tour event in Miami Beach and told the press how much help Mr. Dunphy had been to me. Several weeks later, as I was walking to the eighth tee in the first round of the Masters, Chris approached me, shook hands, and left something in my palm. It was my rumpled $100 check.

Keith Marks

I believe it was in the early 1970s, sometime around the completion of my Frenchman's Creek golf course, that I became acquainted with Keith. He was a tall young golfer from West Virginia, and he came to me seeking advice about his golf swing. Over a period of time, we became fast friends and shared many fine experiences together.

Keith was good with words and had an inquiring mind, and, in the process of picking my brain constantly, I think Keith helped me solidify my beliefs pertaining to a golf swing. As a consequence, Keith became a fine teacher. I know that I taught Keith a great deal of what I knew about a golf swing, and I'm confident that his personal experiences have added a great deal to what I taught him.

Rather strangely to me, Keith is about the only guy who has tried to pick my brain about golf over a period of time. Maybe "they" don't think I know anything, or perhaps "they" knew it all themselves. But Keith, in my opinion, became such a competent instructor that when I had trouble from time to time with my own swing, I didn't go to Lead-better, Haney, or Ballard — I used Keith.

Keith and I made a very nice television film together in New Mexico and did some very successful golf schools for *Golf Magazine*. Keith's been a good friend for a long time, and I will never forget those long nights of listening to good music, tearing apart a golf swing, and sipping a few Dewars.

Mike Manuche

For a "man's man" or a great friend, you just can't beat the great Mike Manuche. Mike formerly ran the best sports bar and restaurant in Manhattan, on Fifty-Second Street, and every sportsman in America seemed to come in for a drink with Manuche when they came to New York.

Mike was such a powerful man that he developed a national reputation for wrist-wrestling. They came from far and wide to test Michael, and always went away with their tails between their legs. One particularly strong man came from Montana with a barfull of money to Manuche's to test Mike. They set up shop on the top of the bar, and on "go"

Mike let this punk have it all. He flipped the guy upside down over the barstool. The guy landed on his head and Mike thought he'd killed him, but up he got and wanted to go again, *left-handed*. Mike declined and sent the guy and his money back to Montana.

Mike was everybody's friend, and he particularly liked Ross Johnson, head of Nabisco. Ross hired Manuche for public relations, and today Mike still runs the Nabisco Dinah Shore Golf Tournament, a job he loves and at which he's damn good. Mike was mainly responsible for my and Lionel Hebert's employment by Nabisco, but that's the kind of thing Mike has done all his life — help others.

Mike is a lover of golf and has had more golf lessons from me and the world's best golf professionals, than anyone could imagine. There have been many times we've almost made a racehorse out of a mule, but so far we haven't quite made The Great Manuche a scratch golfer — but he's scratch with a putter, and both Mike and his beautiful wife, the great Broadway singer Martha Wright, are scratch in my book as great human beings.

Frank Leahy

In the winter of 1954, the legendary football coach of Notre Dame's great football teams, Frank Leahy, decided to retire, and it seemed that golf would take up a large part of Coach Leahy's time in football's place. I was sitting in Ben Hogan's office at Tamarisk Country Club in Palm Springs, California, when Coach Leahy called from South Bend, requesting that Ben spend a great deal of time with him on the lesson tee for a couple of weeks. Ben politely explained to the coach that he *never* taught, but that he would turn him over to his right-hand man, which was me.

Coach Leahy showed up shortly thereafter, and it was not difficult for me to perceive why he had been perhaps

**Gardner with Frank Leahy of Notre Dame (C) and Gus
Henderson of Southern Cal, 1954.**

America's top football coach. He was highly intelligent and
dedicated, and a literal dynamo of energy. His superior
intelligence was apparent in the quick manner in which he
grasped the intricacies of a golf swing, and I could easily
imagine his dissecting other football teams' defenses.

(I understand that Frank Leahy was the first to install
pressbox-to-bench telephones, a common practice today.)

Coach Leahy literally beat balls from the club's opening
until dark each day — for weeks. One day he approached
me rather shyly and finally asked if I would consider meet-

ing him about 6:30 in the morning to begin his golf lessons. He was astounded when I replied, "Sure." But the good coach didn't know that was about the time I sometimes got in from my "tom-catting" at night.

Frank Sinatra

Some time after this, in the early sixties, Frank Sinatra bought and greatly expanded a house on the seventeenth fairway at Tamarisk. Frank obviously liked golf very much, and some of us talked him into playing a little. Several years later, we talked Frank into playing in Bob Hope's Desert Classic. I was in Frank's Tamarisk home when he arrived after the first round. Frank had played much better than he had anticipated, and, when he came in the door, he let out a joyous hoot, flew right past us, and dove into the swimming pool, clothes, golf spikes and all. He was one happy man.

In the middle sixties, my Dad decided to put on a small pro-am event in his hometown of Panama City, Florida. I helped him get such pros as Sam Snead, the Hebert brothers, Johnny Pott, Tommy Bolt, and others. Dad decided to name the event "The Little Tournament of Champions." I told Frank Sinatra about the upcoming tournament and asked him if he'd compete. He said, "Hell yes! Count me in." I could scarcely believe my ears, but I knew he meant it. And he said he'd bring Dean Martin.

About a week before we were to play, I got a call from Frank, who was obviously upset. He was involved in divorce proceedings and said that the judge had forbidden him to leave the state of California until the divorce was final. Therefore, Frank had to decline playing in Panama City. Of course, we were tremendously disappointed, but we understood. The next day, I received a Western Union money order from Frank to the tune of $5,000 with a message saying how sorry he was he couldn't play, but he wanted to donate $5,000 to the purse for "his boys!" Don't say anything bad about Frank Sinatra around our boys.

One night in the 1960s, Frank invited us over to his house for dinner during the Bob Hope tournament. Among the guests were my buddies Lionel and Jay Hebert, Bo Wininger, and Bob Rosburg. Dinner at Frank's was always a big, elaborate deal, and we were all looking forward to it. All of us had partaken of several Scotches, and just before dinner was to be served, Frank's main man-servant came up to me and said that "Mr. Lionel" wanted to see me outside, and was quite sick. I went out and Lionel said that he must go to bed, and requested that I take him back to Thunderbird Country Club, where he was staying. I went back inside and told Frank what I had to do, and he said he was going, too. When we got to Thunderbird, Frank took over, taking Lionel's clothes off and tucking him into bed. Then he hid Lionel's cigarettes and lighter so he wouldn't burn himself up. Well, not many "snockered" guys have had Frank Sinatra tuck them in, but that was Frank's way.

Perry Como

One of the truly genuine celebrities I've ever known is "Mr. C," Perry Como. Perry has lived in our North Palm Beach area ever since I've been down here and is one of the greatest human beings I've ever been privileged to know. Perry, formerly a mid-seventies player, and I have played many a round together, and I've enjoyed every single minute I've been in his presence.

Perry agreed to play one year with us in the Atlanta Open pro-am, and we were greeted on the first tee by 50,000 fans. It was very difficult playing that day, what with the fans

demanding Perry's autograph. As Perry and I approached
the eighth tee, a good-looking, voluptuous lady stuck her
very ample chest out at Como and requested that he sign
her shirt. Perry very quickly quipped that he thought they
should go up in the deep woods before he signed it. Perry hit
fourteen absolutely perfect drives that day, and really enter-
tained the huge gallery on eighteen when he threw his
favorite putter into the greenside lake after missing a short
putt. Despite many, many attempts, nobody to this day has
found Perry's putter in the lake.

Dan Sikes and Tommy Jacobs

These two guys were, to me, two of the greatest friends a
man ever had. I am still today greatly saddened by the demise
of Dan Sikes a couple of years ago. Dan and I, along with
Tommy Jacobs, shared many great moments during our battle
with the club pros and the parent PGA of America. As Tommy
recently wrote to me, "No one can ever know what we sacri-
ficed for the 'guys' during those days." We did, indeed, spend
a helluva lot of time and took a helluva lot of personal risk
for those little cats to turn our business over to the commissioner. I wouldn't do it again, knowing today what I do.

Dan Sikes, a Floridian, attended the University of Florida, played on their fine golf team, attended Florida Law
School, and passed the Florida Bar exams. He turned pro
after graduation but never actually practiced law formally.
On the tour, Dan and I had monumental philosophical
arguments and discussions, but we always ended up friendly, and I think we both learned a great deal as a result. Like
the rest of our group, Dan cared a great deal about the tour
and proved it over and over. His best friends saw Dan turn
to drinking, to help alleviate the pressure, I suppose. We
saw his consumption increase and his personality change,
and we were all deeply saddened when we saw alcohol do

him in at such an early age. To see such a fine mind stilled is indeed tragic — and just when Dan was really becoming one of the tour's best players.

I've spent many a happy hour with Sally and Tommy Jacobs, and, if Tommy told you something, you knew you could take it to the bank. Additionally, "Jake" was, at times, a helluva player. Many thought he should have won the Masters that he lost to Jack Nicklaus in a playoff. Many are even more certain he should have won the U.S. Open at Congressional in Washington, D.C., when Ken Venturi held on to win.

This is only an opinion of my very own, but I'd like to have known just how very good Tommy Jacobs and my pal Johnny Pott might have been if there had not been such a strong pull on them toward home.

Alfred 'Bud' Timbrook

If any of you readers ever have in your lifetime one friend who's as good a friend as Bud Timbrook was to me, you may consider yourself tremendously fortunate. Bud was, indeed, the "salt of the earth" and oh! how I do miss him.

I met Bud in September 1945, when I was a freshman at L.S.U., and Bud was a wounded, recovering Marine Corps paratrooper. We quickly became fast friends and roomed together for four years. A truer friend a man never had, and we played together every day for years and years. Bud had been shot to hell on Guadalcanal, but no one ever heard Bud bitch about it. In his freshman year at L.S.U., I helped Bud rehabilitate a gaping hole in his left thigh from a machine-gun bullet.

I've never been closer to a human being in the world than Bud Timbrook, and I was absolutely slain at his untimely death a couple of years ago from, of all things, lung cancer — and Bud had never smoked. Rest in peace, Bud.

Gardner and Alfred "Bud" Timbrook.

Lewis Keller

When I decided in the fall of 1959 to seek the head pro's job at the old Breakers Hotel course in Palm Beach, I sought the help of a young millionaire friend of mine from Virginia, Lewis Keller. Lewis then enlisted the help of two Breakers members, Paul Carey of New York's Carey Cadillac, and Bernie Gimbel of Gimbel's and Saks Fifth Avenue. Needless to say, I got the job. Lewis and I became fast friends.

One year I invited Lewis, formerly a scratch player at Winged Foot Golf Club in Westchester, New York, to be my partner in the Bing Crosby Pro-Am. The first day, we started at Cypress Point. The previous day, Lewis, by now a six-handicapper, had scored 66 at the Monterey Peninsula course, and he started off at Cypress Point the same way. He birdied numbers one and two with a stroke (for net eagles) and I birdied number three to put us five-under through three holes. Lewis hit a beautiful four-iron on number four but ended up seven or eight feet past the hole on that slick green. I lagged below the hole and two-putted for a par. Lewis had another stroke on number four, so he was putting for another net eagle. I told him he might as well try to make it, since it was downhill and so slick, but he lipped it out and rolled clear off the green. That so unnerved Lewis that I scarcely saw him again the last three rounds.

On Saturday (cut day) at Pebble Beach, Lewis hit a great driver on the eighteenth, but then hit behind his fairway wood and pull-hooked it through the bunker and over the seawall, and presumably into the Pacific Ocean. Since Lewis had a stroke on the hole, I went over and looked over the seawall and saw his ball all teed up on some pebbles on the little retaining shelf below the top. I shouted to Lewis to come over quickly, and we lowered him to the little shelf. He had a nine-iron in his hand, but I told him he could easily knock it on the green with a six-iron.

As he was changing clubs, a gigantic wave approached

and smashed Lewis against the seawall. The only reason Lewis survived at all was that he was holding on to the club I was proffering. Well, you can imagine that his ball had washed away, and we hauled Lewis back up to the fairway — a wet bunch of slacks and cashmere! I did my damndest to hole my birdie putt, but it lipped out and we missed the cut by one, though I made it individually. The end of a "perfect" week for Lewis — and his lovely wife, Rosalie, became pregnant that week, to boot!

As is probably apparent, I have much affection for the Lewis Keller family.

F. Ross Johnson

Ross Johnson, the recently resigned CEO of R. J. Reynolds-Nabisco, had it all to become one of the world's best leaders — indeed, he *still* has what it takes, despite the highly inaccurate book *Barbarians at the Gate*. Ross, a Winnipeg-born Canadian, is possessed of one of the keenest minds I have yet encountered; his opinions on many and varied subjects are better and more astute than yours and mine. He's a man's man and is easy to like instantly.

Through Ross's intelligence and hard work, he rather quickly rode his way up to be the CEO of Standard Brands (the youngest CEO in America). Shortly thereafter, Ross managed to merge with a much larger company, staid old Nabisco Brands. It didn't stay staid very long, when after a few years Ross took over as CEO of Nabisco. The company made record profits and enlarged its market share under his dynamic leadership.

Ross had an affinity for sports celebrities, and he signed up quite a few of them to help advertise Nabisco's products. He later dubbed these celebrities "Team Nabisco," which included Frank Gifford, "Dandy" Don Meredith, Bobby Orr, Alex Webster, Dave Marr, Reggie Jackson, Jay and Lionel Hebert, Nancy Lopez, Pat Bradley, Toney

Ross Johnson's Team Nabisco: (Front row, L-R) Toney Penna, Dinah Shore, Judy Dickinson, (Middle row) Bobby Orr, Lionel Hebert, Pat Bradley, Jay Hebert, Reggie Jackson, Rod Laver, Gardner Dickinson, (Back row) Frank Gifford, Don Meredith, Alex Webster, Nancy Lopez, Dave Marr.

Penna, Rod Laver, and my wife Judy and I.

Some time later Ross signed Jack Nicklaus, Ray Floyd, Fuzzy Zoeller, and Ben Crenshaw. Lots of golfers, huh? You bet! For Ross was a golf nut (and a pretty good player, unlike his successor). He said to me one day, "Golf works for me. Really works. It sells lots of products." Now that the P.G.A. Tour has survived the Karsten case, and if it ever gets into the monument-building business, they should build a rather large Ross Johnson Monument, for he became the Tour's by far largest benefactor.

Ross funded several actual golf tournaments and many attendant side programs, worth millions. He signed very lucrative ten-year long-term contracts with Beman. During the failed take-over attempt, Ross appointed Charlie Hugel of Combustion Engineering as temporary CEO. Somehow Beman became acquainted with Hugel, and once said to me that had it not been for Charlie Hugel, Ross Johnson would still be CEO of R.J.R.-Nabisco! Deane said that Charles had kept his secretary informed of developments during the take-over battle. Perhaps Deane thought Ross represented a threat to take over the tour, but nothing could have been further from the truth.

The idea of a "Super Seniors" was Ross Johnson's idea to attempt to keep out on tour past champions such as Sam Snead, Paul Runyan, Julius Boros, etc., and Ross funded the side-line event. But when Deane took it over, he had it changed from a champion's event each week to a chronological over-60 event, allowing everyone over 60 to compete.

I would guess that when Ross lost out to KKR and hence control of the company, he was spending close to $20 million a year on golf. Thereafter, I'm told that R.J.R.-Nabisco minus Ross paid the tour $21 million to buy out of their tour contract! That's $21 million for which they received absolutely zero in advertising. One must wonder just how smart that was.

Ross did many things for many people, including Nabisco's stockholders. He kept lovely Dinah Shore's name before the public through his Nabisco Dinah Shore L.P.G.A. tournaments, and he personally benefited several team Nabisco members.

Ross was good to both Judy and me, perhaps paying us more than we could have commanded elsewhere; but I'll tell you, I did my damnedest to earn that money, and would have just about done anything in the world for Ross.

The world didn't come to an end for Ross when he lost control of R.J.R.-Nabisco, nor did he go through a lobotomy! He, today, still possesses a very uncommonly keen mind.

But it seems that the Lord does not give anybody everything. Perhaps he left out for Ross the ability to accurately judge all people and that's the only fault that I've been able to lay on Ross. He was good to an awful lot of people, including R.J.R.-Nabisco's thousands of stockholders, when by putting the company into play, Ross caused the stock to rise from $54 to $112!

I have no doubts that if Ross so desires, he'll be back. Look for him!

Mind Wanderings

I recently read where the former director of publicity for Buick, Jerry Rideout, said that the tour should build a monument to Buick, since, he claims, they were the first corporate sponsor to jump on the tour's bandwagon. (This is our same buddy who took Buick *out* of the tour when we had our split with the club pros.)

Jerry must have forgotten about George S. May, who sponsored the first big money event ever at Tam O'Shanter in Chicago. George May was really an iconoclast whose motto was, "You've got to spend money to make money!" And spend it, George did! As a result, his Chicago-based business engineering firm was very successful. Mr. May was also the first sponsor to give the touring pros half-price meals in his great dining room. Of course, George's upstairs slot-machines helped make up for any meal losses. George S. May would be my number one entrant into the tour's Hall of Fame.

I think my number two member would be J. Edwin Carter, hired by the tour in the mid-1950s, and who was most certainly *the* most intelligent person ever to work for the PGA. Ed is the man who put the tour on a business-like basis and although I didn't care for all of Ed's principles and innovations, most of them were pretty damn good. Ed put in a Code of Conduct program, which we certainly needed at the time, and a Player Program for advanced commitments to future tournaments, which the tournament sponsors certainly loved.

He also instituted an incentive program for the players called the "T.T.T. Plan" (Top Ten Tournament Players), in which certain of us participated in a season-ending "Sponsor's" tournament. Ed received a resultant great deal more public attention than did the club-pro officers of the PGA, and, naturally, they stayed after Ed's tail. It took them a long time, but they finally got him (I believe at the Buick Open meeting). In my opinion, we haven't been quite the same since J. Edwin Carter's demise. Ed could get into anybody's office.

Dan Bernheim

My third Hall of Fame member would most certainly be my — and the players' — greatest friend, Daniel Marc Bernheim. How lucky we are that this man lived on this earth just when he did, for I'm certain that had he not, our lives today might be vastly different. Dan owned the Reach-McClinton advertising agency in Manhattan, and the Hebert brothers, Jay and Lionel, and I did some promotional work for him.

During the player revolt of the late sixties, I was heading the tour players and became apprehensive when the PGA officers appeared to be after me personally. I told Dan I needed a lawyer, and he suggested Sam Gates of the firm of Debevoise, Plimpton and Gates on Park Avenue. Dan set up an appointment, and Jack Nicklaus and I met with Sam. Thus began my relationship with one hell of a man, Sam Gates. For almost two years, Sam counselled the players wisely, and, in the end, we finally prevailed (as described in the chapter on Deane Beman, The Political Game).

In the interim, we needed offices and living quarters for our staff and various other things, and Dan Bernheim furnished them for us, as well as much encouragement and advice. In my opinion, the tour could never repay Dan for his contributions, and I still have a most difficult time in accepting Dan's untimely death at age fifty-one.

There are many others deserving of the Hall of Fame, but I shall leave their inclusion to those who may yet come. Time will certainly take care of their accolades.

Gaining Distance

Can the average golfer do anything about increasing his distance? You bet he can. To begin with, he can swing harder.

My recommendation would be to try it first in practice. When I first started as a kid in 1940, I remember my dad asking pro Charlie Miller, "Don't you think the kid is swinging too hard at every shot?"

I remember Charlie replying, "Let him alone. If he's going to be in the rough, I want him to be green high. He's building up his golf muscles, now. I can tone him down later." As a consequence, I was always long, but never as long as I wanted or needed to be.

How could a player ever be too long? How could he ever have arms, hands, wrists or fingers too strong? Frank Stranahan, the fine amateur and a noted fitness buff, suggested the following program to me during a period when I was teaching all day long and, consequently, had little time to play. At the end of each day, go to the range and hit fifty balls with a driver. Swing with all your might and main on each shot. Toss form and caution to the wind. If you swing in balance, you haven't done it violently enough. The first session or two will probably exhaust you, but keep it up on a daily basis for about two or three weeks. When you finally go to the course, swing normally and see if your drives don't fly farther than they previously did. When I tried this, my drives went nearly thirty yards farther than my previous best. I can't think of any way to achieve more distance than to consciously swing harder in practice.

Today's Supercharged Equipment

The other day I watched Larry Mize carry a ball past the hole at the 205-yard seventeenth hole at Warwick Hills in Michigan during the Buick Open — using a six-iron. Does anyone believe that Mize, a fine player of perhaps better-

Gardner tries a radical putter, 1957.

than-average length, can hit the ball any farther than I could, or anywhere near as far as Sam Snead or Lawson Little could? Not on his best day could he do so, yet neither Snead nor Little ever hit a six-iron that far. Do you suppose that modern-day golf equipment has anything to do with this?

Whether the rulesmakers want to acknowledge it or not, we're in an era of supercharged equipment. Years ago, to obtain an extra stiff golf shaft you had to increase the diameter of the shaft so much that the steel weighed about five to six ounces. Today, with the newer graphite materials, you can obtain a super-stiff shaft that weighs only three to three-and-half ounces. So the same player with the same swing can swing the club faster, with less shaft deviation, or twisting. This translates into straighter, longer shots. Thus, today's shafts have almost as much to do with lowering scores as the new golf balls. Almost, but not quite.

The United States Golf Association's technical man, Dr. Frank Thomas, admits that today's golf ball goes eight or nine yards farther than the golf balls of the 1950s, but my own observations — along with the experience of most of the players on tour — lead me to conclude that the golf ball of the 1990s is at least twenty-five yards longer. Of course, you won't hear the pros complaining; like everyone else they love to hit the ball farther. I'm no exception.

When Ben Hogan was experimenting with the line of golf balls the U. S. Royal Company was producing for his new Ben Hogan Company, he would occasionally ask me to try them out. One afternoon he and I were playing a friendly match with Ken Venturi and Mike Souchak at Seminole Golf Club in Florida. He tossed me half a dozen experimental balls and asked me to play them during the match. Well, I found that I could hit it in the neck and still knock my drives twenty-five yards past Souchak, which is something I could not normally do. I whispered to Ben, "Don't let anybody else have any of these; we'll just keep them for ourselves." Venturi went through a dozen balls that afternoon, trying to keep up with our drives. We beat them badly, and when we got to the locker room, Venturi and Souchak threw their money on the table. Ben said, "No, I won't take your money. We cheated you. Gardner and I used some experimental balls, and I know they're too hot."

Frankly, I have no idea how hot they can make a golf ball, but I know it would be much longer if it weren't for the USGA rules governing initial velocity. If we took the limits off, it would be fun for a while just to see how far we could hit it, but, in the long run, it would ruin the game. As it is now, we've practically eliminated fairway woods from the professional game for about half the field.

If the ball is allowed to get any hotter, we better start building par-fours of at least 525 to 550 yards. We can eliminate all of Donald Ross's fine courses from tournament golf, or A. W. Tillinghast's, or William Flynn's, or Dick Wilson's. We might as well send the tour out to Kansas to play Jug McSpaden's Dub's Dread Course, which measures over 8,400 yards, every week. I have no doubt the boys on tour could handle it, and probably score par or better. I know this: As well as these fellows putt, if we continue to give them short irons into the greens week after week — which is what the new equipment is, indeed, giving them — they'll soon be scoring in the 50s with regularity.

Buying a Better Game?

What's the answer? I imagine that the United States Golf Association would have a difficult time trying to reduce the initial velocity of our golf balls, because this country loves power. The golf ball manufacturers are pushing the initial velocity limits, as it is. I suppose it's natural that some balls will come out of the factory slightly over the limit, which, however inadvertently, would make them illegal. Personally, I think the USGA should test some of the tour players' balls on a regular basis. Who's to say that some of those "illegal" balls aren't being shipped — inadvertently, of course — to the tour?

I doubt if the public would stand for banning metal woods. The hollow head of the metal wood, with its attendant perimeter weighting, promotes height. Somehow, this construction makes it much easier to hit the ball up in the air than is normal with traditional, wooden-headed clubs.

The investment-cast process has allowed manufacturers to reduce driver lofts to as low as seven degrees, yet some players can still achieve a high ball flight trajectory with such a club. What an advantage this is when you consider that, all else being equal, the reduced loft allows a golfer to hit the ball farther.

We can acknowledge that today's players have more scientific knowledge of the golf swing, better physical conditioning, and improved practice tools, such as videotape, than the players had in my day. The courses are better conditioned, the mowing is more consistent, and the greens are much better prepared. The players go to bed at night, and most of them drink milk instead of training at all-night bars, as we used to do. Undoubtedly, all of this has contributed to better scoring, but not nearly as much as have the changes in equipment. Are we all, to use that ominous phrase, "buying a better game?"

Why No Dominant Players?

As far as I can tell, the ability to score seems to run in cycles. The scoring today is better overall than, say, three decades ago, but the players are shooting the same scores we did. The only difference is that now there are more of them. We don't seem to have any truly outstanding or dominating players today. Greg Norman comes closest, I suppose, although he doesn't seem to have the killer instinct of a Snead or a Nicklaus in the major championships. Recently, Nick Price has been showing signs he might want the mantle. Before discussing some of today's players, and those of earlier eras, it's appropriate to say a word about the era just ended.

In all the years that Nicklaus dominated the professional game, we tend to forget how many gifted players took a run at him — Palmer, Weiskopf, Miller, Watson, Trevino, among others. Trevino was probably the most successful challenger to Nicklaus, beating Jack several times in head-to-head competition. This surprised some people because no one, to my recollection, ever suggested that Lee had the physical equipment that Nicklaus had. Trevino, though, was a perfect example of what the mind can do, of how much our imagination influences our golf.

Lee felt that he had a psychological edge over Nicklaus; he believed he would find a way to win, and he could imagine himself doing so. When he threw that toy snake at Jack just before the play-off began for the U. S. Open title at Merion in 1971, it was funny, but Lee was also delivering a message. "I'm not scared of you, Jack, and you better play like hell if you want to beat me," he seemed to be saying. In spite of Lee's antics, there is nothing wrong with his head; in fact, he has a pretty sharp mind, with a strong practical streak. "Watching pros putt four-footers for pars day after day reminds me of a dog chasing cars," he says. "Sooner or later, he'll get run over."

Next to Trevino, Tom Watson had the best results against Nicklaus. People talk about what a great scrambler Tom was, what a marvelous putter and wedge player he was, but they forget that he hit a lot of wonderful golf shots. Watson has a beautiful golf swing, probably the best on tour, even today. In his prime, he was one of the three or four longest drivers in the world, although sometimes his drives didn't come down in the same county. He still drives it long. He was blessed with a fine mind, too, though he didn't always control it as well as someone with his intelligence could have; but, then nobody else does, either. I thought that anyone with Tom's intelligence and physical ability might actually be unique, but that combination didn't even make Ben Hogan unique. By the time Ben reached the pinnacle of his powers, he had lost his ability to putt — he couldn't make one from three feet. Watson apparently is headed down the same road. Does anyone doubt that golf is a mental game?

A Shanking Contest

You may have noticed that golfers tend to be superstitious about certain things. Shanking, for instance. Most golfers I know won't mention the word out loud, and consider it a gross breach of golf etiquette to do so. Even to think about it is dangerous, lest it somehow creep into the swing. We professionals don't even like to stand near someone who is shanking, for fear the dreaded affliction might be contagious. Yet two of my colleagues actually challenged each other to a shanking contest one morning on the practice range at the Hartford tournament. The fearless duo was Bob Toski and Porky Oliver, who thought up the contest, they said, just to amuse themselves. Toski and Oliver were both clowns and were always up to something, especially in front of a gallery.

Standing side by side, not far from where I was practicing, they began. *Joing*, came the dreaded sound, and a ball darted across my line of flight. Pretty soon, *Twang*, there went another. The fact is that hitting shanks on purpose is difficult and takes a world of talent. The Mouse and Pork Chops were having a wonderful time and had the gallery falling on the ground with laughter. Neither I nor my fellow pros were amused, however. This went on for some time, and finally we went off to start the tournament.

After the round was over, I'm resting in the locker room when in comes Toski, looking glum. He slumped into a chair. He was not saying a word, just staring into the wall with a glazed expression.

"What's the matter, Blue?" I asked. "Didn't play too well?"

Toski barely shook his head, "No," he moaned, "it was awful."

"What happened?" A long pause.

"There'll be no more of those damn contests," he finally croaked.

"What do you mean?"

"I hit five of those bastards today, that's what I mean," whispered Toski.

As I've mentioned before, Bob was very talented. He could do almost anything with a golf ball, and still can, but I don't believe he tempted the fates with that little trick, anymore. I'm not sure why the shanks stay with you, once you hit one, but I'm sure it's mental, or perhaps emotional. It's fear, I guess, and once that fear gets a lock on your brain, it's such a powerful image that you're a gone goose. I'm not even sure I should be mentioning it.

The Strong Man

I suppose this incident indicates that we had more fun in those days. It doesn't appear to me that the fellows today enjoy the camaraderie of their fellows as much as we did, although we didn't share that much, to be honest about it. We had more fun, though. One of the most popular players when I started on tour was Robert "Skee" Riegel, the former U. S. Amateur Champion. Skee had a tremendous build and was abnormally strong. He used to put his hand under my bottom and do one-armed pushups. Even though I weighed only 127 pounds, that was an impressive feat. His wife, Edie, forbade him to drink in public, and I soon discovered why. We were in Montreal for the LaBatt Open, and the brewery had furnished the players with free beer upstairs in the clubhouse in a bar just off our locker room. About eight of us were sitting around having a few cool ones when in came Skee Riegel.

"Skeezix, come on over and join us for a couple beers," I said. "I was just telling the guys about some of your feats of strength."

"I better not, Gardner. Edie's waiting downstairs, and you know she raises hell if I drink," Skee said.

Was he a man or a mouse, we taunted, and went on

needling him. Finally he said the heck with it and joined in. We continued talking about his strength, and, pretty soon, he was walking on his hands. It appeared that he could do so for as long as he wanted, without falling, and we expressed our admiration.

"That's not tough," said Skee. "Jumping off a table and landing on your hands, without falling, now that's tough. And walking down a flight of stairs takes even greater strength and coordination."

Naturally, we wanted him to jump off the big oak table in the bar, and we began egging him on. When he did it successfully, we screamed for him to walk out the swinging doors on his hands, and proceed down the stairs to the lobby. Skee negotiated the steps without a misstep, crossed the lobby, descended the portico steps, and walked across the putting clock. The last time we saw him, he was still on his hands, scuttling down the first fairway — with Edie in his wake, screaming at him every step of the way.

I think we substituted fun for cash because in those days there wasn't much cash available. When I joined the tour in 1953, we paid money to the top twenty finishers. Except during the summer months when many of the fellows had club jobs, we had fields of 144 players, and if you finished twenty-first or lower you got zip. Each tournament paid twenty percent to the winner, so from a purse of $10,000, which was fairly common, the winner earned $2,000. In those days, it was possible to play the tour for about two-hundred dollars per week — you could find a decent room for twenty-five dollars, the caddie might get fifty, and the entrance fee was one hundred bucks. You could eat on the rest.

Today the tour pays the first seventy spots and, even allowing for inflation, you can see that today's player doesn't need to win tournaments to make a good living. It's pretty obvious that, in my era, there was more incentive — even an imperative — to *win* than there is today. I don't condemn these circumstances one bit because a lot of us fought for years to achieve the financial health the tour enjoys today, but I think the difference may help to explain why we don't see players dominating the game anymore.

In a word, they don't need it as badly.

Rating Today's Players

Of the generation of American golfers that succeeded Nicklaus, Trevino, and Watson, the most that can be said is that they show promise. The leading American players — Fred Couples, Payne Stewart, and Paul Azinger — have the requisite talent, but none has approached the record of either Trevino or Watson, let alone Nicklaus, at a similar point in their careers. In the past few years, foreigners have dominated the game, led principally by Greg Norman, Nick Faldo, and Nick Price. As I mentioned earlier, Norman gives the impression that he might be on the verge of becoming a dominating player, although Faldo has had more success in the majors.

In comparing them, I would say that Norman has more physical talent than Faldo, while Faldo is more of a bulldog. Faldo's swing has not changed much since his early days, but his short game is vastly improved. He's fabulous around the green, and solid from tee to green, too. However, Nick has not exactly torn up the American tour.

After some horrendous disappointments in recent years, Norman was much improved in 1993. There has to be some brain damage, though, from all the things that have happened to him. The odds on one player being victimized by so many impossible shots must be a hundred billion to one. Greg has a very fast tempo, which is not ideal for the pressure situations of tournament play. His swing is very upright, although he has shortened it recently, which is okay for medium irons but not so good for long irons and woods. It didn't seem to bother him when he won the British Open in 1993, but with a backswing that stops short of parallel, you can linger, but you gotta go. It'll get shorter! Long swingers have always been the best and lasted longest, and always will.

Nick Price is strong and has a wonderful attitude. The only thing I don't particularly care for in his golf swing is his tendency to flatten his swing in the transition between the backswing and the downswing. It appears to me that he occasionally tends to lay the club off a little too much. His swing appears to be as fast as Ben Hogan's, although their swings are not as similar as they might appear. Hogan actually didn't have very far to go to flatten his downswing because his backswing dictated a flat downswing. By that I mean that his tailbone went toward the hole during the backswing, and that eliminated any chance of a steep downswing. Steep downswings frequently produce bad golf shots.

Both Seve Ballesteros and Ian Woosnam seem to be fading, although they should be in their primes. Woosnam has a fine swing but appears to have a terminal case with the flat stick. Ballesteros owns one of the finest golf swings I ever saw, just fantastic. He puts the club in an almost perfect position at the top of his swing; from that position, anyone else would have to faint to hit the ball into some of the ugly places he does. Of the younger Europeans, Peter Baker is the most impressive. He has beautiful tempo and is mechanically sound. If he can putt all the time as he did in the 1993 Ryder Cup Matches, he will be something, because I never saw anyone putt better.

Paul Azinger has a pretty ugly-looking grip, but he's living proof that there are no "basic principles" in golf. To me, "basic" means something you *must* have to be a champion golfer. There is no such thing in golf. Basic guidelines, yes, and ideals that might give you a better chance to be consistent, okay, but to say that you "must" hold the club this way or swing that way is just not true. How would you dare teach anyone to grip the club with both hands on one side of the club, as Paul does? But it works for him, and he plays with a world of heart and guts.

Fred Couples is very talented and, I think, will get better. Like another American player, Davis Love III, he is blessed with great length and achieved success fairly early. The American press and public expects great things from both of these players, although things don't always work out the way the press expects. Davis Love puts the club in a good position; it looks nice, but I don't sense any "feel" in his swing. Don't ask me to explain this, but I know what it looks like. I see it in Couples's swing, but not in Love's. Davis reminds me of a marvelous wind-up toy.

Couples puts the club in a magnificent position at the swing's top, although he picks it almost straight up to get it there. Fred has a wonderful effortless-looking tempo, and he can really putt. In my opinion, Freddie's future depends almost entirely on the inside of his head — just what he allows in, or keeps out. He seems to have weathered the Deborah divorce, and he also seems to be playing far fewer slices lately, so I look for Fred Couples to really get it going soon, and he can keep it going if he really wants to. I think only Freddie can stop Freddie.

Greyhounds and Bulldogs

Payne Stewart is kind of puzzling. He's like a greyhound, sleek and smooth, but not always ready. Payne has a very good-looking swing to play as poorly as he does at times, which tells me he doesn't have control of his emotions all the time. Stewart aims too far left, in my opinion, which induces a tendency to push his long shots to the right when the heat is on. This alignment has just the opposite effect with his short irons. He sticks his right leg so close to the line that it almost gets in the way of his swing. The result is that he pulls too many short irons.

You never can tell how a player will turn out because over the long haul, physical abilities by themselves don't make champions. They certainly help, but the mental and emotional skills — desire, composure, thinking, tenacity, concentration, will, attitude — count more heavily in separating a consistent winner from the rest. If Corey Pavin had Payne Stewart's physical abilities, imagine what he might accomplish. Of course, he makes up for it with his marvelous wedge play and just about the best putting stroke on tour. It's strange how often this seems to happen, by the way. Pavin has an unorthodox golf swing, and is a good deal shorter than most of his peers, but he's an absolute bulldog.

He reminds me a lot of Jerry Barber, a tenacious marvel of my era, who was even shorter than Pavin. His golf swing looked so bad we would avert our eyes, but from 150 yards in, he was murder. And could he putt! Just ask Don January, whom he beat in a play-off to win the PGA Championship in 1961 after holing putts of twenty, forty, and sixty feet on the last three holes at Olympia Fields in Chicago. Jerry played golf differently from the rest of us. He might top his drive, hit two more ugly shots, then hole a fifty-footer for par. A bad shot never bothered him.

Barber was forty-five years old when he won that tournament, having started late in competitive golf, but has continued to compete for more than forty years. Today, he may be the best 78-year-old player in the world. He still competes on the senior tour and regularly shoots six to seven shots under his age. The PGA Tour is trying to run him off the senior tour, which I think is a mistake because he's a great inspiration to club golfers and the public might like to see him in action.

Scoring with Funny Swings

In the same vein, I can recall players like Dave Stockton and Bob Charles. We used to turn our heads when they made a swing, because we couldn't bear to watch. I even hated to listen to their shots: *Sklurk!* It sounded awful, but they could score. Stockton won two PGA Championships, and Charles became the best left-hander in history, winning five U. S. tournaments and the British Open. Both of these men, as everyone who follows golf knows, were among the finest putters of their day. Believe me, they had to be. Charles, a very tall man, takes the club straight up, like a man hammering a post in the ground. He must be very talented to be able to find the ball on his downswing from that position. Stockton's swing is kind of a hitch, a lurch, and a recovery. Yet there they are, still out on the senior tour winning tournaments and, at least one year, leading the circuit in money winnings.

Of all the players who reached the top ranks, Raymond Floyd appeared to have the most unorthodox swing. He joined the tour at the age of nineteen, and even then he was cocky, brash, and had a world of talent. He was long, too. I nicknamed him "Humphrey," after the strong man featured in the comic strip "Joe Palooka." He was always physically strong, although his plumpness tended to fool you about his power. "Humphrey" had just one speed — wide open. He didn't see many of the fairways, but, after his drives, he rarely had far to go to reach the greens. When he got near or on the greens, he was fabulous, and still is.

Raymond was never a shrinking violet, on or off the course. Some of us thought he might have done much better as a youngster had he not believed that it was his sole duty to romance every attractive woman in America and consume all the beverages within reach.

Ray Floyd never had what you'd call a classic swing. His club was laid off at the top, which means it pointed into the left rough, but, with diligence, he worked on this until he had an effective, if not graceful, swing. He learned how to play knock-down shots and gradually improved his driving consistency, and his short game seemed to improve like good wine. To date, Raymond has won four majors and twenty-two tour events spread over four decades, and has been chosen to eight Ryder Cup teams. Raymond never paid much attention to, nor cared about, how he looked. He cared about making low numbers, and, to that end, was fearless and relentless. In professional golf, that's really all that matters.

Pretty Swings Don't Make Champions

The other side of this coin is that pretty golf swings don't always produce champions. Tom Weiskopf appeared to have as much physical ability as anyone I've seen. The only thing I didn't like about Tom's set-up was his grip. It always looked rather awkward to me. I do know this: In the cool of an evening, when Tom was coming down the stretch, you could look to the right because that's where he was apt to hit it. Guys who play with some part of their body — shoulders, legs, hips, or whatever — instead of playing with the head of the club, have this tendency.

Other than that, you had to love his golf swing, and many people expected Tom Weiskopf to challenge Nicklaus, or at least win half a dozen majors and thirty or so tournaments, instead of the fifteen tournaments and one major that he actually won. He had that kind of talent. Tom was runner-up four times in the Masters and once in the U. S. Open. In 1973, the year he won the British Open, he captured four U.S. tournaments, but every time he was on the verge of breaking through to the top, something seemed to snap. I think he had the desire, and he certainly had the physical ability, but he didn't have Jack's mental or emotional toughness.

Another player who puzzled me was Tommy Aaron. Tommy had a long, flowing swing, the kind that holds up forever, and seemed to have a good temperament for the game. He hit the ball far enough, his mechanics were sound, and he was a wonderful putter. His swing was gorgeous to watch. You never sensed that he rushed a shot; every one seemed to be executed with the same beautiful tempo. With all this going for him, it's always mystified me that he won only two tournaments in his career. Of course, one of them was the Masters, and that's a nice one to win, but Tommy never seemed to have enough fire in the belly to win more. In professional golf, they don't give prizes for being nice, and Tommy Aaron is such a nice man that perhaps he backed away from the rough and tumble needed to be a consistent winner.

Superstitions

I'm not sure that professional golfers are any more superstitious than players in other sports, but we do have our fair share. For a long time, Gary Player would wear black-only outfits on Sunday in the belief that it made him stronger. "White reflects the sun's rays," he explained, "but black attracts light, and so I get strength from the sun." I suppose there's a grain of truth in that, but I noticed that Gary won plenty of tournaments wearing white, or some other color. As for myself, I just hated to play with balls bearing the number "four" and always chose to play with number "threes." Maybe I thought I would score more birdies, I dunno, but it was mental. The great putters, with the possible exception of Bobby Locke, rarely would admit their prowess on the green. Jack Burke and Arnold Palmer, two of the best putters I've seen, would howl in protest if a writer asked them about their phenomenal putting. "Man, go talk to Finsterwald or Mangrum," Burke would whine. "I can't buy a putt." Of course, Jackie collected more long snakes than the Miami Serpentarium. They didn't mind bragging about their long games but never their putting skills. They never knew when the touch would vanish. Superstition? Probably so,

Gardner Dickinson doffing the famous hat.

although few of us would have been willing to admit it.

We tended to be partial to our hats. In those days, we didn't have all those corporate logos and such. Sam Snead used to wear fedoras, but he switched to straw hats in the forties and wore them the rest of his life. Probably thought it would help his putting. Ben Hogan wore fedoras, too. But he had switched to his familiar white caps by the early fifties, and never again wore anything else. Naturally, I copied Hogan and wore white caps most of my career. Fellows like Dutch Harrison and Clayton Heafner wore wide-brimmed straw hats. Heafner was a big, broad-shouldered redhead from North Carolina, and I'm sure he needed those wide-brimmed hats to protect his fair skin from the sun.

On the Monday after the 1953 Western Open at Bellerive in St. Louis, a bunch of us were out trying to qualify for the U. S. Open, which was scheduled to be held that year at Oakmont. About midway through the second nine, I was on the green, about to putt, when big Clayton Heafner suddenly appeared. Clayton, playing in another group, was crossing behind the green on his way to an adjacent tee and called out "How you fellows doing?"

My playing partner, Al Zimmerman, replied, "Sarge, I'm not doing much, but the kid here is seven under!"

Heafner stopped in his tracks. "Be damned," he snorted, then strode onto the green, nearly trampling on my line, until he reached me. He reached over, grabbed my white cap, and placed it on his huge head. On him, it looked like an aspirin. Then he jammed his huge straw hat on my head, which promptly disappeared. I could barely see. "I'll wear this for a while, and maybe I'll start playing like Hogan, too," declared Heafner. And he marched away.

Well, I had just received that cap from Cavanaugh, the Park Avenue, New York, company that made them for Ben Hogan, and had paid $25 for it. In those days, that was extravagant, but, of course, I had to have one. I waited for my hat to arrive at the eighteenth green, and fortunately, Sarge hadn't scored that well, so he returned it. It wasn't only the money, you see; I was convinced I played better when wearing that cap.

Some of the things we do are more habit than supersti-

tion, although it might not always seem that way to specta-
tors. When players like Billy Casper or Jack Nicklaus go
through their disciplined pre-shot routines, they might
appear, if not superstitious, then ritualistic. If interrupted,
Nicklaus will step back and begin his routine again; Casper
would go so far as to replace his club in the bag, then start
over by once again drawing the club from the bag. Each
player has his own way of concentrating on the shot, and
this was theirs.

Good habits, like these, take a while to form. Bad habits
are hard to break, especially if you have somehow managed
to overcome them while achieving success.

A Heavy Load

I don't mean to pick on Cary Middlecoff, because he is a
friend, a former neighbor, and among a handful of our
greatest players. But, the truth is that Doc was not a very
good bunker player.

Cary Middlecoff was a great player long before he
joined the tour; he had beaten all the big guns in the 1945
North-South Open, as an amateur, and kept right on winning after he turned pro. By the mid-1950s, he'd won two
U. S. Opens and the Masters, and by the 1960s he had
won about forty tournaments and was reckoned one of the
game's top players. So it was a pretty heavy load that Jay
Hebert and I took on one morning in the early 1960s,
while practicing at the Lost Tree Club in North Palm
Beach, Florida, for an upcoming Masters Tournament. We
had agreed to play Middlecoff and Hogan for two days,
and, naturally, a few bob were on the line. The first day,
we played pretty even and, as I recall, everything was riding on the last hole, a par-five that Doc Middlecoff could
reach with an iron. He puts his second shot in the right
bunker, leaving a clean lie from a shallow bunker; if he

gets down in two, they win the hole and tie us.

Middlecoff's ball airmailed the green and continued right on out to the street. You should have seen Hogan's face as the ball sailed by. Well, we tied and the next day, the same thing happened. Doc put his second in the bunker, except this time, if he could get it down in two, they would collect all the money. Wouldn't you know, Doc pooped the shot and left it in the bunker. Then he hurried over and rushed his next, and knocked this one out on the street, too. It was pitiful, but that was how bad a bunker player Doc had become.

Actually, in his earlier days Middlecoff was not that bad. But his sand play had, indeed, become a heavy load to bear, and I believed I had discovered one of the reasons for his trouble. Doc was a tall man, about six feet two, yet his arms were particularly short in relation to his height. This would make bunker play difficult for anyone. If I had to grip down on my bunker club six or seven inches — which, in effect, is what Middlecoff had to do — I don't believe I could play bunker shots very well, either. So I had a bunker club that was about five inches over standard made up for him at the Toney Penna plant.

"My God," said Doc when he saw the club, "it's longer than my driver." I told him it would be just fine, once he grew accustomed to standing more erect. I suggested he play the ball more forward in his stance, just opposite his left toe, or even in front of it, if he could. This opened his shoulders the correct amount, so that now he could use his own back-swing without consciously trying to take the club back outside. Finally I suggested he pull his right leg back out of the way so that his right thigh would not get in the way as he swung the hands back.

Doc began experimenting, and pretty soon he was popping the ball up in the air. After a while, he was landing most of his shots by the hole. Middlecoff was, after all, a proven genius with a golf stick in his hands; all he needed was equipment that fitted him properly. We played that afternoon, and Doc played several excellent sand shots, and he even holed one. It was a spectacular improvement, so I'm thinking to myself I've performed a miracle. Well, I went back out to play the tour for about three weeks, and when I returned, Doc was back playing with his little old short bunker club, and playing the ball back in his stance. I never said another word. The only reason I could think of was that Doc had been too long in the habit of using that old bunker club of his, and just couldn't get used to the change.

Hookers Have More Fun

Most players on tour are natural hookers. By that, I mean that their natural ball flight pattern moves from right to left. The reason for this is easily explained. Because golfers stand to the side of the ball, a solid, square contact imparts some counter-clockwise spin to the ball, causing the ball to curve gently in flight from right to left. We call this action a draw, which, if overdone, can make the ball curve quite sharply, which we call a hook. A fade, or slice, spins just the opposite, in a clockwise direction, and moves in a left-to-right flight pattern. Again, because golfers stand to the side of the ball, to hit a slice, or fade, the club face must be open, if only slightly, at the moment of impact. You can readily see, then, that a ball with hooking spin is the most powerful shot in golf.

Not many golfers would wish to give up this power, and those who are natural slicers rarely see the kingdom of the tour. A few champions have learned to fade the ball in order to tame an uncontrollable hook — Lee Trevino and Ben Hogan, to name two — but be assured that either man could produce a hook on command, when he needed one. In his early days, Hogan had a savage hook and often had trouble getting the ball in the air. "If this had not been the case, would you have gone to such trouble to learn to fade the ball?" I asked him once.

"Of course not," he answered.

But, as some of us know, the cure for a hook is a slice, and that was Hogan's. On many occasions Hogan went back to a draw with his driver, and his increase in distance was dramatic. Hogan was long, even with his fade, but anyone who purposely slices or fades the ball is giving up distance.

Billy Casper is another top player who learned a fade when he came on tour, but he was a natural hooker who eventually went back to it when he joined the Senior Tour, because he needed the distance. Dow Finsterwald was another who liked to move the ball from left to right, and in recent years both Jack Nicklaus and Craig Stadler adopted that flight pattern to bring their long games under better control. As long as they hit their drives, they could afford it. Fellows like Paul Runyan, Jerry Barber, Deane Beman, Dave Marr, and Corey Pavin, today couldn't afford a fade. They were too short, as it was. All of these players had the ability to "work" the ball, to bend it right-to-left, or left-to-right at will, when the circumstances required such a shot.

If a golfer is doomed to play one type of shot forever, whether a hook or a slice, it not only takes much of the fun from the game, it also restricts that golfer's ability to play certain holes. For example, if a hole calls for a right-to-left shot, and all you have is that nice old slice, you'll have very few options for how you can play the hole. In effect, it takes half the golf course away from you, even before you tee off. I would encourage any aspiring golfer to learn how to bend the ball both ways, to know how to hook it and slice it on purpose. The main reason is to be able to rescue yourself on the day when all you can do is hit slices or hooks. At the Tournament of Champions in Las Vegas one year, I found that I could not hook a ball to save my life. I sliced the first drive across the "Strip," out-of-bounds, and only when I tried to snap-hook the ball could I extricate myself from my predicament.

Even then, all I managed was a little fade, or a straight shot, but had I not known how to hook, I'd have been a basket case.

On the professional tour, you'd better know how to bend the ball in either direction, or else pack it in and hop a bus to the next town. I've been accused of teaching "hooks," but I firmly believe that to be a good golfer, let alone a great one, a player must be able at all times to start a ball in the right rough and hook it back into the center of the fairway, if he so desires. A good player must know how to draw or hook the ball on any swing, with any club. I managed to win thirty-seven amateur tournaments playing a ten- to fifteen-yard hook, but since I knew it was coming, it was just as easy to aim that hook as it was to aim a straight shot. It was not until sometime later, during my professional career, that I found out how to play a reliable fade. I could always count on my ability to draw a shot, and that's very comforting in the heat of competition, but it was just as comforting to know I could fade the ball when I needed that shot.

Tricks of the Trade

In all my years on the professional tour, I've yet to see anyone who can hit straight shots on purpose. Byron Nelson was probably the straightest player in history, yet he always played with a slight draw — unless he was playing a special type of shot. Ben Hogan said he had no idea how to hit a ball straight. When he wanted to try, he explained, he would set up everything at address for a slice, then try to hook the ball during his swing. Hogan said he always tried to move the ball one way or the other because he wanted to control its flight and reach the safest part of the fairway. He would no more "turn a ball loose," he said, than fly to the moon.

"You don't have to know exactly where your golf ball is going, but you better know where it's *not* going," Hogan once told me. How much lower our scores might be if we all followed this simple yet profound advice.

This business of shaping your shots applies equally to approach shots played to greens. I've often heard it said that a fade produces more backspin than a draw, but don't you believe it. I've never seen anyone get more backspin on his approach shots than Howard Creel, the former National Left-Handed Champion from Colorado, and Howard drew every shot. In my experience, a drawn shot spins every bit as much as a faded one, perhaps more.

Another reason for learning to bend shots is to enable you to hit "hold-up" shots when playing in crosswinds. The idea is to use the spin of the ball to counteract the force of the wind. With the wind blowing left-to-right, for example, you might play a little draw; the spin of the ball wants to take it left, but the wind moves it to the right. You are "holding" the shot into the wind, with the result, you hope, that it will go straight. The opposite would be true when playing in a right-to-left wind: Play a little fade, and hope the wind will cause the ball to fly straight. Admittedly, this is a graduate school technique, but the knowledge and mastery of these shots is absolutely necessary for a golfer aspiring to play among the best. Wind conditions vary greatly, as will the amount of hook or slice needed to hold a ball in the wind. Mastery comes only from practice and experience, and, even then, it's sometimes an educated guess.

Personally, I would almost always try to work the ball against the wind with my irons, but with a driver, I seldom tried to join the wind if it was blowing left-to-right. I felt confident I could handle a "hook" wind, but in a "slice" wind I could never be sure just how far left I should aim. Besides, I figured if the left-to-right wind was strong enough, my ball was apt to be traveling straight before it had gone much more than a hundred yards.

Master of the Fade

The all-time master of the fade was Jimmy Demaret. Jimmy must have been a hooker in his youth, though, because he could hit every kind of shot you've heard of, and a few you haven't. Demaret had a magnificent pair of hands, thick and strong, yet he played with extraordinary feel and touch. Growing up in East Texas, Jimmy learned to play in the wind and, by the time he turned pro, he was a master. The boys on tour considered him the best wind player in the world. In fact, they considered him a fantastic player, period.

Demaret is badly underrated, because he could really play you some golf. He was such a funny man, with such a warm personality, that people sort of skip over his record. Jimmy was good enough to win three Masters titles, the first man ever to do so, and along the way he won thirty-one tour victories. In the history of the tour, only twelve men have won more. Jimmy loved the high life and the company of happy souls, it's true, but just ask Ben Hogan or anybody else in Texas if Demaret could play. Of his friend Demaret, Hogan said, "This man played shots I hadn't even dreamed of. I learned them, but it was Jimmy who showed them to me first."

Through much of his career, Demaret was a great driver, long and straight, and had a wonderful swing until he started slicing the ball too much, a flight pattern that he referred to as his "fade." He changed his strong, three-knuckle left-hand grip to a weak one that showed only one knuckle, and became a predominately left-to-right player. It didn't seem to matter, though, because he still could play better than most everyone else. He was a wizard with an old laminated four-wood, a club he had wheedled out of Toney Penna, Macgregor's great club designer. Playing that patented fade of his, I promise you, he could eat with that club.

In the late 1950s, I was paired with Jimmy the first two

(L-R) Jimmy Demaret, Gardner, and Bing Crosby.

rounds of the San Diego Open at the Stardust course. In those days, San Diego was the last regulation tournament before the Bing Crosby Pro-Am. The final hole is a 225-yard par-three with a driving range bordering the left side, which was out-of-bounds, and a rather deep, clay bunker on the right edge of the green. Usually it played into the wind, so it was double-tough. Anyone scoring a three was tickled pink. When we reached this hole, Demaret hauled out his trusty four-wood and started his tee shot out over the driving range and we watched it fade back to the green, where it finished about four feet from the hole. The following day, Jimmy played precisely the same shot, only this time it faded up to within two feet of the cup.

"Guess you don't think this hole is too tough," I said, after complimenting him on the shot.

"Son, if they scrapped all the other holes on this course and just played this one seventy-two times, the rest of you fellas might just as well head for Pebble Beach and get ready for the Crosby."

How good a player was Demaret? The first time I saw him was at the Masters in 1950, before I had turned pro. My buddy, Jack Gillon, and I had hitchhiked to Augusta to watch the pros and had taken a room at the old Bon Aire Hotel, a magnificent rat-trap. On Saturday night we were in the ballroom listening to the band, when in walked Demaret, feeling no pain. I should point out that Jimmy was leading the tournament after three rounds. He grabbed the mike and began singing "Where or When," along with several more ballads. Demaret had a fine singing voice, but people gasped at the sight of the tournament leader out drinking and carousing so late. I think he closed up the joint later.

The next morning, Jack and I were watching the pros on the putting clock, and here comes Demaret, bouncing jauntily, as he always did, but looking a little green around the gills. He stroked two or three putts, then dashed away behind Bob Jones's cottage and flipped up his breakfast, along with a bottle of Scotch. He reappeared, teed off with no apparent difficulty, shot 69, and won the Masters for the third time.

Demaret's Fast Quips

Jimmy Demaret surely enjoyed the nightlife and parties and good companions as much as his golf, and rarely did he let one interfere with the other. He loved color and clothes, and wasn't afraid to mix the two in outrageous combinations. The ladies loved him, and I think the feeling was reciprocated. He was a master of the fast quip.

Demaret and his partner, Jack Burke Jr., built the Champions Golf Club in Houston, a beautiful thirty-six-hole facility that hosted the 1967 Ryder Cup Matches. Demaret, Burke, Hogan, and I were having lunch in the clubhouse prior to the

Old Warriors: Gardner and Jimmy Demaret.

afternoon matches, when in walks Don Cherry. Don was a native Texan, a buddy of Demaret's and Burke's who was a fine popular singer as well as an accomplished amateur golfer. Cherry breezed over to the table sporting a bald head and a heavy red beard, which, I gather, he had grown for a movie. Hogan hated beards, and for a while he completely ignored Cherry. Demaret broke the tension.

"Don, you look great, but you have your head on upside down." Everyone laughed, except Hogan.

"What I can't understand is why the hell an intelligent man would take the club back no farther than waist high," said Ben, finally, referring to Cherry's extremely short backswing.

"Hell, Ben, anyone around this place could tell you why," quipped Demaret. "Don keeps all his money in his right hip pocket, and he never lets his hands get very far from his cash."

The Champions' Desk

When Jackie Burke and Jimmy Demaret built the Champions Club, they designed one of the finest locker rooms in America, a spacious room with comfortable alcoves, a friendly bar, large tables and stuffed chairs, all surrounded by beautifully-finished wooden lockers. This and Seminole's, in North Palm Beach, Florida, are just about the best locker rooms in golf. They also designed a spacious office that they shared, featuring one of the biggest and most magnificent mahogany desks I've ever seen. They shared the desk, too, but after a while, as business flourished, they decided to purchase separate desks. Demaret was in the office when the new desks arrived. Jimmy supervised the placement of his own desk, and when the delivery man asked where Mr. Burke's desk was to be placed, Jimmy said, "Why, just put it out there on the driving range, since that's where Jackie spends all his time." And that's just what they did.

Jack Burke Jr. is known for his quick wit, his youthful good looks, and a sharp mind for business. Although he lacked a formal college education, Jackie is possessed of a large native capacity for knowledge. He knows as much about golf, and the golf swing, as anyone I know. His father, Jack Burke Sr., was one of America's fine players and premier teachers, so Jackie came by it naturally. Young Jack took to the game quickly and turned professional at the age of nineteen. When he was introduced to Bing Crosby as a golf pro, Crosby said, "Yeah? Golf pro where, at Boys Town?" The name stuck.

"Boys Town" became one of the finest players of his generation, winning both the Masters and the PGA Championship, and about twenty tour titles. Not many people remember that he was the last man to win four tournaments in a row, a feat he accomplished in 1954.

Like his father, Jackie was an accomplished teacher as well as player, and was much sought-after by tour pros when their swings went off the track. Jackie loved to teach, and most weeks would go up and down the practice range passing out tips to players, and, along the way, hitting half their practice balls.

In those days, tournaments didn't provide practice balls. We had to bring our own. Jackie would saunter out of the clubhouse and stroll over to one end of the range, where he would interrupt whoever was there.

"Say, Lionel, you're not swinging as smoothly as you should, are you? Here, let me show you what I mean." Burke would hit a few shots with a nine-iron, then he'd move to the next fellow.

"Say, Arnie, you look a little ragged with those short irons," and he would proceed to hit some eight-irons with Arnold's practice balls.

By the time he'd worked his way down the whole line, Burke had gone through his entire bag, from short irons to driver, and he was nicely warmed up. Jackie didn't need any practice balls, because he hit ours. I always suspected that he tried out his new theories on us, and, if they worked, he'd incorporate them into his own game; but his help was always welcomed by those of us, myself included, who needed it.

The Colorful Mr. Bolt

During my time, I've seen some wonderful players, but without any doubt one of the premier ball-strikers of all time was Tommy Bolt. Tom was also quite a character and one of the tour's most colorful but tasteful dressers. Tom spent a fortune on clothes. A writer once asked Tommy what he thought of Doug Sanders' outfits. "Doug Sanders? Why, hell, my caddie dresses better than he does," Bolt replied.

Tommy Bolt could really play. I remember a particularly mean and blustery day in San Diego when Tom shot 62 on a day most of us had trouble finishing. I had to wonder what course he had played. Ben Hogan admired Bolt very much as a player but liked to "put him on." Tom was always complaining about his clubs, and Ben told him it was because he never had a decent set. So Tommy asked Ben to make him a full set of clubs, exactly like Ben's. Bolt's new clubs were delivered the morning before the Colonial National Invitational in Fort Worth, and we all played a practice round together. On the first tee, Bolt hit a big push-slice with his driver, which sailed out-of-bounds. The second attempt almost went out, too. Tom went on this way for a while before he realized that the grips on his new clubs were slipping and turning. Apparently Ben had not allowed enough time for the glue to set. Tommy turned to Ben, told him the grips were turning, and asked if he could borrow Ben's clubs while the grips dried.

"Hell, no," said Ben, giving me a wink. "With that lousy grip you take on the club you'd rip the grips right off any club."

Tommy complained, but Ben stuck to his guns. I was laughing so hard I finally had to whisper to Tom that Ben was putting him on, and I let him use my clubs for a couple holes.

In the late 1950s we hired J. Edwin Carter to run our tour. Ed Carter was a businessman with promotional skills, and, in my opinion, was the only man who ever held that position who had any brains. Carter reorganized and improved our schedule, worked hard to increase our purses, and established new rules and procedures. One of the first pros he ran into was Tommy Bolt. It seems that Tom had had a bad night before a tournament and was paired the first day with Bob Rosburg. Tom's stomach was raising cain, loudly, and it appeared to Rosburg that Tom was not making much effort to control himself. The intermittent reports of his passing gas were, unfortunately, audible to the large gallery. Rossie admonished Bolt, but Tom suggested that Bob mind his own business, and continued his rather loud behavior. When the round was over,

Rosburg reported the behavior, citing Carter's new rules pertaining to "conduct unbecoming a professional golfer." Bolt was fined $100. Of course, the press got wind of this, if you will pardon the expression. Though the writers wouldn't touch this story, they nevertheless asked Tommy if it were true that he'd been fined $100 for "passing gas."

Replied Bolt, "Hell, yes! They're trying to take all the *color* out of the game!"

Earlier I mentioned that Bolt was one of the premier shot-makers of all time. Let me give you an example. During the Memphis Open, held at the Colonial Country Club, I had shot some fabulous scores in the first three rounds and was paired in the last group on Sunday with Tom Bolt and Don Fairfield. I was nervous and wanted to get on with things, but old Tom was playing the gallery for all he was worth. As a result, he was dragging Don and me around the course. The ninth hole at Colonial was a very long par-three with a small green flanked by clay bunkers on the left and out-of-bounds near the right edge of the putting surface. Typically it called for a long iron or fairway wood. Some weeks prior to the tournament, the ninth green had been closed for repairs and members had been forced to play to a little rock-hard temporary putting surface just short of the true green.

Well, it didn't take us long to figure out that balls hit with a four-iron or five-iron would land short, onto the hard patch where the temporary green had been, and roll onto the regular green. When we reached this hole on Sunday, I bounced a four-iron onto the preferred patch and watched my ball run up there about twenty feet from the hole. Fairfield did the same. Now, Bolt stood there for what seemed an eternity, and when I asked him what was wrong, he said, "I ain't got no damn club for this hole."

"And why not?" I asked.

"I can't hit no hot hooks up there like you turkeys," said Tom, "and I can't carry no two-iron far enough to reach it."

"Well, then, I guess you'll have to hit a four-wood," said I.

"Are you crazy? I ain't gonna hit no wood on this hole with that S.O.B. on the right edge," said Tommy.

What Bolt did was this: He hit a beautiful, high two-iron that landed softly on the hard temporary green and rolled on, stopping about ten yards short. Bolt turned to me: "See what I mean, G. D.?"

Greatest Golf Shots — IV

This was a great shot, all right, but only one of many struck by Tommy Bolt. There is no question in my mind that he played the greatest single pressure shot I have seen. Again, I was paired with Tom in the last round, this time at the Colonial National Invitational in Fort Worth the year Mike Souchak won. We were both near the lead most of the day, but Tommy had decided quite early in the round that the gallery was intent only on "harrassing ol' Tom."

"Look at all them S.O.B.s," he would mutter to me. "Every last one of them's hoping ol' Tom's gonna double-bogey every hole." Owing to his state of mind, Tom didn't play quite as well as he might have, and, as a matter of fact, neither did I. By the time we reached the final hole, we were both out of it — or, so it seemed.

Souchak had fired a closing round of 65, and, as we walked off the eighteenth tee, I remarked to Tom what a remarkable round this was. Dumbfounded, Bolt exclaimed, "A 65? Souchak didn't shoot no 65 on *this* damn course." But I assured Tom that he had, which meant that Tom had to hole his second shot for a deuce just to tie Souchak. We both had hit good drives, Tom's a little shorter than mine, so I had to wait for him to play his second. I waited a good while, and, when it finally appeared that Tom might pass, I walked over to his golf bag, took out his six-iron, and stuck it back in the bag so that he would notice it. Tom strolled back to his bag, saw the six-iron sticking up, and grabbed it. With his eyebrows raised inquiringly, he announced that the six-iron was the right club.

As I walked away, Tom settled himself to the shot and let her fly. The ball went directly at the flagstick, pitched just short, grabbed, and appeared to go straight in. The huge gallery surrounding the green let out a thundering roar, a blast that I imagined could be heard in New Orleans. The ovation continued while I played my second, and the applause lasted until we arrived at the green. Tom's ball lay directly behind the hole, with a fraction of it hanging over the lip. Mike Souchak was standing beside the green, and when Tommy's ball hit by the hole, a friend of mine told me, Souchak turned white. What a stroke it was, and Tom *knew* he had to hole it. Over the years, Tommy Bolt has had his critics, but in my book, American tournament golf has been enriched by Tom's presence and performance, and he goes down in my book as one of golf's good guys.

Match Play

Match play is the poorest test of a golfer's ability. When you can make an eight on a hole and still beat a guy who never scores more than a five all day, then something's wrong with that. The total round, counting all the strokes, should always count more than any single hole, in my opinion, and, obviously others share that opinion. That's why we don't have any more match-play tournaments on the pro tour. I suppose you could have a match-play event, provided you played all eighteen holes and counted the medal scores. But just playing for holes, son, that just won't get it. If you can make twelve on just one hole, and only lose one hole in the match, I fail to see why anyone could consider match play a test of anything, and certainly not of golf.

The Competitive Urge

Professional golfers play mostly for money, it's true, but they play for something else, too. Call it ego, or competitive instinct, or what you will, when the tournament is on the line, something happens. If you're aggressive by nature, the adrenalin starts pumping, the ego begins to swell, the brain may go numb, and the muscles and tendons grow taut. At times like these, patience and composure are hard to muster, because all you want to do is beat the other fellow.

At the 1971 Atlanta Open, I was having one of those weeks when things were going my way. Playing the last round, I was tied for the lead with Jack Nicklaus as we both reached the last hole. Playing just behind him, I watched Jack birdie the par-five eighteenth to take a one-stroke lead. I knew I must birdie the hole to tie him. My drive, struck a little in the neck, was shorter than I hoped. When we reached my ball, my caddie, Herman Mitchell, told me I had 256 yards to the front edge of the green. Since my wedge game at the time was just ordinary, I decided against laying up. Mitch handed me my strong three-wood, and I nailed it right at the flag, but not as high as I had hoped. The ball pitched on the grassy bank and rolled back into the bunker about thirty feet from the hole.

"There won't be any damn playoff," I muttered to Mitch. "I'm going to hole this shot." I thought I had when it hit the hole, but it rolled by and I had to tap it in for a birdie. I headed for the first tee and the play-off with Big Jack, where about forty thousand people surrounded us. I was pumped up when I won the toss and elected to drive first. When I felt my club drop into the ideal slot at the top of the backswing, I told myself, "Just let 'er rip." I swung with all my might and caught it on all four screws. The ball sailed about forty yards farther than my drive had at the same hole earlier that day, which had been a good one. The gallery cheered, and I grinned at Jack as I went over to my bag.

Gardner embraces Jack Nicklaus after winning sudden death play-off in Atlanta Classic, 1971.

"Your shot, Jackson," I quipped.

Jack smiled back: "You bad guy."

He stood over that drive for what seemed an eternity, then swung harder than I had ever seen him swing before. His ball landed just to the right of mine. The officials were going to measure to see who was away, but I said I'd go first. I felt itchy-nervous, but confident, too. Where earlier I had hit a six-iron, now I played a pitching-wedge, and the ball never left the flag. The green was elevated, so we couldn't see where the ball landed, but from the roar of the gallery, I thought maybe I'd holed out. I'm sure Jack thought so, too. The buzz from the gallery continued even while Jack played his second, which flew straight over the flag and over the green. I'm certain he was trying to hole out.

We climbed the hill to the green, where someone told me my ball had rimmed out. It lay three or four feet from the hole. Jack played a fine chip to about three feet, so I had only to hole my putt for the victory. But it, too, rimmed out, so I went to the back of the green, put on my glove, and turned my thoughts to the par-five second hole. Just about the time I was thinking that I could reach the green in two, Jack astonished me, and everyone else, by missing his little three-footer with a seemingly disinterested stroke. Just that suddenly, the victory was mine. I walked over, put my arm around him, and asked if he'd missed the putt on purpose. Jack knew the win would mean much more to me than it would to him, but, champion that he is, he replied, "I like you, Gardner, but I wouldn't do that for you."

The Other Side of the Coin

In professional golf, it is not enough to have that strong competitive urge, even when accompanied by a reliable swing. Equally important are the mental and emotional factors which, to such a large extent, govern our behavior —

confidence, for one, and, perhaps more valuable still, the ability to compose yourself, especially when faced with adversity or pressure. In the big events, the importance of these psychological factors are magnified. In my own case, I had chances to win several major championships but always managed to invent ways to take myself out of the picture.

One such event was the 1961 U. S. Open played on the fabled South Course designed by Donald Ross at Oakland Hills Country Club outside Detroit, perhaps the toughest par-70 in golf. In fifty years, this course had yielded only one truly great round — the stunning 67 by Ben Hogan in the final round when he won the 1951 U. S. Open. He had called the course a "monster," because of revisions made to it by course architect Robert Trent Jones. Few other courses in American golf have so many tough par-fours, all of which demand long, straight driving and accurate irons. To this, add the fact that the greens were wickedly fast, as they were again in 1961.

In the first two rounds, I played quite well and drew sweet-swinging Gene Littler, one of my favorite playing partners, in the pairings for Saturday's 36-hole grind. In those days, we played the final two rounds of the U.S. Open the same day. During the morning's third round, I hung close to the lead, then opened the afternoon round with a birdie, and followed that with an eagle at the second hole. I had picked up three strokes in two holes and was told I now had the lead.

The third hole is an innocuous looking three-par, perhaps a middle iron, with two yawning facing bunkers in front of the green. During the practice rounds, Hogan had cautioned me to aim for the grassy opening between these bunkers, no matter where the pin might be placed. But I was hitting it so pure that I disregarded Ben's advice. I aimed right at the flag, which was cut over one of the bunkers. I thought I had struck the shot perfectly, but my ball pitched on the front of the green and spun back into the bunker. When I reached the ball, I saw it sitting on the upslope. All week I'd been knocking my bunker shots practically stiff, so I didn't fear this one. Digging in with my feet, I found plenty of sand, but when I hit down behind the ball, there was virtually no sand at all. Consequently, I bladed the ball badly, sending it over the gallery's heads behind the green. It settled in rough deep enough to bury a dog in. My subsequent quadruple-bogey seven completely deflated me, and I let it take me right out of the tournament.

I played the last fifteen holes in one-over par to post a 75, but I was finished. On the back nine, I began rooting for Littler, who was in the midst of a great round. On the fourteenth hole, I had outdriven Gene by an obvious amount but was on the other side of the fairway. This was one green a player could not afford to overshoot because of out-of-bounds close behind it. When I saw "Litt" take out a four-wood, I shouted across to him that I'd play first. I hit a five-iron onto the middle of the green, then remarked loudly to my caddie, "That was the best five-iron I've hit in the tournament." Littler promptly changed to a middle iron, put his shot on the putting surface, and, I believe, holed the putt for birdie. Had he used the four-wood and flown the green, he might easily have made double-bogey.

Joe Dey, the USGA's observer for our pairing, looked at me rather sternly but said nothing. Gene went on to win the championship with a final round 68, which beat Bob Goalby and Doug Sanders by a stroke. As far as I was concerned, it couldn't have happened to a finer man than Gene Littler, and since I had blown my chance, I was happy for him.

Blowing Another Big Chance

I blew another chance to win the Open, at Baltusrol in 1967, but it took me all day Sunday to do it. Baltusrol is a Tillinghast course in New Jersey with two long par-fives at the end. The 620-yard seventeenth gained notoriety during the 1993 U.S. Open when John Daly became the first man to reach it in two shots. In the practice rounds, Ben Hogan had remarked to me, disgustedly, "They'll break the tournament record this week." The high, U. S. Open-length rough Ben had been practicing on the previous three weeks had been cut down. His prediction proved to be accurate, as usual, when Jack Nicklaus shot 275, lowering Hogan's own record of 276, which was set at Riviera in Los Angeles in 1948.

Entering the final round in 1967, I stood two strokes behind the leader, Marty Fleckman, who was an amateur and a prodigious hitter. But nobody thought Fleckman would hold on, and he didn't, shooting 80 in the last round. A stroke behind was the trio of Arnold Palmer, Jack Nicklaus, and Billy Casper, the defending Open champion. I was only a stroke behind this group and felt certain that they were the ones to beat. I was looking forward to it because I was striking the ball so well. But that little devil inside up and grabbed me again. Almost always, the part of one's game that is least sound seems to come unglued in pressure situations, and that part of my game, I believed, was putting.

True to form, I three-putted one of the greens early in the round. From then on, the harder I tried to hole one, the more helpless I became. It was not a lack of physical talent; I had holed my share of putts during the first three rounds. But I couldn't buy one in that final round. It just burns your tail when you play like a genius with thirteen other clubs, then mess it up with the flat stick. As I look back, it's obvious that my mind was producing those awful results. I was a dejected young man when I knocked my second shot onto the eighteenth green, then three-putted it, too, for a score of 73. In that round, I had hit all eighteen greens in regulation, the par-five eighteenth in two, and had shot three-over par. It was the sorriest damn thing you ever saw.

The large IBM scoreboard told the world that Jack Nicklaus and I had tied for the lead in the number of greens hit in regulation for the entire tournament, although I may be the only guy who remembers that. Nobody else gives a damn, nor should they. I won the following week's tournament, the Cleveland Open, and while all tour victories are great, I felt I was a week late.

Reduced to an Onlooker

This had become an all too-familiar pattern for me in the major championships. The 1965 PGA Championship was held at Laurel Valley near Arnold Palmer's hometown of Latrobe, Pennsylvania. The tournament began amidst controversy. The tour players were engaged in a knock-down fight with the parent PGA of America. The club professionals were determined that the players would not run the tour by themselves.

Dave Marr was our leader at the time, and chairman of the PGA Tournament Committee. With our backing, Dave was standing up to the club pros, and he made several statements to the press that the PGA of America officers didn't like. At a committee meeting prior to the tournament, they determined that Dave Marr would be stripped of his PGA membership immediately following the Championship. That made all of us hot as hell.

For the first two rounds, I drew Ben Hogan and George Knudson as playing partners for the third straight week. Ben put on his customary, magnificent tee-to-green display, along with some of the most pitiful putting any of us had witnessed. So, for a change, I outscored Ben. I opened with a round of 67, a stroke behind the leader Tommy Aaron, and, after a mediocre second round, came back with a 69, the low round of the day. This put me three-under for the tournament and a stroke behind the two leaders, Aaron and Dave Marr.

Paired with Marr on Sunday, I managed to take myself out of contention with a big hole somewhere, although I can't remember which one. The mind finds a way to forget unpleasantries. In effect, I'd been reduced to an onlooker again, and, as I did at Baltusrol, I began rooting for my playing partner. By the time we reached the final hole, Casper and Nicklaus had climbed back into contention and were breathing down Marr's neck. When he drove into the left fairway bunker, things began to look interesting because of a pond resting below the elevated green between his ball and the pin. As he was discussing the shot with his caddie, I overheard Dave mention a wood club. When he walked up the fairway to size up the terrain, I was horrified that he might actually try to hit the fairway wood, so I strolled over to Marr's caddie, took his four-wood and shoved it back in his golf bag — upside down!

I have no idea if Dave noticed my gesture, but he elected to lay up short of the pond, then pitched his third cold-stiff. He tapped in the putt to become the PGA Champion. I, on the other hand, three-putted the eighteenth and missed qualifying for the Ryder Cup team, the end of a perfect day. Even though I had butchered another opportunity in a major championship, it wasn't a total loss, however. You see, nothing more was heard about kicking Dave Marr, or anybody else, out of the PGA.

A Hard Lesson

There's a lesson to be learned from these experiences. In professional tournament golf, success is not measured by your ability to conquer your opponent, or even the golf course. Nor can we say that competitive urges alone are decisive. The hard truth is that success is measured by your ability to conquer yourself. It's an old truth, as old as the game itself. I wonder why it takes some of us so long to learn it?

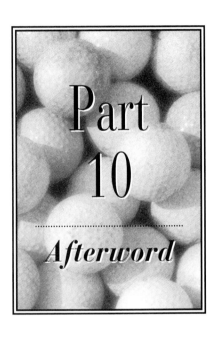

Part
10

Afterword

The Dickinsons: (L-R) Spencer, Judy, Barron, Gardner.

Endgame

After having played golf for over fifty-two years, and having taught it for nearly forty of those years, why in the world would I sit down and write a book? During those fifty-two years, I've read only two books — Henry Cotton's *My Golfing Album* and Ben Hogan's *The Modern Fundamentals of Golf* — which I thought even came close to making a contribution to golf, though some others are admittedly entertaining. Lord knows, there are enough of them, books by fine players trying to write down how they *think* they play, or books by the inexhaustible supply of "experts" who can't play but *think* they know how the good players play — and therefore, how *you* should play.

I can assure you that I have no desire to add another dusty volume to your shelf of golf books, for if I did, I have, indeed, invested too much of the precious time I have left to me. I'm aware that my sweet nostalgia is not necessarily as dear to everyone else's heart as it is to mine. My intention has been to make a record of a lifetime's experience in golf that might help golfers, of all ages, gain some practical knowledge of a golf swing and, hopefully, real insights into their own games.

In various parts of the book, I'm sure you've found many of my opinions expressed rather forcefully at times. Well, that's the way I am, as any of my golfing peers can tell you. I will state, quite candidly, that my opinions on golf technique change from time to time, for I believe that we can, and do, find easier ways to do the same old things essential in a golf swing, and I don't apologize for that. In writing about many of my well-known golfing friends, I've tried to describe things about them you might not have known, using incidents that I hope you will find interesting.

Though I haven't done so here, perhaps someone should study the aging process as it pertains to one's golf game. Having been blessed with the gift of outstanding coordination in my youth, it's tremendously frustrating not to be able to make my body do, anymore, the things I once did so beautifully and effortlessly. I shall fight the aging process until I die, for I abhor every facet of aging — except for the comfort of realizing that I now understand things so much better than once I did.

After middle age, it's virtually impossible to find a golfer who has actually gotten better, although for the life of me, I can't see why it couldn't be done. In my own case, I know my scoring ability has declined — but, I certainly can't blame it all on physical decline. My mind is so much stronger than it was when I was a kid, I feel I should be able to make up for most of my diminished physical capacities. Perhaps that's a good place to start again. Perhaps that's the message of this book, one that every golfer, including me, can take to heart.

For who knows what lies ahead and beyond? I rather hope the poet was correct who wrote:

> *For the plan would be imperfect*
> *Unless it held some sphere*
> *That paid for the toil and talent*
> *And love that is wasted here!*

And, just in case you're wondering, should there be another volume, there'll be "No More Mr. Nice Guy!"